NAVIGATION FOR PILOTS

J. E. HITCHCOCK

NAVIGATION FOR PILOTS

Airlife
England

First published in the UK in 1997
By Airlife Publishing Ltd

British Library Cataloguing in Publication Data
A catalogue record for this book
is available from the British Library

ISBN 1 85310 803 0

Typeset by Phoenix Typesetting, Ilkley, West Yorkshire
Printed in England by Livesey Ltd, Shrewsbury

Airlife Publishing Ltd

101 Longden Road, Shrewsbury SY3 9EB, England

ACKNOWLEDGEMENTS

The author wishes to acknowledge the assistance of the following people in the preparation of this book. Mr A du Feu of Flight Crew Licensing 2 at the CAA for his advice on publications relating to Licences for Pilots and sources of related training materials. Mr D P Smith of the Aeronautical Charts section of the CAA for permission to reproduce certain charts. The Controller, Her Majesty's Stationery Office for permission to reproduce pages from the *Air Almanac*. Mr R Pooley of Pooley's PLC (formerly trading as Airtour International) for permission to use illustrations of the Airtour CRP-5 navigation computer. Except where otherwise credited all illustrations are by the author.

CONTENTS

PREFACE

I hope that student pilots who read this book will find it of use when preparing themselves for their written examinations and that some of the practical ideas may be of help as well, even though they do not form part of the examinations.

As someone whose entire working life has been at the sharp end of aviation, (initially as servicing ground crew, then as aircrew and finally for many years as a senior lecturer in navigation subjects at one of Europe's top commercial civil aviation schools), I have at times encountered problems with some text books. One particularly bad trend that appears all too often is text written, supposedly for beginners, where the author has assumed that the reader already has as much background knowledge as he or she! Aviation text books are not the only ones guilty of this sin, quite a few so called basic computer manuals are incomprehensible to the layman, as many of you may have discovered.

In preparing this book I have tried to avoid any assumption of subject knowledge in my readers. As a result, some of you may feel that there is too much 'dotting of i's and crossing of t's'. To you I say, please be patient and remember that not everyone may have the same background as yourself.

Modern education at both primary and secondary level in schools has encouraged the use of pocket calculators and desktop computers to the detriment of mental calculation. This is fine as long as an electronic calculator or computer is available, functioning correctly, and the operator keys in the right information. If any one of these three parameters is missing all that is left is the computer we were all issued with at birth, *brains*. Throughout this book the reader is encouraged to develop an automatic mental checking system *before* programming up any type of computer, i.e. to determine parameters within which the correct answer must lie. This has a twofold benefit:

(1) It will immediately indicate a nonsense answer from the computer, usually due to faulty information entered by the operator.
(2) It will in time and with practice develop a mental ability to cope with navigation problems in flight without recourse to any form of computer aid, a great asset during single pilot operations especially in helicopters and light aircraft.

To the aspiring pilot, at whatever level, I would like to say, 'May you be successful in your studies and get as much enjoyment out of flying in the future as I have in the past'.

JE Hitchcock, Abingdon

xi

ABOUT THIS BOOK

The purpose of this manual is to provide a complete study pack for the subject of Navigation as applicable to a whole range of aircraft pilot licences. It is as well to point out that the subject of Navigation is only one of a group of subjects which together constitute 'Navigation Subjects' for licensing purposes. The other subjects are Meteorology (Theory and Practical), Flight Planning, Aviation Law, Instruments, Radio Aids and Human Performance. Candidates for pilot licences will have to study all these subjects to the level required by the Licensing Authority. In the case of the United Kingdom this is the Civil Aviation Authority (CAA), other Countries having their own regulatory bodies.

In the UK various Pilots' Licences are available, these being:

1. The Private Pilot's Licence   (PPL).
2. The Private Pilot's Instrument Rating   (PPL I/R).
3. The Basic Commercial Pilot's Licence   (BCPL).
4. The Commercial Pilot's Licence   (CPL).
5. The Airline Transport Pilot's Licence   (ATPL).

The first three of these licences exclude the right to fly for hire and reward as an Airline Transport Pilot, the BCPL only being eligible to fly for reward as a flying instructor (private pilot training) or crop sprayer. All of these licences have a requirement for ground studies and an appropriate set of written examinations. The text in this book covers the navigation element for *all* these licences. All student pilots, Private or Commercial, will need to study fully Chapters 1 to 8 and 13. Private pilots will need to also study Chapters 9, 10 and 11 but will not need to get involved in the various calculations. Commercial pilots need to study the whole text, candidates for the CPL normally being required to carry out a more basic plot than that demonstrated in this book.

Also included in the text are items that are not in the written examinations. These illustrate practical applications and tips that are not always pointed out to pilots, especially at private pilot training establishments. These items are indicated in the text as hints and it is up to you to decide whether or not to make use of them.

For some time now discussions between European Aviation Authorities have been underway with the aim of producing a Joint European Airline Transport Pilot's Licence. The current proposals under consideration for this European Licence are in many ways similar to the UK ATPL.

Certainly the proposed Navigation aspects are almost identical to the current UK licence requirements which are covered in this book. The idea behind a common European Licence is to ensure standardisation of training and qualification of Airline Transport Pilots within Europe. It is proposed that when this European Licence comes into force it will only be obtainable via full time integrated flying and ground studies at an approved training establishment.

A final but very important point is that of the form which the Licence examinations take. The CAA use 'multiple-choice' questioning. A word of warning to anyone thinking that this form of examination is easy! Firstly the standard choice is from four possible answers with a penalty system (in most cases of minus one third) for any incorrect selection. So a candidate indicating a wrong selection for a question worth six marks would end up with no marks for the question and a loss of two marks from the total score on that paper. In other words the odds are loaded against guessing! Furthermore the examiners have vast experience in writing multiple-choice questions and many of the incorrect answers offered are derived using known common errors made by candidates. If you make a common error, the chances are your answer will match up with one of the given wrong answers!

SECTION 1

THE EARTH

Navigation is the art of finding one's way around. Before the subject can be developed it is necessary to explain the standard methods used to identify position, denote direction and measure distance. Since navigation is carried out over, or, in the case of air navigation, above the surface of the earth, the shape and form of our planet is the logical starting point of these studies.

The earth is not quite a perfect sphere, being approximately 42 kilometres smaller at its polar diameter than at its maximum diameter which is at a point not quite half way between its poles, (which means it is also slightly pear shaped). Since the average diameter of the earth is 12,740 km it can be seen that these deformities in the shape of the earth are of the order of 0.33% and can be ignored *for most practical purposes*. Unless stated otherwise, from this point on the earth will be considered to be a perfect sphere.

CHAPTER 1

POSITION

1.1 Identifying position on the surface of a sphere is not easy since a sphere has no obvious natural datum points (such as corners) to which a position can be related. Some form of graticule needs to be constructed on the surface of the sphere along with a system of locating any position on this graticule. Before any such graticule can be constructed, some unique feature of the earth must be identified to which the graticule can be associated.

THE CARDINAL POINTS

1.2 The unique feature that fulfils this requirement is the direction of rotation of the earth. This rotation takes place about two points on the earth diametrically opposite to each other known as **The Poles**, the axis of spin passing through the centre of the earth. The two poles are known as the **North Pole** and the **South Pole**. To distinguish between them it is necessary for an observer to face in the direction of the earth's rotation (towards the rising sun), the North pole will then be on the observer's left hand and the South pole on the observer's right hand. The direction of rotation of the

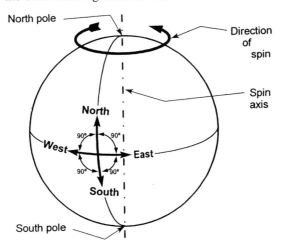

Fig. 1–1.   The Cardinal Points.

3

earth is known as **East** and the opposite direction to East is known as **West**, both of these directions being at a right angle to the North/South spin axis.(see Fig. 1-1). The four basic directions of **North (N), South (S), East (E)** and **West (W)** are collectively termed the **Cardinal Points.**

THE EARTH GRATICULE

1.3 Having established the presence of the poles and the basic direction references of North (N), South (S), East (E) and West (W) these can now be used to construct a graticule on the surface of the earth. If a circle could be drawn on the surface of the earth so that it passed through the position of both the poles, the direction that such a line defined would be N/S. It would also have its centre co-incident with the centre of the earth and a diameter the same as the earth's, such a circle is the largest that can be drawn on the surface of the earth and is known as a **Great Circle (GC).** Since the poles are diametrically opposite to each other on the earth, it follows that an infinite number of GCs could be drawn to pass through the poles each one defining N/S. Each Semi-GC joining the poles is termed a **Meridian** and forms part of the graticule used in establishing positions. The Semi-GC that shares the other half of GC with a meridian is known as the meridian's **Anti-meridian.**

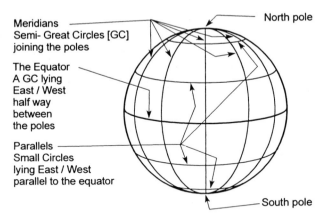

Meridians
Semi- Great Circles [GC]
joining the poles

The Equator
A GC lying
East / West
half way
between
the poles

Parallels
Small Circles
lying East / West
parallel to the equator

North pole

South pole

Fig. 1–2   The Earth Graticule.

1.4 With the meridians defining N/S it is necessary to imagine lines running E/W to complete a graticule system on the earth's surface. Such E/W lines would appear as circles around the earth at right angles to the meridians. Only one of these circles (exactly half way between the two poles) is a GC, having the same centre and diameter as the earth. All the other E/W lines are of varying lesser diameters and collectively are known

4

as **Small Circles**. The E/W GC described above is termed the **Equator**; it divides the earth in two. Since all the E/W Small Circles are running parallel to the Equator they are termed **Parallels**. (see Fig. 1-2)

LATITUDE (lat)

1.5 The equator is the only line defining E/W direction that is a GC. This unique property plus the fact that it also divides the earth into two hemispheres provides one of the datums used in establishing position on the earth. The first thing that can be stated is whether or not a position is N or S of the equator, thus eliminating half of the earth from the reckoning.

1.6 The next thing to be specified is the parallel running through a position; this will narrow the search down to all places along that parallel. The centre of the earth is used as the point of origin of the equator and parallels, the equator being described by the rim of a flat disc, the parallels by the rims of the bases of a series of cones and the poles by points at right angles to the equator. The angle between the equatorial flat disc and the cone describing a particular parallel is termed the **Latitude (lat)** of that parallel, (see Fig. 1–3).

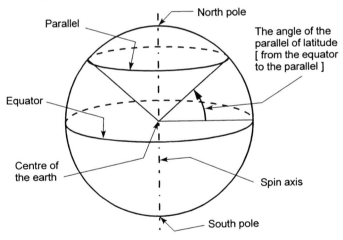

Fig 1–3   Parallel of Latitude

1.7 The means of angular measurement used is the established international system whereby a circle is divided into 360 degrees, each degree into 60 minutes and each minute into 60 seconds. Thus the equator becomes 0° of lat, since it is the dividing line between the hemispheres and is neither N nor S. The poles become 90° of lat but must be specified by hemisphere, the N pole being 90° N; similarly the S pole becomes 90° S.

In aviation, intermediate parallels are usually expressed in just degrees and minutes. However, many documents give airfield and ground radio installation positions to a higher degree of accuracy which includes seconds as well. Thus London (Heathrow) is shown as lying on the parallel of 51°28'11"N and Strasbourg (Neuhof) as on the 48°33'16"N parallel (see Fig. 1–4.) Note the use of ° to denote degrees, ' to denote minutes and " to denote seconds. It is common practice to leave these out, thus Neuhof's lat may be written 483316N. This form of notation may be further modified in some documents to conform with the way certain pieces of advanced navigation equipment have their computers programmed. Thus the lat of Strasbourg (Neuhof) could be shown as N4833·27 with no °, ' or " and the 16 seconds being expressed in a decimal form as ·27 of a minute.

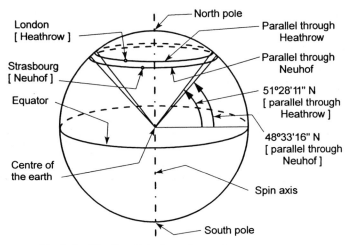

Fig. 1–4   The Parallels through Heathrow and Neuhof.

LONGITUDE (long)

1.8   Having established the parallel on which a position lies, its exact position can be given by identifying the meridian which passes through the position. It has already been stated that there are an infinite number of meridians, so there is no one meridian that is an obvious datum. Nonetheless, one meridian has to be nominated as the datum, or **Prime Meridian**, and here the choice of the meridian passing through **Greenwich** came about as a result of an International Conference held in Washington in 1884 to decide which of several options to adopt as the World standard. The meridian through the observatory set up at Greenwich in 1675 had long been the most likely choice. This was because of the publication in 1766 of a Nautical Almanac, the development of a reliable nautical

chronometer by John Harrison (1693–1776) and the establishment of
Greenwich Mean Time (GMT) (now renamed **Co-ordinated Universal Time
(UTC))**. A major factor in the final selection was that the chosen prime
meridian would also become the datum for universal time, with the date
changing on crossing its anti-meridian which would be known as the
International Date Line. Obviously such a Date Line needs to be through
as much open ocean as possible. Any country having the Date Line running through it would be presented with the administrative problem of
always having two different dates operating within its boundaries.
Fortunately the choice of Greenwich as the prime meridian does not cause
too much of a problem with the Date Line, only a couple of detours in the
line being needed to avoid going through countries. There is more of this
in Chapter 16.

1.9 Having established Greenwich as the prime or 0° meridian, other
meridians can be identified by horizontal angular measurement E or W of
the 0° meridian up to a maximum of 180° either way. Again the centre of
the earth is the point of origin, the angle being measured horizontally from
a line joining this point of origin and the prime meridian at the equator to
a similar line joining the same point of origin to the meridian being identified, (see Fig. 1–5). This angle is termed the **Longitude (long)** of the meridian
and it must also specify in which 180° arc E or W of Greenwich it is to be
found. In paragraph 1.7 it was stated that Strasbourg (Neuhof) is on the
483316N parallel of lat. The meridian that passes through Neuhof is
07°46'41"E of the Greenwich meridian, this normally being written as

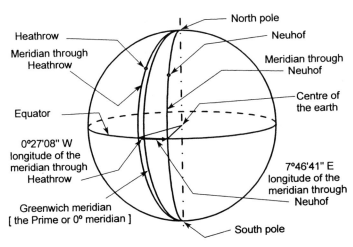

Fig 1–5   The Meridians through Heathrow and Neuhof

7

074641E. The combination of a position's lat and long are unique to that position, so Neuhof's location is expressed as 483316N 074641E. Note that lat is always given before long and in this case a 0 is written in front of the long to signify that there is no hundred or tens in front of the 7. In a similar way 0 would be use where necessary in quoting minutes and seconds. For instance the long of London (Heathrow) is 002708W, meaning it is zero degrees twenty seven minutes and eight seconds of long W of the Greenwich meridian. In the alternative computer form Neuhof's position is given as N4833·27 E00746·68 the extra 0 in the long being required by the computer which is programmed to expect up to 180° of long, Heathrow's position becomes N5128·18 W00027·13 under this system. Unless otherwise stated the non-computer form of lat and long reporting will be used from here on in this book.

1.10 The speed with which most aircraft change position means that to try and give position reports to within seconds of lat and long is impractical. Apart from documents giving the positions of airfields and various ground located radio aid installations it is common practice, on purely practical grounds, not to give position to an accuracy greater than to the nearest minute of lat and long. Using this system Heathrow's position would be given as 5128N 0027W and Neuhof's position as 4833N 0747E.

DIFFERENCE IN LAT AND LONG BETWEEN PLACES

1.11 It is sometimes required to know the difference in lat and long between two positions. This is termed **d'lat** (short for difference in lat) and **d'long** (short for difference in long) or alternatively **ch'lat** and **ch'long** (for change in lat and long). They both mean exactly the same thing! All levels of Pilot Licences are liable to include questions involving the calculation of d'lat and d'long so here are some ground rules and examples:

d'lat rules:

If both places are in the *Same* hemisphere *Subtract* the smaller lat from the larger, (remember that one degree has 60 minutes in it).

If the places are in *Opposite* hemispheres *Add* the lats together.

The direction of the change will be either North or South *From* the first given place *To* the second place.

d'long rules:

If both places are on the *Same* side of the Greenwich meridian *Subtract* the smaller long from the larger.

If the places are on *Opposite* sides of the Greenwich meridian *Add* the longs together. Now check the answer. If it is 180° or less, that completes the calculation. *If however it is more than 180°, it means that the d'long is less going the other way around the world.* To calculate this lesser value just *Subtract* the answer found from 360°.

The direction of the change will be either East or West *From* the first given place *To* the second place *by the shorter route.*

Example:

Calculate the d'lat and d'long from 'A' 5643N 2716W to 'B' 0552N 6918W.

Answer:

Both 'A' and 'B' are in the same hemisphere and West of the Greenwich meridian, so subtract the smaller from the larger in both cases.

Latitude 5643N 'A'   Longitude 6918W 'B'
    -0552N 'B'   -2716W 'A'
d'lat 5051 Southward   **d'long 4202 Westward**

d'long <180°, so is the correct answer (see Fig 1–6a).

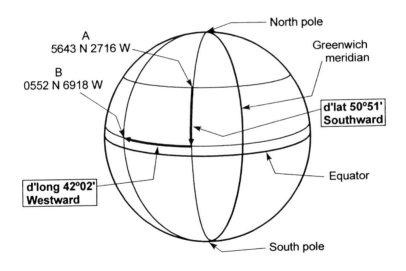

Fig.1–6a   D'lat and D'long

Example:

Calculate the d'lat and d'long from 'A' 1435S 12754E to 'B' 7149N 16628W.

Answer:

'A' and 'B' are in opposite hemispheres and on opposite sides of the Greenwich meridian, so add the values in both cases.

9

Latitude 1435S 'A'   Longitude 12754E 'A'
+7149N 'B'   +16628W 'B'
d'lat 8624 Northward   **d'long 29422 Westward**

d'long > 180° , so subtract from 360° and reverse direction of change.

36000
-29422 Westward
d'long 6538 Eastward

(See Fig. 1–6b)

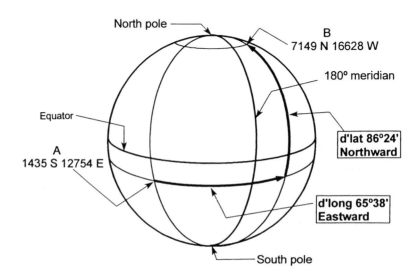

North pole

B
7149 N 16628 W

180° meridian

Equator

d'lat 86°24'
Northward

A
1435 S 12754 E

d'long 65°38'
Eastward

South pole

Fig. 1–6b   D'lat and D'long

Example:
Calculate the d'lat and d'long from 'A' 2128S 5619W to 'B' 4952S 2103E.

Answer:
'A' and 'B' are in the same hemisphere but on opposite sides of the Greenwich meridian, so subtract the smaller latitude from the larger and add the longitudes together.

Latitude 4952S 'B'   Longitude 5619W 'A'
-2128S 'A'   +2103E 'B'
d'lat 2824 Southward   **d'long 7722 Eastward**

d'long < 180° , so the answer is correct. (See Fig. 1–6c)

10

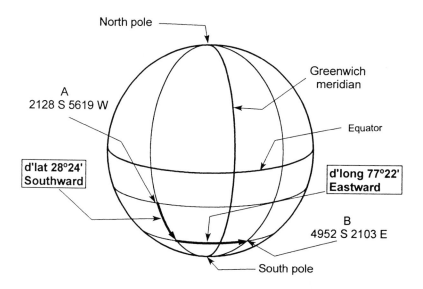

Fig. 1–6c   D'lat and D'long

MORE GREAT CIRCLES

1.12 Meridians and the equator are not the only GCs that can be drawn on the earth. GCs can be drawn at any angle to the latitude and longitude graticule and there is only one particular GC that can be drawn to pass through any two selected positions on the earth (the one exception to this being places, like the Poles, that are geographically opposite each other where the number of possible GCs joining them is infinite). The shorter arc of the GC passing through any two places will represent the most direct route between them. This gives rise to the rule that:

'The shortest distance between two points on the earth is along the shorter arc of the GC passing through them.'

Since radio waves travel by the most direct route from transmitter to receiver it can be seen that they will be following a GC route. As will be shown later this can influence the choice of chart projections for some tasks.

1.13 Fig. 1–7 shows the earth with the GC drawn on it passing through New York and Paris. Also indicated are the angles that this GC makes rela-tive to the meridians it is crossing, in this case the angles get larger as movement is made from New York to Paris.

The only cases where GC directions remain constant along their length are up or down any meridian (due N or S), or along the equator (due E or

*Fig. 1–7   GC passing through New York and Paris showing the
change in the (T) direction along it.*

W). To summarise, the shorter arc of a GC joining two places on the earth gives the shortest distance between them but, apart from up or down a meridian or along the equator, the direction will not be constant. The reason for this is because the meridians which are parallel to each other at the equator converge to meet at the poles thus changing their direction *relative to one another*, this is dealt with in detail in Chapter 2.

RHUMB LINES

1.14 Fig. 1–8 shows the same GC joining New York and Paris as in Fig. 1–7. Also shown drawn between New York and Paris is a curved line which maintains a constant direction relative to the meridians it crosses. Such a constant direction line is called a **Rhumb Line (RL)**.

Meridians and the equator, which are GCs, also have constant direction so by definition they are RLs as well as GCs, (in fact they are the only GCs that are also RLs). In all other cases, such as in Fig. 1–8, the RL does not coincide with the GC joining two places on the earth and, since the GC arc is the shortest distance between the points, it follows that the RL distance between the points *must* be greater.

*Fig. 1–8   The Constant (T) direction Rhumb Line (RL)
between New York and Paris*

1.15 Apart from the meridians and equator cases where GC and RL coincide:

Flying along a GC between two places has the disadvantage of changing direction but the advantage of the shortest distance.

Flying along a RL between two places has the advantage of constant direction but the disadvantage of greater distance.

Over short distances these differences are not of any great significance. For instance a GC drawn from W to E across southern England only changes direction over its length by about 4° and a similarly drawn RL is less than 1% greater in length. Over great distances the differences can be considerable and influence the choice of route to be flown. For instance from New York to Paris (see Fig. 1–8) the GC changes direction by some 54° and the RL is around 10% longer than the GC . With modern airliners equipped with navigation aids capable of automatically flying along GC routes the saving in fuel and time by selecting the GC route for such a journey is obvious.

1.16 It is of interest that when Charles Lindbergh (1902–1974) flew from New York to Paris solo in 33 hours back in 1927 the route he chose approximated to the GC. A study of the GC route (see Fig. 1–8) shows that it follows the North American and Canadian coast up to Newfoundland and this he flew in a series of short RLs. He then crossed the Atlantic to southern Eire using a pre-calculated sequence of timed single headings to keep him approximately on the GC until landfall when it was back to a further series of rhumb lines across the Celtic Sea, Cornwall, Plymouth, the English Channel and France to Paris. Had he chosen the single RL route he would have been over open ocean for most of the way and have needed at least three more hours of flying time!

CHAPTER 2

DIRECTION

360° NOTATION

2.1 In Chapter 1 the four cardinal points of N, E, S and W were introduced. Using the same 360° notation for direction as is used for lat and long and going in a clockwise direction starting from N, the angular values of the cardinal point are:

North	=	000° (or alternatively 360°)
East	=	090°
South	=	180°
West	=	270°
North	=	360° (or alternatively 000°) (see Fig. 2–1).

Note how three figure groups are used throughout, 0 signifying no hundreds or no tens as appropriate. This is to reduce the chance of errors

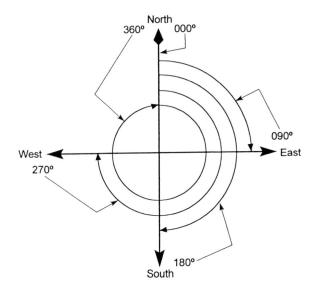

Fig. 2–1   The 360° notation

15

being made when transmitting information by whatever means, particularly in the case of Radio Telephony (R/T) transmissions if reception conditions are poor. For example, if a pilot is instructed to steer 026° but only hears 26 there could be a 0,1,2 or 3 in front of the 26 or any number from 0 to 9 after it. So three figure groups are *always* used for directions and if less than three figures are clearly received a repeat of the message *must be requested and confirmed to clarify the situation.*

TRUE DIRECTION, MAGNETIC DIRECTION AND VARIATION

2.2   The directions so far mentioned are relative to the geographical cardinal directions on the earth. These directions are said to be **True Directions** and are suffixed **(T)**. Unless an aircraft is fitted with sophisticated navigation equipment, such as an Inertial Navigation System (INS), it will not normally have immediate means of finding (T) direction and recourse to a magnetic compass is necessary. The earth has a weak magnetic field which can be sensed in the horizontal plane by a suitably designed compass system (the Instrument part of the licence syllabus covers earth magnetism and compass systems in some detail). Navigationally the main problem with **Magnetic Direction (M)** is that the axis of the earth's magnetic field is not in line with the earth's spin axis, the N (M) pole being situated in the vicinity of Victoria Island, Northern Canada and the S (M) pole on the edge of Antarctica not quite geographically opposite the N (M) pole. As a result the lines of the magnetic field vary in direction when compared to the meridians (which define N (T)). This difference between the (T) direction and the (M) direction at any point on the earth is known as **Magnetic Variation** or **Variation (varn)**. The value of varn is different from place to place (anything from 0° to 180°) depending on the relative directions of the (T) and (M) poles from the observer's position on the earth, the direction of N (M) as defined by the magnetic lines of force may be either E or W of the N (T) direction.

2.3   If (T) direction is to be derived from (M) direction, or vice versa, the value of the local varn has to be applied in the correct sense. The values of local varns are displayed on topographical, plotting and radio navigation charts by lines joining all places having the same value of varn; these lines are called **Isogonals**. Unfortunately due to movement of the Magnetic poles varn values are not constant, this movement although very slow means that charts need updating every few years, the value of change being different from place to place. When consulting a chart to extract the value of local varn always check that the chart is up to date; the isogonals will be labelled with the degrees of varn, whether it is E or W of (T) and the Year. Thus an isogonal bearing the label **19E (1996)** is saying that in 1996 all places along that isogonal had a varn of 19°, the (M) direction lying to the E of (T) direction (see Fig. 2–2a.)

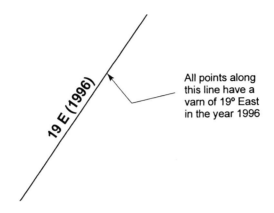

All points along this line have a varn of 19° East in the year 1996

Fig. 2–2a   An Isogonal.

2.4   Fig. 2–2b shows in plan view the relative directions of N(T) and N(M) at a place on the earth where variation is 19E. Also shown is a line representing the direction an aircraft is pointing in (known as its **HEADING (hdg))**. From the Figure it can be seen that the aircraft hdg when measured from N (M) will be 19° less than when measured from N (T). When variation is E, (M) direction is always *Less* than (T) direction and conversely when variation is W, (M) direction is always *More* than (T) direction (see Fig. 2–2c).

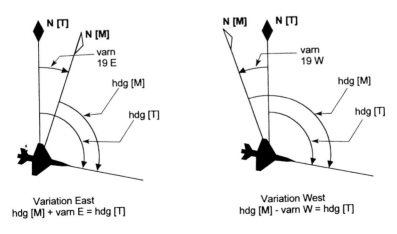

Variation East
hdg [M] + varn E = hdg [T]

Variation West
hdg [M] - varn W = hdg [T]

Fig. 2–2b   Variation East   *Fig. 2–2c   Variation West*

MAGNETIC DIRECTION, COMPASS DIRECTION AND DEVIATION

2.5 It would seem that all that has to be done is to install a magnetic compass in the aircraft and read hdg (M) from it, extract the variation from the chart and apply it in the correct sense to get hdg (T). Unfortunately it is not quite as simple as that, because magnetic fields within the aircraft structure also affect magnetic compasses causing the reading to be deflected from the hdg (M), the resultant indications being known as **Compass Headings (hdg (C))**. The difference between the hdg (C) and the hdg (M) is called **Deviation (dev)** and its value varies with the hdg of the aircraft. Like varn, the dev is given in degrees E or W, only in this case it is the number of degrees the hdg (C) is lying to the E or W of the hdg (M). Similar rules for converting hdg (C) to hdg (M) and vice versa apply as were used between hdg (M) and hdg (T), (see Fig. 2–3.)

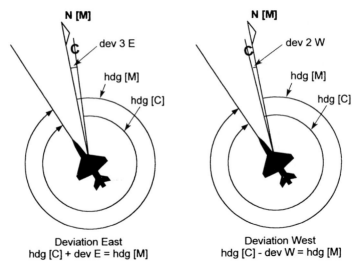

Deviation East
hdg [C] + dev E = hdg [M]

Deviation West
hdg [C] - dev W = hdg [M]

Fig. 2–3   Rules for applying dev to hdg (C).

The derivation of compass dev and methods of correction forms part of the instrument syllabus and will not be dwelt on here. Amounts of dev present once a compass has been corrected should normally be no more than 3° though in practice slightly larger values are sometimes encountered. Uncorrected compasses have been known to display very large amounts of dev due to such things as the fitting of extra fuel tanks in the rear fuselage for ferry purposes. Because no two aircraft have precisely the same amount or disposition of magnetism in their structure and no two compasses will be precisely identical in performance, it follows that values of dev will be different for every individual magnetic compass installation as well as varying with the hdg of the aircraft. Dev cards are displayed beside magnetic compass indicators giving the necessary correction to convert hdgs (C) to hdgs (M).

2.6 Conversions between (C), (M) and (T) in both mathematical and diagram form are given in the following examples:

Example:
hdg 097 (C), dev 3E, varn 17W. Calculate hdgs (M) and (T).

Answer:
dev 3E means hdg (C) < hdg (M) by 3°.
varn 17W means hdg (M)> hdg (T) by 17°.
hdg 097 (C), + dev 3E = hdg **100 (M)**,– varn 17W = hdg **083 (T)**
(see Fig. 2–4a).

Example:
hdg 342 (T), varn 21E, dev 2E. Calculate hdgs (M) and (C).

Answer:
varn 21E means hdg (M) < hdg (T) by 21°.
dev 2E means hdg (C) < hdg (M) by 2°.
hdg 342 (T), – varn 21E = hdg **321 (M)**, – dev 2E = hdg **319 (C)**
(see Fig. 2–4b).

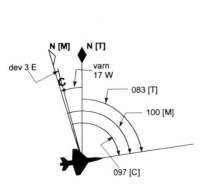

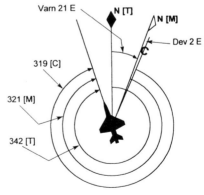

Fig. 2–4a
hdg 097 (C), dev 3E, varn 17W.

Fig. 2–4b
hdg 342 (T), dev 2E, varn 21E.

Example:
hdg 006 (M), dev 1W, varn 8W. Calculate hdgs (T) and (C).

Answer:
dev 1W means hdg (C) > hdg (M) by 1°.
varn 8W means hdg (M) > hdg (T) by 8°.
hdg 006 (M), + dev 1W = hdg **007 (C)**.
hdg 006 (M), – varn 8W = hdg **358 (T)**.*
*(006° – 8° = – 2° from 000 / 360° = 358°) (see Fig. 2–4c).

Example:
hdg 053 (T), varn 49W, dev 3E. Calculate hdgs (M) and (C).

Answer:
varn 49W means hdg (M) > hdg (T) by 49°.
dev 3E means hdg (C) < hdg (M) by 3°.
hdg 053 (T), + varn 49W = hdg **102 (M)**, – dev 3E = hdg **099 (C)**
(see Fig. 2–4d).

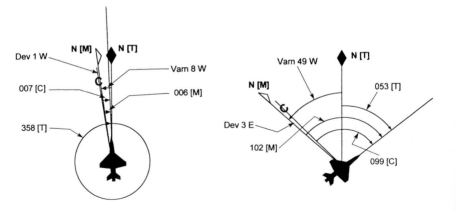

Fig. 2–4c	Fig. 2–4d
hdg 006 (M), dv 1W, varn 8W.	*hdg 053 (T), dev 3E, varn 49W*

Note: Figs. 2–4a, b, c and d highlight the point that there is only one aircraft but its heading can be measured from more than one datum. It is therefore essential always to annotate a direction with its applicable datum.

CONVERGENCY

2.7 A look back at Fig. 1.7 shows that the meridians start off parallel to each other along the equator but converge towards each other to meet at the poles. This leads to a problem with N (T) for apart from along the equator or up/down a meridian the *relative direction* of N (T) varies from place to place. This change in direction is known as **Convergency (conv)** and is a factor that affects many aspects of navigation.

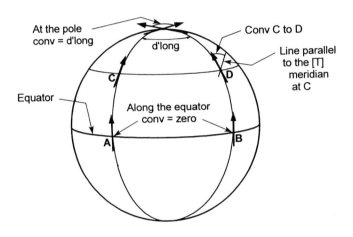

Fig. 2–5   Convergency.

2.8 Fig. 2–5 compares the direction of N (T) at various places on the earth:

At 'A' and 'B' on the equator N (T) is in the same direction although there is a considerable d'long between them, (conv at the equator is 0°).

If the meridians through 'A' and 'B' are followed up to the N pole it can be seen that they converge by the amount of d'long between the meridians, (conv at the poles is maximum = d'long).

'C' and 'D' are on the same meridians as 'A' and 'B' but they are at a lat some way from the equator and the value of conv is somewhere between 0° and d'long.

To summarise, conv is zero at 0° lat and maximum (d'long) at 90° lat. Since sine 0° is zero and sine 90° is 1 (maximum) it follows that conv varies as the sine of the lat and is equal to its maximum value × sine of the lat. In navigation the value of conv is often required between places at different lats and the formula used is:

Convergency = d'long (in degrees) × Sine of mean lat

By *mean* lat is meant the lat half way between the two places *in the same hemisphere*. This can be calculated by either one of two methods:

Either   Work out the d'lat, halve it and add to the lower lat (or subtract from the higher lat).

Or   Add the two lats together and halve the result.

2.9 As will be shown later the sense in which conv is applied in the southern hemisphere is the opposite to that in the northern hemisphere. Calculation of conv between places on either side of the equator has to be carried out in two steps, from one place to where the equator is crossed and from that point on to the second place in the other hemisphere. Calculations of this nature are not usually found in the licence examinations but if set would give the candidate the long of crossing the equator to enable the two separate parts to be resolved, the final answer being the algebraic sum of the two parts.

2.10 In Chapter 1 the route New York to Paris was discussed with regard to GC and RL differences and it was stated that the direction of the GC changed by some 54° along this route. This is due entirely to the conv between New York and Paris. In round terms their positions are New York 4100N 7400W and Paris 4900N 0200E; this gives a mean lat of 4500N and a d'long of 76°, (apply the rules from paragraphs 2.8 and 1.11). Putting these facts into the conv formula gives:

$$\text{Conv New York to Paris} \quad = 76° \times \text{Sine } 45°$$
$$= 76° \times 0.7071$$
$$= 53.7396° \text{ or approximately } \mathbf{54°.}$$

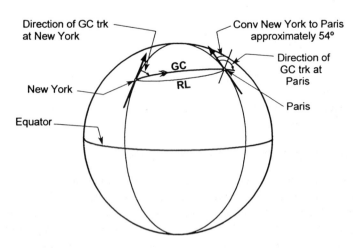

Fig. 2–6   GC direction change from New York to Paris.

Fig. 2–6 illustrates this example and shows a line parallel to the meridian through New York drawn through Paris. The angular difference between this line and the meridian through Paris is the conv between New York and Paris i.e. 54°. It is apparent from Fig. 2–6 that direction of the GC measure from the (T) meridian at Paris is greater than the direction of the GC measured from the (T) meridian at New York by the amount of conv between the two places. In the northern hemisphere going Easterly along a GC the (T) direction increases by conv from the departure point, going Westerly it will decrease. Fig. 2–7 shows the southern hemisphere case where the (T) direction decreases with Easterly movement and increases with Westerly movement, (also shown is the RL appropriate to the GC illustrated).

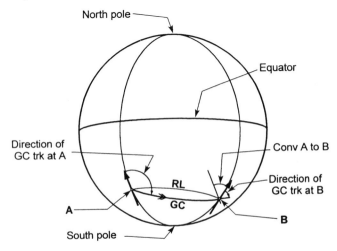

Fig. 2–7   Convergency in the Southern Hemisphere.

Figs. 2–6 and 2–7 highlight another fact. Apart from the equator and the meridians (where GC and RL coincide) the RL *always* lies on the equatorial side of the GC, or conversely the GC path between two places *always* lies on the polar side of the RL path.

GRID DIRECTION AND GRIVATION

2.11 For long distance flying, particularly in high lats, a technique known as **Grid Navigation** is sometimes employed, the idea being to draw a squared grid over the top of the lat and long grid with one axis of the squared grid being denoted as the **Grid North (N (G))**. In some cases the grid may be aligned with N (T) at the point of departure, at other times it may be offset so that the planned route will in general stay close to N (G) (see Fig. 2–8).

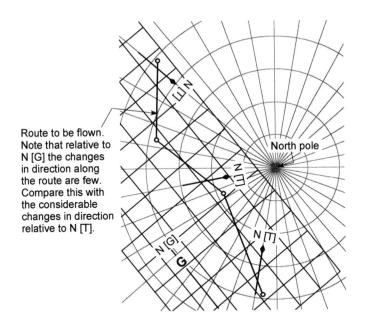

Fig.2–8   A Grid Overlay on a Polar region chart showing Grid North (N(G)).

Navigation is now carried out with reference to the squared grid and N (G), the effect of conv between N (G) and the local N (T) is combined with local varn to give a correction known as **Grivation (griv)** which is applied in a similar way as varn but in this case it is used to convert hdg (G) to hdg (M) and vice versa.

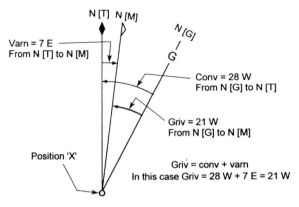

Fig. 2–9   Calculation of Grivation (griv).

2.12 On grid navigation charts all points having the same griv are joined by lines known as **Isogrivs**. These are annotated in the same way as the isogonals are for denoting lines of common varn. An example of how griv is calculated is given in Fig. 2–9.

At position 'X' the conv between N (G) and N (T) is 28W (*always* measured *from* N (G) *to* the local N (T)), local varn (*always* measured *from* N (T) *to* N (M)) from the isogonal is 7E, therefore griv at 'X' is conv (between N (G) and N (T)) plus varn = 28W + 7E = 21W. As already stated griv is applied in the same sense as varn, so at position 'X' the 21W griv is added to hdg (G) to give hdg (M) or subtracted from hdg (M) to give hdg (G).

CHAPTER 3

DISTANCE

3.1 Through the ages there have been many units used for measuring distance, most of which have long been forgotten. Currently there are three predominant standard units of measurement in use in the world and all have found their way into aviation. Until such time as some universal standard is agreed it is necessary for aviators to know something about the origins of these three units of measurement and, most important of all, how to convert from one to another.

THE STATUTE MILE

3.2 The first of these units of measurement is the **Statute Mile (st m)**. The name 'statute' gives the origin away, it derives from a Royal statute, or law, of Queen Elizabeth the First of England (1535–1603). This law was introduced standardising weights and measures throughout the country, the units being developments and modifications of existing empirical units. The st m is 5280 feet (ft) = 1609 metres (m) long.

THE NAUTICAL MILE

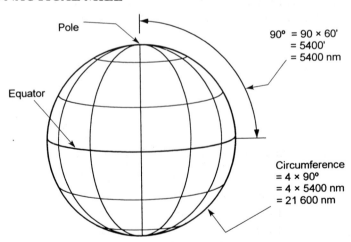

$$90° = 90 × 60'$$
$$= 5400'$$
$$= 5400 \text{ nm}$$

Circumference
$$= 4 × 90°$$
$$= 4 × 5400 \text{ nm}$$
$$= 21\,600 \text{ nm}$$

Fig. 3–1   Nautical Miles on the Earth.

26

3.3 The next unit of measurement is the **Nautical Mile (nm)**. As the name implies the origin is a nautical one, this being a unit of measurement originally derived for navigation at sea. It was evolved as a unit of measurement to tie in directly with the latitude graticule. The nm is the *average* length of the arc of 1 minute of latitude at the earth's surface measured up, or down, a meridian. Since a meridian encompasses 90 degrees from the equator to a pole and each degree has 60 minutes in it, it follows that there are 90 × 60 = 5400 minutes of arc from equator to pole which gives 5400 nm, so the full circumference of the earth is four times this distance i.e. 21 600 nm, (see Fig. 3–1). The nm is 6080 ft = 1852 m long.

THE KILOMETRE

3.4 The final unit of measurement is the **Kilometre (km)**. This unit has its origin in the metric system initiated by Napoleon Bonaparte (1769–1821) and like the rest of that system has 10 as its root. Metrification intended to replace the 360 degrees in a circle with 400 metric degrees, giving 100 metric degrees in a right angle. Furthermore each metric degree was to have 100 metric minutes in it thus giving 10,000 metric minutes in a right angle. The km is the *average* length of the arc of 1 metric minute at the earth's surface measured up, or down, the meridian through Paris. Since there are 10,000 metric minutes in a right angle there must be 40,000 in a full circle, which means that the circumference of the earth is 40,000 km. The km is 1000 m = 3280 ft long. Metric degrees were never universally accepted because of a fundamental flaw; figures like isosceles triangles that occur naturally in trigonometry do not have a straightforward number of metric degrees to their internal angles. For example 60 standard degrees converts to 66.66666 (recurring) metric degrees turning quite simple trignometrical problems into number crunching nightmares.

CONVERSION BETWEEN STANDARD UNITS

3.5 Because of the direct relationship between the nm and a minute of latitude the nm is the favoured unit of measurement for navigation with many countries, but not universally so. It is therefore a requirement of pilots to be able to convert from one standard to another. This may be achieved by straight mathematics using the following conversion factors:

$$1 \text{ nm} = 6080 / 5280 = 1.152 \text{ st m}$$
$$1 \text{ nm} = 6080 / 3280 = 1.854 \text{ km}$$
$$1 \text{ st m} = 5280 / 6080 = 0.868 \text{ nm}$$
$$1 \text{ st m} = 5280 / 3280 = 1.61 \text{ km}$$
$$1 \text{ km} = 3280 / 6080 = 0.539 \text{ nm}$$
$$1 \text{ km} = 3280 / 5280 = 0.621 \text{ st m}$$

This can be a rather tedious chore and there are many electronic navigation calculators on the market that are pre-programmed to do these conversions, *unfortunately the use of such calculators is not allowed in the licence examinations!* A close study of the rules governing the use of electronic calculators in all examinations is strongly advised. At the time of writing they are not allowed at all for the navigation paper and only non-programmed or nonprogrammable electronic calculators are allowed for other papers. Since the rules governing examinations can change, candidates should check the current rules pertaining prior to sitting any examinations.

THE CIRCULAR SLIDE RULE

3.6 The use of a navigation computer such as the Airtour CRP–5 Computer is allowed in all the examinations. The circular slide rule side on such computers has index marks for the full range of measurement, weight, and volume conversions that a pilot may have to make. Circular slide rules, or straight slide rules come to that, are not often taught in schools these days, the electronic calculator having taken over the number crunching role

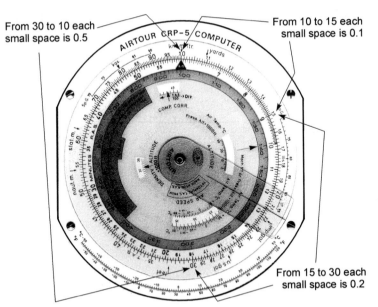

From 30 to 10 each small space is 0.5

From 10 to 15 each small space is 0.1

From 15 to 30 each small space is 0.2

From 10 to 30 each whole number is marked but from 30 on as the scale contracts only each fifth number is marked

Fig. 3–2   The CRP-5 Circular Slide rule showing the spacing and numbering of the scale.

in most cases. For anyone unfamiliar with slide rules a few points regarding layout and procedures now follow, even the experts may like to refresh their memories!

3.7 The circular slide rule is basically a device for solving ratio problems. In fact it is a scalar form of logarithms but no knowledge of the theory and use of logarithms is required in its use. There are however two aspects of the scale that need to be clearly understood; these are the way in which the scale is spaced out and how it is numbered. Reference to Fig. 3–2 shows:

Spacing. This is not constant, closing up as the numbers get larger.

Numbering. The actual numbers printed go from 10 to 95, with some omissions due to compression of the scale. Computers like the Airtour CRP – 5 have a rotatable cursor and by moving this around the graduated scale it is possible to select any value from 10 to 99·9. Since only whole numbers are printed on the scale any decimal point has to be mentally inserted. This may seem to be a drawback when compared to an electronic calculator but in fact it gives the circular slide rule great flexibility. By mentally moving the decimal point to the right or the left a selected number on the scale can be used to represent any one of a whole range of numbers. For instance half way between the third and fourth small division to the right of 22 can be used to represent 22·7; 2·27; 22700; 0·227; 0·00227 etc.

3.8 When carrying out calculations on the circular slide rule particular care has to be taken when positioning the decimal point in the *final* answer. To ensure the correct positioning of the decimal point when reading off answers on the scale *carry out a rough check of the expected answer **before** programming the computer*. This is one of the golden rules when using *any* computing device from abacus through to a main-frame computer and reduces the chance of a nonsense answer being accepted as gospel. Nonsense answers are invariably the result of incorrect inputs to the computer by the human user. Examples of the rough checking procedure will be found throughout this book.

3.9 Reverting to distance conversions on the computer: On the outer scale of the circular slide rule at 10 will be seen **km – m – ltr** with a small vertical index line under the **m**, this being the index mark used for km input or readout during conversions involving km, nm and/or st m. The index marks for **naut m** and **stat m** will be seen at approximately 54 and 62 respectively, (see Fig. 3–3).

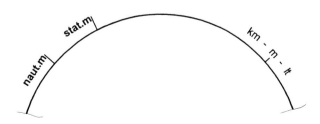

Fig. 3–3
Computer distance
conversion datums.

3.10 Suppose it is required to convert 972 nm into st m and km. First carry out a rough check of the expected answers. These do not have to be very precise, the aim being to make sure the decimal point goes in the correct place in the final answer. Referring back to paragraph 3.5, the conversion factors show 1 nm = 1·152 st m = 1·854 km, for the rough check the use of 1·1 and 2 respectively is good enough and in the example given 972 can be rounded up to 1000. Thus the rough check for 972 nm is 1000 × 1·1 = approximately 1100 st m and 1000 × 2 = approximately 2000 km. The computer is now programmed by turning the inner scale round until the known number (972) of nm is lined up with the **naut m** index on the outer scale. Use of the rotatable cursor can be of great assistance in both lining up with and reading off from index marks. Fig. 3–4 shows the computer set up.

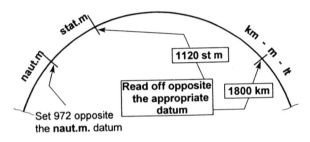

Fig. 3–4   Example of distance conversions.

Reading off opposite the **stat m** index gives 112, since the rough answer expected was 1100 the correct answer is therefore **1120 st m**. Opposite the **km** index is 18, rough answer 2000, therefore the correct answer is **1800 km**. *For rough working of distance conversions the following factors will give answers close enough for the correct positioning of the decimal point in the final answer:*

1 nm	= 1·1 st m	= 2 km
1 st m	= 0·9 nm	= 1·5 km
1 km	= 0·5 nm	= 0·6 st m

DEPARTURE

3.11 From the definition of a nm it follows that any N or S movement up or down a meridian will give a change of 1' of latitude for every nm moved. Conversely every minute of d'lat results in 1 nm of movement N or S. Movement due E or W is not quite so straightforward. Along the equator, which is a GC, a similar relationship exists as for up and down the meridians, that is to say 1' of d'long = 1 nm (of E/W movement). Due to the meridians converging towards the poles, at all lats other than the equator 1' of d'long < 1 nm (of E/W movement), becoming 0 nm at either pole (see Fig. 3–5). This is a Cosine relationship, being 1 (maximum) at 0° latitude and 0 at 90° latitude. E/W distance is given the title **Departure (Dept)** and it is derived from the formula:

Dept (nm E/W) = d'long (in minutes) × Cosine lat

Provided two of the elements are known the third can easily be resolved. This formula has several applications in navigation and will appear from time to time in this and other text books. It should be learnt by all licence candidates.

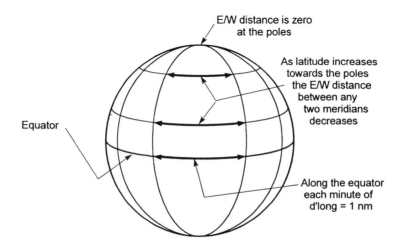

Fig. 3–5   E/W Distance between Meridians.

Example:

An aircraft sets out from 5347N 0928W. It is flown 275 nm due S followed by a further 124 nm due E. Calculate its position at the end of this flight.

Answer:

275 nm due S = 275' d'lat = 4° 35' d'lat S.

lat at end of first leg = 5347 N – 4° 35' = **4912 N.**

Dept = 124 nautical miles E at 4912 N.

124 = d'long (in minutes) E × Cosine 49° 12'.

124 / Cosine 49° 12' = d'long (in minutes) E.

124 / 0·6534 = 190' d'long = 3° 10' E d'long.

long at end of second leg = 0928 W – 3° 10' = **0618 W.**

Position at end of flight = **4912N 0618W** (see Fig. 3–6)

31

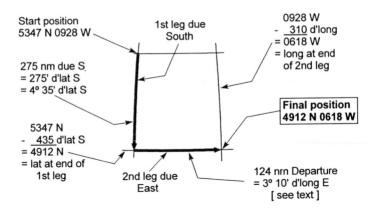

Start position
5347 N 0928 W

1st leg due
South

0928 W
- 310 d'long
= 0618 W
= long at end
of 2nd leg

275 nm due S
= 275' d'lat S
= 4° 35' d'lat S

Final position
4912 N 0618 W

5347 N
- 435 d'lat S
= 4912 N
= lat at end of
1st leg

2nd leg due
East

124 nm Departure
= 3° 10' d'long E
[see text]

Fig. 3–6   Change of position using d'lat and departure.

CONVERSION BETWEEN METRES AND FEET

3.12 Calculations to convert **Metres (m)** to **Feet (ft)** and vice versa mostly arise in problems concerned with altimetry and the selection of safe cruising levels, such problems are common in the meteorology and instrument papers. From time to time the navigation paper also comes up with a problem needing conversion between m and ft and candidates are advised

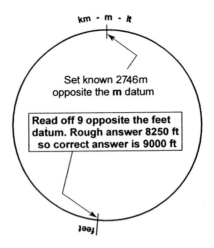

km - m - ft

Set known 2746m
opposite the m datum

Read off 9 opposite the feet
datum. Rough answer 8250 ft
so correct answer is 9000 ft

feet

Fig. 3–7   Conversion between Metres and Feet.

to be on the lookout for the need to convert from one to the other as needed. Conversion is carried out on the circular slide rule in the same way as the nm, st m and km conversions, the **m** at the 10 on the outer scale and the **feet** datum line near 33 on the outer scale being the appropriate index marks. There are 3·2808333 ft in a m so for the initial rough check multiply the number of m by 3 to approximate the answer in ft, similarly divide the number of ft by 3 to approximate the answer in m.

Example:
Convert 2746 m to ft.
Answer:
Rough check 2750 × 3 = approximately 8250 + ft.
Set 2746 on the inner scale of the circular slide rule opposite the **m** index on the outer scale.
Opposite the **feet** index on the outer scale read off 9 on the inner scale.
Rough check 8250 + ft therefore the correct answer is **9000 ft** (and not 900 ft or 90,000 ft), (see Fig. 3–7)

CHAPTER 4

SPEED

4.1 Speed is rate of movement. It can be expressed in many ways and different units of measurement. This chapter will only be dealing with those aspects of speed applicable to aircraft navigation.

AERONAUTICAL UNITS OF SPEED

4.2 Rate of movement is how much distance is being covered in a specified time. In aviation it is most commonly expressed in units of distance per hour. Chapter 3 introduced the distance units of nm, st m and km. Speeds expressed in these units per hour have their own names:

Nm per hour are known as **Knots (kn)**, a nautical derivative from the days of sailing ships when a rope with knots along its length was trailed behind the ship. The faster the ship went more of the rope was visible from the stern and the number of knots revealed indicated the speed of the ship through the water.

St m per hour are known as **Miles per hour (mph)**.

Km per hour are known as **Kilometres per hour (kph)**.

Since these units of speed are based on the standard units of distance, the ratios for conversion are the same. The same index marks on the navigation computer used for conversion of distances are used for speed conversions. Just imagine each index mark has 'per hour' added to turn it into a speed index. The same rules of rough checking before setting up the computer apply.

SPEEDS USED IN AVIATION

4.3 In aviation the measurement of speed can be expressed in several different ways. These are:

> Indicated airspeed (IAS)
> Rectified airspeed (RAS)
> True airspeed (TAS)
> Equivalent airspeed (EAS)
> Ground speed (GS)
> Mach number (M No)

34

Apart from GS all of these are explained in detail in the instruments syllabus, nonetheless some level of clarification is needed before proceeding with navigation proper. Note: In American aviation the equivalent of RAS is known as Calibrated Airspeed (CAS).

4.4 The Air Speed Indicator (ASI) measures the difference between the Pitot (or Total) pressure and the Static pressure, this difference being the Dynamic pressure due to forward movement of the aircraft. Dynamic pressure is generated by the number of air molecules that collide with the forward faces of the aircraft as it moves through the air and will therefore vary with air density and the true speed of the aircraft through the air (its TAS). The ASI is calibrated to indicate speed on the assumption that air density has a fixed value of 1225 grams/cubic metre. This causes it to give the same readout for a given amount of dynamic pressure no matter what combination of air density and TAS has produced it. Since the control of an aircraft is directly related to dynamic pressure, this means the ASI reading required for any manoeuvre will be the same at any altitude. Although this makes for ease of control it means that the TAS is rarely the same as the speed shown on the ASI. Since the density of air decreases with the decrease in pressure as an aircraft climbs to altitude, it follows that in the majority of flight conditions the TAS will be greater than the IAS displayed on the ASI. TAS is fundamental to navigational and fuel requirement problems and the procedures for calculation of TAS on the navigation computer are given in the following paragraphs. Note: 1225 grams/cubic metre (g/cub m) is the *assumed* **mean sea level (msl)** air density in the **International Standard Atmosphere (ISA)** which is used in the calibration of pressure instruments.

4.5 The 'raw' reading on the face of the ASI is the IAS and has first to be corrected for any errors in sensing of the Pitot and Static pressures (position error) as well as any anomalies in the individual instrument (instrument error). These two errors are usually calibrated together and a correction table produced over the operating speed range and for various flap and landing gear configurations. These corrections are usually quite small and when applied to the IAS give the corrected speed known as RAS. RAS is used in conjunction with the **Correct Outside Air Temperature (COAT)** and the pressure altitude to solve for TAS on the Navigation computer. Note: Differences in inputs and procedures found on many American Navigation computers are briefly covered in paragraph 4.8.

CONVERSION OF RAS TO TAS (TAS < 300 kn)

4.6 Rotate the inner disc of the circular slide rule to align the **COAT** on the outer edge of the **AIR SPEED** window with the pressure altitude (altitude with 1013 mb set on the altimeter sub-scale) inside the window.

Opposite the value of the RAS on the inner circular slide rule scale read off the value of the TAS on the outer slide rule scale. Use of the rotating cursor, where available, will make for easier alignment and read off.

Example:
Pressure altitude 21,000 ft. COAT -32 C. RAS 174 kn. What is the TAS?
Answer:
In the **AIR SPEED** window set 21 (pressure altitude × 1000 ft) opposite -32 C on the **COAT** scale. Position the cursor through the RAS of 174 kn on the inner scale and read off the **TAS of 238 kn** on the outer scale (see Fig. 4–1).

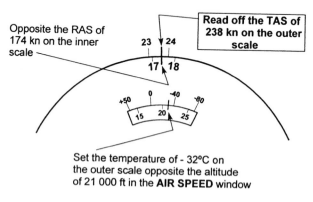

Opposite the RAS of 174 kn on the inner scale

Read off the TAS of 238 kn on the outer scale

Set the temperature of - 32°C on the outer scale opposite the altitude of 21 000 ft in the **AIR SPEED** window

Fig. 4–1   RAS to TAS (TAS>300kn).

Note:- As an aide memoir the AIRTOUR CRP-5 computer has a **red RAS** on the inner slide rule scale between 35 and 40 and a **red TAS** in the same position on the outer scale. Most makes of navigation computer have some similar form of reminder on them.

CONVERSION OF RAS TO TAS (TAS > 300 kn)

4.7 At high TAS air becomes compressed causing an extra pressure over and above normal Pitot pressure to be sensed by the ASI. In the ASI a modification to the calibration formula eliminates this error at the calibration density of 1225 g/cub m, but this correction does not hold good above 300 kn TAS when flying at levels where the air density is less than 1225 g/cub m. The uncorrected residual error is non-linear and gets larger the higher and faster the aircraft is being flown. This uncorrected compressibility factor results in the TAS found on the computer coming out at a higher value that the correct TAS. Any time the conversion of RAS to TAS on the computer results in an initial TAS in excess of 300 kn a *subtractive* correction has to be made using the

COMP.CORR. (compressibility correction) window on the computer as follows:

Having calculated RAS to TAS (as described in paragraph 4.6) and arrived at an initial TAS in excess of 300 kn, apply the TAS found into the formula printed by the **COMP.CORR.** window, i.e. **TAS/100 – 3 Div.**

The answer this gives is the number of divisions that the arrow pointing at the **COMP.CORR.** window has to be moved to the *left* against the scale visible in the window. This scale varies and has large spacing at high altitudes and very close spacing at low altitudes, in fact at msl it is at infinity.

Rotating the inner scale to the left to reposition the pointer will align the RAS opposite a lower value of TAS on the outer scale, this being the correct TAS to use for navigation purposes.

Example:

Pressure altitude 33 000 ft, COAT -50 C, RAS 266 kn. Calculate the correct TAS.

Answer:

In the **AIR SPEED** window set 33 (pressure altitude × 1000 ft) opposite -50 C on the **COAT** scale. Opposite the RAS of 266 kn on the inner slide rule scale read off the initial TAS of 450 kn on the outer scale. Since this is over 300 kn enter the 450 kn initial TAS into the formula giving 450/100 – 3 Div = 1·5 Divisions. Moving the inner disc to the left 1·5 divisions in the **COMP.CORR.** window repositions the RAS of 266 kn opposite the correct **TAS of 435 kn** (see Fig. 4–2).

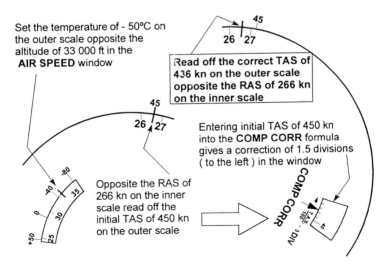

Fig. 4–2   RAS to TAS (TAS >300kn)

4.8 Most American navigation computers are labelled **CAS** as opposed to RAS (see paragraph 4.2) and programmed to use **Indicated Air Temperature (IAT)** instead of COAT. COAT is, as its name implies, the actual temperature of the air surrounding the aircraft. COAT is also known as the **Static Air Temperature (SAT)** and IAT as the **Total Air Temperature (TAT)**. As the aircraft moves through the air its forward faces are striking air molecules which release kinetic energy in the form of heat. This leads to temperature rises on, amongst other things, the external air temperature probe feeding the Air Temperature Gauge. The IAT shown on the gauge will therefore be warmer than the COAT, the actual amount of heating varies with the TAS, a fairly accurate rule of thumb goes:

$$\textbf{Kinetic heating temperature rise} = \textbf{(TAS / 100)}^2 \, \textbf{°C}$$

An accurate scale of Temperature Rise v TAS is to be found on many navigation computers. A check against such a scale shows only small discrepancies in this rule of thumb. The use of IAT on a computer means that in flight the IAT reading of the temperature gauge can be used to input the computer directly. It does mean however that pre-flight planning require the meteorology forecast temperatures (which are expected COAT) to be modified for expected temperature rise to give an IAT for planning purposes. Another difference often found is in the way compressibility is corrected. Instead of a **COMP.CORR.** window a correction factor table is supplied. This may be printed on the slide of the computer or within the computer handbook. The table is entered with the pressure altitude and the CAS and a correction factor (of less than one) extracted. The initial TAS is then multiplied by this factor to give the correct TAS.

MACH NUMBER (M No.)

4.9 This is the ratio of the aircraft's TAS to the local speed of sound (the local speed of sound at msl is in the region of 660 kn, varying with changes in the COAT). The significance of M No on the handling of the aircraft at high speed and high altitude is covered in detail in the Instrument syllabus. The Navigation examination is only concerned with the conversion of M No to TAS on the navigation computer. The previous examples of RAS to TAS problems employed the **AIR SPEED** window of the circular slide rule. M No to TAS uses the same window but it has to be rotated clockwise until the highest pressure altitude indicated on the scale in the window has been passed (on the CRP-5 this is 75,000 ft) to reveal an arrow head labelled **Mach No. Index** pointing at the **COAT** scale. To convert M No to TAS align the **Mach No. Index** with the COAT at the level being flown, locate the M No on the inner scale of the circular rule and read off the TAS opposite it on the outer scale. (see Fig. 4–3.)

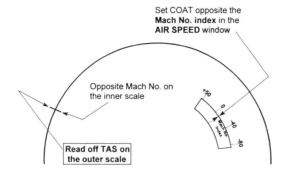

Fig. 4–3   COAT, Mach No. and TAS set up on the Navigation Computer.

Setting the **Mach No. Index** opposite COAT + 50 and reading off against Mach 1·0 the TAS is seen to be 700 kn whereas at COAT – 80 the TAS opposite Mach 1·0 is only 541 kn. At Mach 1·0 the TAS = local speed of sound and the above two calculations show how the local speed of sound varies with the COAT. If the same two settings are repeated it will be seen that the **COMP. CORR.** window is empty in both cases, the inference being that no correction is required for compressibility effects even though the TAS is greater than 300 kn. This is in fact correct as compressibility error is calibrated out in the mechanism of the Machmeter itself. With a fixed index and three variables if any two of the variables are known the computer will solve for the unknown third variable.

Example:
COAT – 46 C, M 0·8. What is the TAS?
Answer:
Align the **Mach No. Index** opposite the COAT of – 46 C. Opposite M 0·8 on the inner circular slide rule scale read off the **TAS of 468 kn** on the outer scale. (see Fig. 4–4a.)

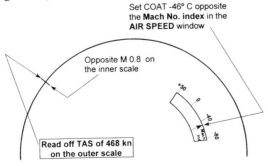

Fig. 4–4a   Finding the TAS from Mach No and COAT.

Example:

COAT – 20 C, TAS 390 kn. What is the Mach no?

Answer:

Align the **Mach No. Index** opposite the COAT of – 20 C. Opposite the TAS of 390 kn on the outer scale of the circular slide rule read off **M 0·63** on the inner scale (see Fig 4–4b).

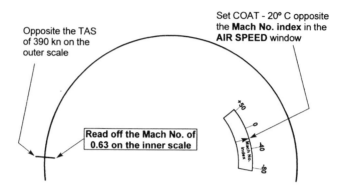

Fig 4–4b   Finding the Mach No from COAT and TAS.

Example:

If M 0·78 gives a TAS of 445 kn what is the COAT?

Answer:

Align M 0·78 on the inner scale of the circular slide rule with the TAS of 445 kn on the outer scale. Read off the **COAT** of – **57 C** opposite the **Mach No. Index** (see Fig. 4–4c.)

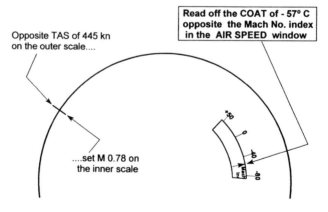

Fig.4–4c   Finding the COAT from Mach No and TAS.

GROUND SPEED (GS)

4.10 This is, as its name implies, the speed of the aircraft relative to the ground surface over which it is flying. GS and the actual track of the aircraft are the end results of the wind effect on the hdg and TAS of the aircraft. This is covered in depth in Chapter 5.

SPEED, DISTANCE AND TIME

4.11 The relationship between speed, distance and time is a major factor in both the planning and execution of any flight:

If an expected GS is calculated, how long will it take to cover a known distance?
If a known GS is flown for a given time, how far will the aircraft fly over the ground?
If a known distance is covered in a measured time interval, what is the GS?

All are questions that can arise many times in planning or in flight. It was stated in Chapter 3, paragraph 3.7 that the circular slide rule of the navigation computer is basically a device for solving ratios. Any relationship that can be expressed in the form A / B = C / D can be set up on the circular slide rule in the way shown in Fig. 4–5 and provided the value of any three of the variables is known the value of the fourth can be read off.

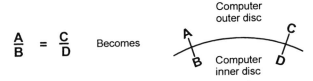

$$\frac{A}{B} = \frac{C}{D} \quad \text{Becomes}$$

Fig. 4–5   Setting up a ratio on the Navigation Computer.

4.12 The relationship between speed, distance and time is one that lends itself to solving for unknowns by this method. GS is the distance travelled over the earth's surface in 60 minutes (mins), or 1 hour (hr), so in 30 mins (half the time) it will cover half the distance it would have covered in 60 mins (i.e. half the GS). That is to say the distance covered is in the same ratio to the GS as the time gone is to 60 mins. This can be written in the ratio form:

$$\frac{\text{Speed}}{60 \text{ (min)}} = \frac{\text{distance}}{\text{time (min)}}$$

If the speed used is GS then the distance will be ground distance. Similarly if the speed used is TAS then the distance will be air distance and if the speed used is wind speed the distance will be wind distance. It is also important to remember that speed in kn goes with distance in nm, speed in mph goes with distance in st m and speed in kph goes with distance in km.

Avoid mixing units, *always* compare like with like! In the same way note that the times in this ratio are quoted in mins. This is because on a slide rule the use of hrs would require mins to be converted to a decimal part of an hr (i.e. 1 hr 47 min would have to be entered as 1·783333 hrs!) it is quicker and more accurate to work in mins (1 hr 47 mins = 107 mins).

4·13 In the ratio mentioned in paragraph 4.12 the number 60 is a constant, it is also a constant for other navigational calculations as will be seen in later Chapters. Because it is such an important constant it is highlighted on the inner scale of the circular slide rule of all navigation computers, usually by a triangular pointer as on the AIRTOUR CRP-5 COMPUTER. Many computers also have an hrs and mins scale inset on the inner scale to help with quick conversion into mins (see Fig. 4–6.)

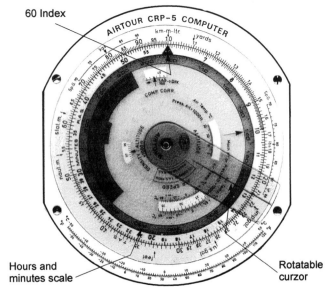

Fig. 4–6 The CRP-5 Circular Slide Rule showing the 60 Index and Hours and Minute Scale.

4.14 The ratio in paragraph 4.12 is set up on the circular slide rule as shown in Fig. 4–7. Provided any two of the variables is known the third can be solved.

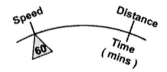

Fig. 4–7 Distance, Speed and Time ratio set up.

42

Example:
GS = 285 kn, distance to go 346 nm. How long will it take?
Answer:
Rough check. Calling it 350 nm at 300 kn; 350 nm at 5 nm / min gives a rough answer of 70 mins.

Rotate the inner scale to align **60** with the GS of 28(5) kn on the outer scale. Locate the distance of 34(6) nm on the outer scale and read off 7(3) opposite it on the inner scale. The rough check puts the answer in the region of 70 mins, therefore the correct answer is **73 mins** = 1 hour 13 mins (see Fig. 4–8.)

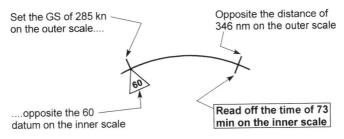

Fig. 4–8   *Computer set up to solve for Time*

Example:
GS 196 kn, what distance will be covered in 17 mins?
Answer:
Rough check. Calling it 15 mins (0·25 hour) at 200 kn gives a rough answer of 50 nm.

Rotate the inner scale to align **60** with the GS of 19(6) kn on the outer scale. Locate the time of 17 mins on the inner scale and read off 55(5) opposite it on the outer scale. The rough check puts the answer in the region of 50 nm therefore the correct answer is **55·5 nm.** (see Fig. 4–9.)

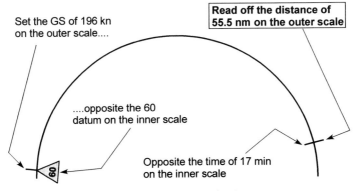

Fig. 4–9   *Computer set up to solve for Distance.*

Example:
An aircraft covers 154 nm over the ground in 21 mins. What is its GS?
Answer:
Rough check. Calling it 150 nm in 20 mins (a third of an hour) gives a rough answer of 450 nm in 60 mins or 450 kn.

Rotate the inner scale to align the known time of 21 mins on the inner scale with the known distance of 15(4) nm on the outer scale. Opposite the 60 (mins) datum on the inner scale read off 44(0) on the outer scale. The rough check put the answer in the region of 450 kn therefore the correct answer is **440 kn GS.** (see Fig. 4–10.)

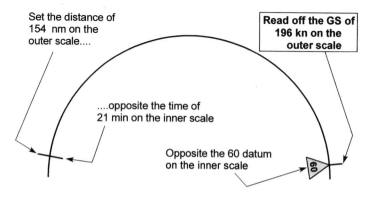

Set the distance of 154 nm on the outer scale....

Read off the GS of 196 kn on the outer scale

....opposite the time of 21 min on the inner scale

Opposite the 60 datum on the inner scale

Fig. 4–10   Computer set up to solve for GS.

4.15 One mistake that can be made, especially by newcomers to the circular slide rule, is that of reading the answer off in the wrong direction. For example if, in the first of the three examples above, having set **60** on the inner scale opposite 285 on the outer scale the distance of 346 nm had been erroneously located on the inner scale a very wrong answer of 16(4) would have been obtained on the outer scale! Such an error should be instantly detected *provided the rough check had been carried out first.* As a further help most computers have mind joggers on them. For instance the CRP – 5 has the word **minutes** printed in red between 30 and 35 on the inner scale to remind users that the inner scale is for time entries, leaving the outer scale for (in this case) distances and speeds.

Section 2

Basic Navigation Techniques

Aircraft fly in air which is itself moving relative to the earth. Movement of the air, better known as wind, is variable in both direction and speed depending on the weather situation. The path and speed of an aircraft relative to the ground over which it is flying (known as the track and groundspeed) is the end product of the vector generated by the heading and true airspeed of the aircraft and the local wind velocity vector. Knowing how to use these vectors during both the planning of a flight and the conduct of the flight itself are fundamental to navigation and flight safety.

Unless an aircraft is equipped with means of in-flight refuelling (mainly a military requirement) it has to be operated within the available fuel in the tanks at start up. Knowledge of the fuel load carried and the monitoring of its consumption are vital cockpit functions.

In some circumstances cockpit workload and lack of space call for simplified navigation techniques, this is especially true of single pilot operations in light aircraft or helicopters. This leads to a form of navigation known as Pilot Navigation which requires careful preparation of maps before flight and uses visual map reading and rules of thumb (based on logic) when in flight. Professional pilots also employ many of these techniques on the flight deck of large aircraft using information from sources other than visual ones.

This section is concerned with the basics of these techniques.

CHAPTER 5

THE TRIANGLE OF VELOCITIES

THE THREE BASIC VELOCITY VECTORS

5.1 In the introduction to this section three vectors were briefly mentioned. These constitute what is known as the triangle of velocities. They are:

Aircraft Heading and True Airspeed (hdg / TAS) relative to the air.
Aircraft Track and Groundspeed (trk / GS) relative to the earth.
Wind Velocity (WV), the wind direction and speed of the air relative to the earth.

Unlike the hdg and trk of an aircraft, which are always expressed as the direction *towards* which movement is taking place, wind directions are always given as the direction *from* which the wind is blowing (another inheritance from the days of sailing ships). This sometimes confuses newcomers to navigation but with usage it soon becomes second nature. The vector of WV is added to the vector of hdg / TAS to give the resultant vector of trk/GS. Fig. 5–1 shows an example of a vector triangle.

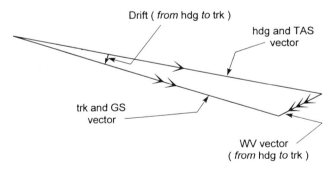

Fig.5–1   The Vector Triangle

This Figure also introduces the conventional symbols used for the three vectors:

A single arrow-head for hdg/TAS.
Two arrow-heads for trk/GS.
Three arrow-heads for WV.

The point of the arrows indicates the direction of movement in each case, the length of each vector represents the speed (all to a common scale).

DRIFT

5.2 Also illustrated in Fig. 5–1 is **Drift**, this is the angle between the hdg of the aircraft and its trk over the earth. Drift is *always* measured *from* hdg *to* trk and *never* the other way round! Fig. 5–2a shows a hdg of 049 (T) and a trk of 045 (T) giving a drift of 4° to the left or **Port**. Fig. 5–2b shows a hdg of 284 (T) and a trk of 295 (T) the drift in this case being 11° to the right or **Starboard**.

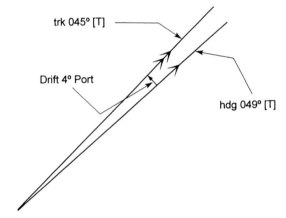

Fig. 5–2a   Port Drift.

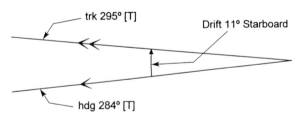

Fig.5–2b   Starboard Drift.

Once again the nautical origins of navigation arise with the use of the terms Port and Starboard, terms which unfortunately must be mastered. A useful mnemonic is the one about the customer enquiring of the wine merchant:

'Have you any RED PORT LEFT ?'

Red being the navigation light which is carried on the **Port** or **Left** wing of an aircraft. Drift angle is often expressed by a number followed by P or S, thus in the two cases already cited drifts are 4P and 11S respectively, the use of the degree sign in the case of drift angles seems to have become optional. It is of interest to note that electronic computers on equipment such as Inertial Navigation Systems have adopted **L** and **R** for Left and Right drift in place of P and S.

5.3 There are three situations when the drift angle will be 0° and the trk will be the same as the hdg:

When there is no wind at all, i.e. flat calm. In such a case the GS will be the same as the TAS. (see Fig. 5–3a).

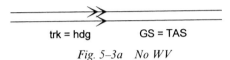

Fig. 5–3a   No WV

When the aircraft is heading directly into the wind, i.e. a headwind. In such a case the GS = TAS – Windspeed.(see Fig. 5–3b).

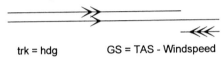

Fig. 5–3b   Headwind.

When the aircraft is heading directly downwind, i.e. a tailwind. In such a case the GS = TAS + Windspeed. (see Fig. 5–3c).

Fig. 5–3c   Tailwind.

It follows that the GS must *always* fall somewhere within the range of TAS – or + Windspeed. Any time there is a tailwind element GS > TAS and with a headwind element GS < TAS. These basic facts should always be used to check for possible errors in GS due to programming mistakes on the slide side of the navigation computer (how this is done is explained later in this Chapter). Another point that Figs. 5–1 & 5–2 highlight is that apart from the 0° drift cases the *trk always lies downwind of the hdg.*

5.4   In Fig. 5–4a an aircraft is shown flying on a hdg of 269 (T) at a TAS of 170 kn, the WV is 150 (T) / 30 kn giving a trk of 277 (T) at a GS of 187 kn the drift being 8S. Although the diagram shows all the vectors of the triangle of velocities the actual movement of the aircraft is along the trk / GS vector with its nose pointing towards 269 (T). Fig 5–4b illustrates this showing the 8S drift *from* hdg *to* trk and the trk lying downwind of hdg.

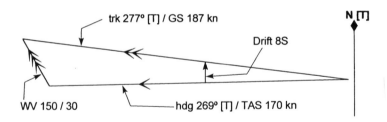

Fig. 5–4a   Vector Triangle with values.

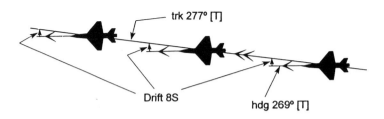

Fig. 5–4 b   Aircraft flying down the trk showing drift angle.

THE BASIC VECTOR TRIANGLE PROBLEMS

5.5   In any vector triangle there are six elements, three directions and three speeds. Provided any four of these elements are known it is possible to solve for the other two. Considering the navigation vector triangle the elements are:

hdg / TAS (signified by a single arrow-head).
Trk / GS (signified by two arrow-heads).
WV (signified by three arrow-heads).

In practical navigation terms there are only three cases of solving for two unknowns that need to be considered, these are:

Finding WV from known hdg / TAS and trk / GS.
Finding trk / GS from known hdg / TAS and WV.
Finding hdg and GS from known WV, TAS and desired trk.

How these problems are solved will first be illustrated in the rather long (and in one case cumbersome) method of drawing out the complete vector triangle of velocities. The slide side of the navigation computer will then be introduced to show how the same problems are solved on this instrument in simpler and faster ways.

50

GEOMETRICAL SOLUTIONS

5.6   Finding the WV. WV varies with altitude, time and place and it is these continual changes that generate the majority of navigation problems. A pilot knows from his instruments what the hdg/TAS is. If the current trk/GS is also known the WV can be solved by the vector triangle. Many aircraft still carry equipment known as 'Doppler'. Doppler is a radio aid that measures and indicates the drift and GS. The drift readout enables the trk to be calculated from the present hdg so the pilot of an aircraft fitted with Doppler has continual access to all the elements needed to find the WV. Any time an examination question quotes a Doppler drift and GS, candidates are in effect in a position to solve for trk/GS plus WV. Other techniques for finding current trk/GS are given in later Chapters.

Example:
hdg 157 (T) / TAS 145 kn ; trk 151 (T) / GS 130 kn. What is the WV?
Answer:
Fig. 5–5a shows the hdg/TAS and trk/GS vectors plotted to scale from a common start point. Drift from hdg to trk is 6P and since GS < TAS there is an element of headwind. Fig. 5–5b shows the same two vector with the WV vector drawn in blowing *from* hdg *to* trk. Using the same scale the length of the WV vector gives 21 kn as the windspeed and measurement of the angle shows the wind to be blowing *from* 198 (T). Answer: **WV is 198/21.**

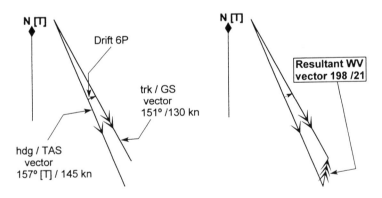

Fig. 5–5a   hdg/TAS and trk/GS vectors   Fig. 5–5b   Resultant WV Vector.

Note: Since wind speeds given by the Meteorological Office are in degrees (T) it is common practice to ignore quoting the (T) for winds based on (T) direction. Some navigation techniques employ winds based on (M) directions. In such cases (M) is written in after the direction to avoid possible errors. In the same way wind speeds are assumed to be in kn unless otherwise stated. These practices will be used throughout the rest of this book.

5 7   Finding trk/GS. Trk/GS are the end product of the hdg/TAS and WV vectors.

Example:
hdg 293 (T), TAS 210 kn, WV 165/30. What is the resultant trk / GS?
Answer:
Fig. 5–6a shows the hdg/TAS vector.

Fig. 5–6b has the WV vector added with the arrows following on from the end of the hdg/TAS vector.

The resultant vector of trk / GS is now drawn in from the start of the hdg/TAS to the end of the WV vector as in Fig. 5–6c. Measurement of this vector gives a trk of **299 (T)** and a **GS of 230 kn**. It also shows the drift to be **6S**.

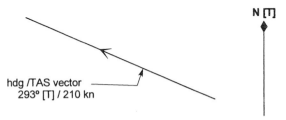

Fig. 5–6a   hdg/TAS vector.

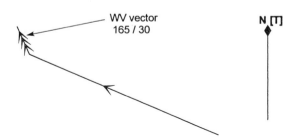

Fig. 5–6b   Added WV vector

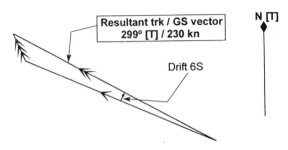

Fig. 5–6c   Resultant trk/GS vector

5.8 Finding hdg to steer and GS. Finding hdg to steer to make good a desired trk (using the aircraft's TAS and a known, or forecast WV) is both a basic pre-flight planning requirement and an in-flight navigation technique. The solution of hdg will complete the vector triangle enabling the expected GS to be measured. Because the unknowns are from different vectors the procedure for drawing the diagram has to be changed. This is illustrated in the following example.

Example:

Required trk 018 (T), TAS 300 kn, WV 150/80. Calculate the hdg (T) to steer and the resultant GS.

Answer:

Draw a line in the direction of the desired trk and mark with two arrows. GS is not known, it cannot be greater than TAS plus wind speed 300 + 80 = 380 kn, or less than TAS minus wind speed 300 – 80 = 220 kn (see paragraph 5.3). Make the length of the vector slightly longer than the greatest possible GS (see Fig. 5–7a).

At the end of the trk vector draw the WV vector blowing in towards the trk (see Fig. 5–7b).

From the beginning of the WV vector strike off an arc with a radius equal to the TAS so as to cut the trk vector near its beginning (see Fig. 5–7c).

Join the point where this arc cuts the trk to the beginning of the WV vector with a straight line to form the hdg/TAS vector and mark it with a single arrow-head pointing to the beginning of the WV vector (see Fig. 5–7d).

Measuring the direction of the hdg vector gives a **hdg of 029 (T)** and the length of the trk vector gives a **GS of 350 kn**. The drift works out as **11P**.

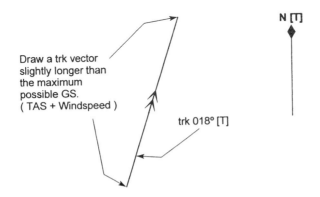

Fig. 5–7a   Vectorial solution to find hdg and GS. Step 1.

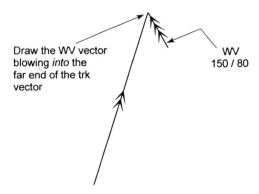

Draw the WV vector
blowing *into* the
far end of the trk
vector

WV
150 / 80

Fig. 5–7b   Vectorial solution to find hdg and GS. Step 2.

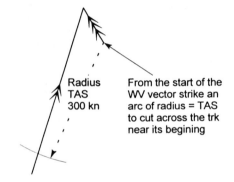

Radius
TAS
300 kn

From the start of the
WV vector strike an
arc of radius = TAS
to cut across the trk
near its begining

Fig. 5–7c   Vectorial solution to find hdg and GS. Step 3

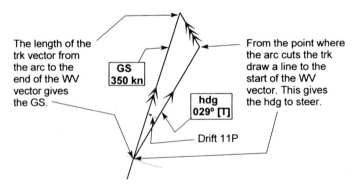

The length of the
trk vector from
the arc to the
end of the WV
vector gives
the GS.

GS
350 kn

From the point where
the arc cuts the trk
draw a line to the
start of the WV
vector. This gives
the hdg to steer.

hdg
029° [T]

Drift 11P

Fig. 5–7d   Vectorial solution to find hdg and GS. Step 4.

5.9   The above geometrical solutions of vector triangle problems are tedious and for the number of calculations involved in the preparation and execution of a flight would consume large quantities of paper and time.

Navigation computers have been developed in a variety of ways to speed up this calculation process. The simplest and most widely used system is a transparent direction plate backed by a speed and drift angle slide (see Fig. 5–8).

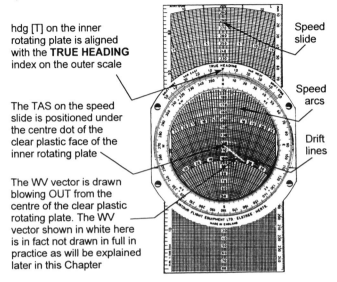

hdg [T] on the inner rotating plate is aligned with the **TRUE HEADING** index on the outer scale

Speed slide

Speed arcs

The TAS on the speed slide is positioned under the centre dot of the clear plastic face of the inner rotating plate

Drift lines

The WV vector is drawn blowing OUT from the centre of the clear plastic rotating plate. The WV vector shown in white here is in fact not drawn in full in practice as will be explained later in this Chapter

Fig. 5–8   A Typical navigation computer showing the rotating transparent direction plate and Speed and Drift Slide.

The navigation computer solution of the triangle of velocities concentrates on that part of the triangle where the WV vector is. Since the pilot is directly in control of hdg and TAS, computers are designed to have this vector displayed running up to the centre of the transparent disc, the triangle being correctly set up when:

The disc is rotated to have the hdg aligned with the **TRUE HEADING** index.
The slide is moved to set the TAS under the centre dot of the disc.
The WV vector is drawn blowing **Out** from the centre of the disc.

Under the end of the WV vector the GS can be read off against the speed arcs and the drift angle read off against the drift lines, hdg + S drift or – P drift giving the trk.

5.10 Reworking on the computer of the three previous examples is given below but beforehand a *word of warning* . There are a number of well meaning, but misguided, people around who advocate a different 'short cut' method for solving the hdg and GS problem which involves reversing the WV and switching the other vectors around. In the case of inexperienced students this frequently leads to confusion. In over a quarter of a century of teaching professional pilots, the author has had to spend a lot of time curing problems that have emanated as a result of trainees being introduced to this and other 'short cuts' before they had a sound grasp of the basics. Remember 'short cuts' are for the experts. Until you are an expert leave them alone!

5.11 Before demonstrating the computer techniques for solving the vector triangle problems take a look at the speed and drift angle slide. Most computers have a double sided slide, these may vary slightly in detail, the AIRTOUR CRP-5 COMPUTER being typical of the majority in its layout. The CRP-5 slide has a low speed side (marked **L** at the top right) with speed arcs 40 to 300 and a high speed side (marked **H** at the top right) with speed arcs from 150 to 1050. The **L** side has a squared section at the bottom which is used to calculate head and cross wind components on runways (covered in paragraph 5.16). Both sides of the slide have drift lines. Below the 100 speed arc on the **L** side and below the 300 speed arc on the **H** the lines are 2° of drift apart. At the higher speeds on each side the drift lines are 1° apart. Care must be taken not to read the 2° lines as 1° and vice versa. Fig. 5–9 illustrates both sides of the CRP-5 slide and highlights another feature common to most computer slides – the speed scale on the **L** side is more than double the speed scale on the **H** side.

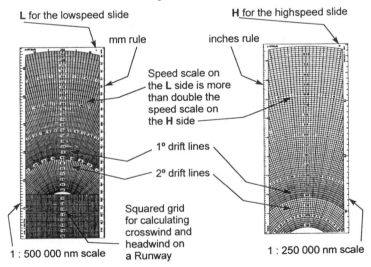

Fig. 5–9   The Low and High speed sides of the Navigation Computer Speed Slide.

This means that a WV vector marked on against the scale on one side of the computer will have to be remarked against the new scale if the slide is reversed during a calculation. This of course should not happen if the procedures for selecting the correct side of the slide are carried out as in the reworked examples that follow.

SOLUTIONS ON THE NAVIGATION COMPUTER

5.12 Finding the WV. Paragraph 5.6 had the example: hdg 157 (T) / TAS 145 kn, trk 151 (T) / GS 130 kn. What is the WV?

TAS is 145 kn and GS is 130 kn so select the **L** side of the slide and with the **L** on the slide and the **TRUE HEADING** index both uppermost move the slide up until the speed arc 145 kn (the TAS) is lying under the centre dot of the disc.

Now rotate the transparent disc to align the hdg of 157 (T) with the **TRUE HEADING** index. The hdg/TAS vector is now in place.

With hdg 157 (T) and trk 151 (T) the drift (*from* hdg *to* trk) is 6P. The trk of 151 (T) will be seen to be to the left of the **TRUE HEADING** index opposite the 6 division on the scale labelled **DRIFT PORT**, this confirms the drift already calculated.

Making certain not to move the hdg/TAS settings, take a soft lead pencil and mark a cross on the transparent disc over the point where the 6P drift line intersects the speed arc of the 130 kn GS (see Fig. 5–10a). The centre dot is the start of the WV vector and the pencil cross the end of it.

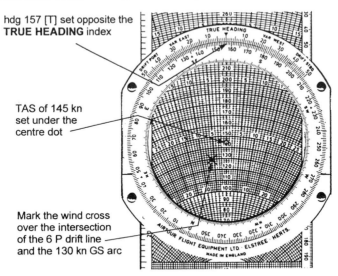

hdg 157 [T] set opposite the **TRUE HEADING** index

TAS of 145 kn set under the centre dot

Mark the wind cross over the intersection of the 6 P drift line and the 130 kn GS arc

Fig. 5–10a   Finding the WV from hdg/TAS and trk/GS. Step 1.

To measure this WV vector rotate the disc to place the pencil cross on the centre (0° drift) line *below* the centre dot of the disc, The direction under the **TRUE HEADING** index is the direction from which the wind is blowing and the length of the vector measured along the speed scale gives the wind speed (Fig. 5–10b.) In this case the **WV** read out is **198/21** the same as the answer found previously in paragraph 5.6.

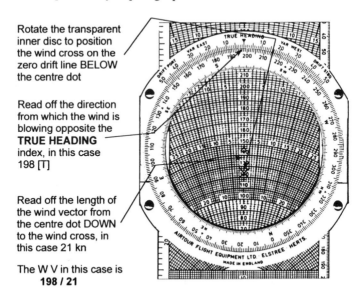

Rotate the transparent inner disc to position the wind cross on the zero drift line BELOW the centre dot

Read off the direction from which the wind is blowing opposite the **TRUE HEADING** index, in this case 198 [T]

Read off the length of the wind vector from the centre dot DOWN to the wind cross, in this case 21 kn

The W V in this case is **198 / 21**

Fig. 5–10b   Finding the WV from hdg/TAS and trk/GS. Step 2.

5.13 Finding trk/GS. Reworking the example from paragraph 5.7 on the computer requires the WV vector to be marked on first once the correct side of the slide has been selected. Here is the problem again: hdg 293 (T), TAS 210 kn, WV 165/30. What is the resultant trk/GS?

Checking the limits of the GS gives 210 – or + 30 kn, a range of 180 to 240 kn which could go on either the **L** or the **H** side of the slide. In such a case it is advisable to use the **L** side as its larger scale makes for greater accuracy. Insert the **L** slide into the computer but do not set the TAS under the centre dot just yet.

To set the WV vector, rotate the disc to align the wind direction of 165 (T) under the **TRUE HEADING** index and with a soft pencil mark in the end of the WV vector with a cross the appropriate number of speed units *below* the centre dot. The speed arcs can be used as a guide here; for instance in this case a vector of 30 units is required, if the 130 speed arc is positioned under the centre dot the cross is drawn over the point where the 100 speed arc intersects the centre line (see Fig. 5–11a).

With the wind cross marked now move the slide to position the speed arc of 210 kn (the TAS) under the centre dot and rotate the disc to align the hdg of 293 (T) under the **TRUE HEADING** index, the hdg/TAS vector is now set with the WV vector blowing *out* from its end (see Fig. 5–11b).

The wind direction of 165 [T] is set opposite the **TRUE HEADING** index

The wind cross is marked in on the zero drift line 30 kn BELOW the centre dot. In this case the 130 kn and 100 kn speed arcs are used as a means of ensuring that the vector length is correct

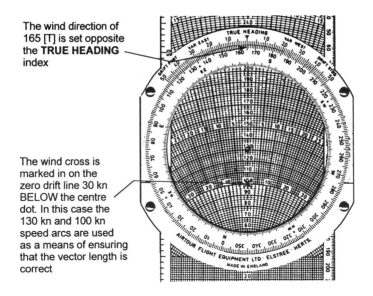

Fig.5–11a   Finding trk/GS from hdg/TAS and WV. Step 1.

The wind cross is seen to be lying over the intersection of the 6S drift line and the 230 speed arc. Going to the **DRIFT STBD** scale to the right of the **TRUE HEADING** index opposite the 6S mark read off the trk (T) of 299 (T) on the disc scale. Answer **trk 299 (T), GS 230 kn**, the same as found in paragraph 5.7.

hdg 293 [T] set opposite the **TRUE HEADING** index

TAS 210 kn set under centre dot

Under the wind cross read off the **GS 230 kn** and the drift 6° S

Opposite the 6° mark on the **DRIFT STBD** scale to the right of the **TRUE HEADING** index read off **trk 299 [T]**

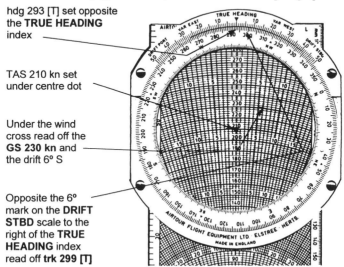

Fig.5–11b   Finding trk/GS from hdg/TAS and WV. Step 2.

59

5.14 The worked examples in paragraphs 5.11 and 5.12 illustrate the way the computer appears with all the vectors set on correctly as mentioned in paragraph 5.9:

The TAS is under the centre dot with the hdg opposite the **TRUE HEADING** index.

The WV vector is blowing **out** from the centre of the disc. (The whole vector is not needed, a cross marking the end of the vector being sufficient).

The GS lies under the end of the wind vector as indicated by the cross with trk lying along the drift line under the cross.

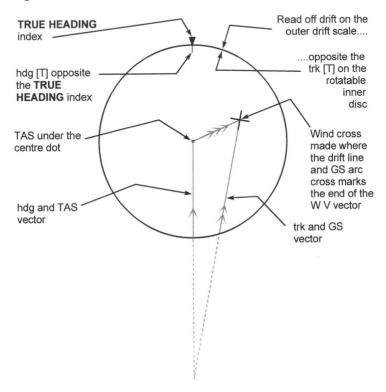

Fig. 5–12a   Appearance of the Navigation Computer set up solving for the WV.

Figs. 5–12a and b show, in a simplified form, this standard method of setting up the computer to solve triangle of velocity problems. In the two examples so far given two complete vectors were used to solve the third vector. The third problem is not so straightforward and requires a simple piece of logical drift balancing to achieve the standard set-up. It is at this point that an alternative 'short cut' method is sometimes advocated which involves plotting the WV vector in reverse, it also involves switching the other two vectors around and is altogether non-standard! Unlike the standard layout which can be used to solve *all* known vector triangle problems this alternative layout is limited in its uses and has been proven time and time again to be the prime cause of many pilots having problems, with basic navigation. This book will only deal with standard methods as used by professionally trained pilots. Readers are advised to learn the basics properly and not to get seduced into trying 'quick fix' methods.

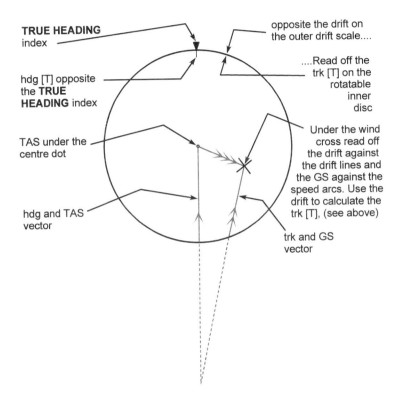

TRUE HEADING index

opposite the drift on the outer drift scale....

hdg [T] opposite the **TRUE HEADING** index

....Read off the trk [T] on the rotatable inner disc

TAS under the centre dot

Under the wind cross read off the drift against the drift lines and the GS against the speed arcs. Use the drift to calculate the trk [T], (see above)

hdg and TAS vector

trk and GS vector

Fig. 5–12b   Appearance of the Navigation Computer set up solving for trk (T) and GS.

5.15 Finding hdg to steer and GS. Here is the problem from paragraph 5.8 again:

Required trk 018 (T), TAS 300 kn, WV 150 / 80. Calculate the hdg (T) to steer and the resultant GS obtained.

GS range is from 300 – 80 kn to 300 + 80 kn = from 220 to 380 kn therefore select the **H** side of the speed slide.

With the wind direction of 150 (T) aligned under the **TRUE HEADING** index mark the wind cross 80 speed units **below** the centre dot.

Move the slide to position the 300 speed arc under the centre dot. The WV vector and TAS are now set.

The logic now goes like this, 'If drift were 0° the hdg would be the same as trk. So set trk direction opposite the **TRUE HEADING** index and see if drift is 0°. If it is not, rotate the disc *towards* the cross until the drift line under the cross is the same value as drift reading opposite the trk direction on the disc scale'. This is best illustrated by following the problem through.

Rotate the disc to align the desired trk direction of 018 (T) with the **TRUE HEADING** index (see Fig. 5–13a.) It is clear that drift is not 0° but 10P and if 018 (T) were steered it would result in a track of 008 (T)!

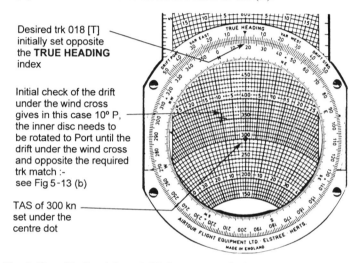

Desired trk 018 [T] initially set opposite the **TRUE HEADING** index

Initial check of the drift under the wind cross gives in this case 10° P, the inner disc needs to be rotated to Port until the drift under the wind cross and opposite the required trk match :- see Fig 5-13 (b)

TAS of 300 kn set under the centre dot

Fig. 5–13a   Finding hdg and GS from required trk WV and TAS. Step 1.

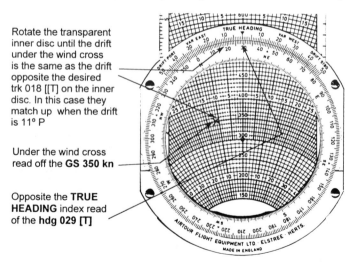

Rotate the transparent inner disc until the drift under the wind cross is the same as the drift opposite the desired trk 018 [[T] on the inner disc. In this case they match up when the drift is 11° P

Under the wind cross read off the **GS 350 kn**

Opposite the **TRUE HEADING** index read of the **hdg 029 [T]**

Fig. 5–13b   Finding hdg and Gs from required trk, WV and TAS. Step 2.

By rotating the disc towards the cross (anticlockwise for P drift) bring the trk direction under the 10P mark on the scale to the left of the **TRUE HEADING** index.

Check to see if the drift angle under the cross is still 10P. If it has changed, move the disc until the drifts under the cross and opposite the trk direction are identical. In this case they match up at 11P, the computer is now set-up in the standard way and the problem is solved (see Fig. 5–13b).

The **hdg** under the **TRUE HEADING** index is 029 (T) with the 11P drift giving the desired trk of 018 (T). At the same time the **GS of 350 kn** can be read off the speed arc under the cross. This is the same answer as in paragraph 5.8.

This explanation may seem longwinded but with very little practice this routine can be completed in seconds.

5.16 Finding the WV at a turning point. The slide side of the computer has other things to offer. It is possible to find the WV from a series of drifts found on different widely spaced headings, with no knowledge of the GS being available. This was a technique in common use before the advent of today's sophisticated aids. Although no longer considered a prime navigation technique it is still employed as a back-up check and occasionally the solution of a plotting question on the examination paper requires the candidate to exhibit knowledge of this technique.

Example:

An aircraft is approaching a turning point on a hdg of 327 (T) at a TAS of 156 kn with a drift of 7S (drift can be assessed in several ways, both visually and from various radio aids, the actual method is not relevant to this

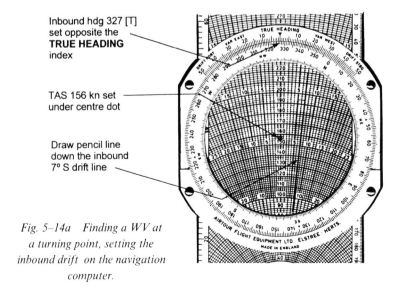

Inbound hdg 327 [T] set opposite the **TRUE HEADING** index

TAS 156 kn set under centre dot

Draw pencil line down the inbound 7° S drift line

Fig. 5–14a Finding a WV at a turning point, setting the inbound drift on the navigation computer.

example). At the turning point hdg is altered to 044 (T) with TAS unchanged. Once settled down on the new hdg the drift is checked and now found to be 3P. What is the WV in the vicinity of the turning point?

Answer:

With a TAS of 156 kn select the **L** side of the speed slide and position the speed arc for the TAS under the centre dot.

Rotate the disc to position the inbound hdg of 327 (T) opposite the **TRUE HEADING** index and with a soft pencil draw a line down the 7S drift line (see Fig. 5–14 a).

Now rotate the disc to position the outbound hdg of 044 (T) under the **TRUE HEADING** index, the TAS being unchanged leave the speed arc of 156 under the centre dot. (Had there been a change in the TAS on altering hdg the new TAS should be set at this point).

The outbound drift is now drawn in down the 3P drift line so as to cross the inbound drift line (see Fig. 5–14b).

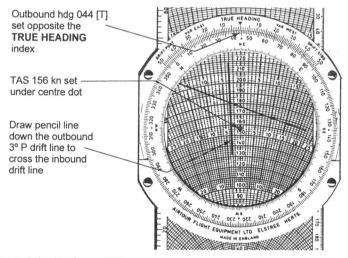

Outbound hdg 044 [T] set opposite the **TRUE HEADING** index

TAS 156 kn set under centre dot

Draw pencil line down the outbound 3° P drift line to cross the inbound drift line

Fig. 5–14b   Finding a WV at a turning point, setting the outbound drift on the navigation computer.

The intersection of the two drift lines is the wind cross marking the end of the wind vector. Rotating the disc to put this cross on the centre line *below* the centre dot enables the wind direction to be read off opposite the **TRUE HEADING** index and the wind speed to be assessed from the speed scale, the answer being a **WV of 202 / 26** (see Fig 5–14c).

The use of only two drifts to find a WV requires the hdg change to be large enough to give drift lines that cut at 90° + or – 20°, accuracy falling off rapidly with shallower cutting angles. The classic multi-drift wind finding method was to fly a 60° / 120° / 60° dog-leg (see Fig. 5–15). taking visual drifts on each leg, and adding time to the **Estimated Time of Arrive (ETA)** at the next turning point to correct for time lost on the diversion. All right at low level over the open sea but not practical over land in today's crowded and restricted airspace.

Rotate the transparent inner disc to position the wind cross formed by the drift lines on the zero drift line BELOW the centre dot

Read off the direction from which the wind is blowing opposite the **TRUE HEADING** index, in this case 202 [T]

Read off the length of the wind vector from the centre dot DOWN to the wind cross, in this case 28 kn

The W V in this case is **202 / 28**

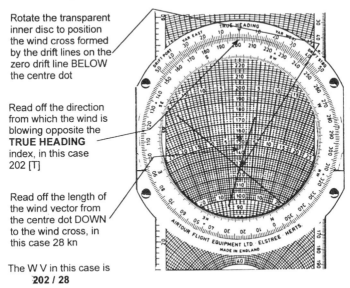

Fig. 5–14c   Finding a WV at a turning point, reading off the WV.

The drift is taken on all three hdgs and the W V found in the same way as described for finding the W V at a turning point, the three hdgs and drifts making for greater accuracy

Flying two sides of an equilateral triangle adds time to the ETA equal to the time spent on one leg

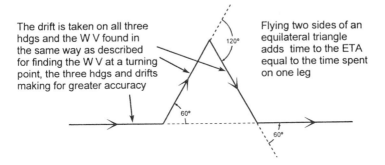

Fig. 5–15   The classic dog-leg method of finding a WV by multiple drifts.

HEAD AND CROSS-WIND COMPONENTS ON A RUNWAY

5.17 The squared grid (found at the bottom of the **L** side on the speed slide of most navigation computers) is used to calculate the headwind and cross-wind components for take off and landing to check that these are within the limits for the type of aircraft being operated. Because **Runway (RW)** directions are given to the nearest 10° (M) the aerodrome air traffic control always pass surface WV for take-off and landing in degrees (M) and kn. This is the only WV passed in degrees (M), WVs at all other levels are passed in degrees (T). Since RW direction and surface WV direction are both in (M) they can be directly compared with one another to check the head and cross-wind components (this can be achieved by using the **TRUE HEADING** index as if it were a **MAGNETIC HEADING** index). If the surface WV were passed in (T) it would be necessary either to convert it to (M) or the RW to (T) before they could be compared. (This is a non-standard element that is sometimes introduced in examination questions – so beware!)

To calculate the wind components start by moving the slide to position the centre dot over the top horizontal line of the squared grid and rotate the disc to align the surface wind direction opposite the **TRUE HEADING** index.
Mark in a wind cross below the centre dot using the scale of the squared grid.
Rotate the disc to align the RW direction opposite the **TRUE HEADING** index.
Using the squared grid read off the wind components from the top and centre lines.

Example:
RW 22 (i.e. 220 (M)), surface WV 260/25. What are the wind components on the RW?
Answer:
With centre dot over the top line of the grid, rotate the disc to align the wind direction of 260 with the **TRUE HEADING** index and mark in the wind cross 25 unit below the centre dot (see Fig. 5–16a).

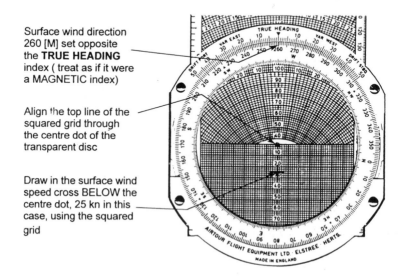

Surface wind direction 260 [M] set opposite the **TRUE HEADING** index (treat as if it were a MAGNETIC index)

Align the top line of the squared grid through the centre dot of the transparent disc

Draw in the surface wind speed cross BELOW the centre dot, 25 kn in this case, using the squared grid

Fig. 5–16a   Finding the wind components on a RW. Step 1.

RW direction 220 [M] set opposite the **TRUE HEADING** index (treat as if it were a MAGNETIC index)

The surface wind cross is displaced to one side showing there are both head and cross wind components in this case

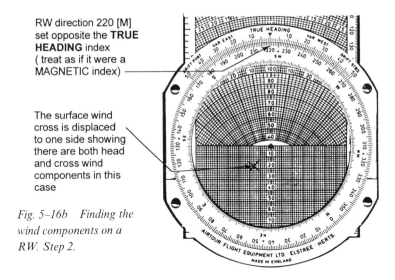

Fig. 5–16b   Finding the wind components on a RW. Step 2.

Now rotate the disc to align the RW direction of 220 with the **TRUE HEADING** index (see Fig. 5–16b).

Reading vertically down from the top line to the cross gives the **headwind** as **18 kn** and reading horizontally from the centre line to the cross gives the **crosswind** as **16 kn** from S (right) to P (left) (see Fig. 5–16c).

Reading across from the centre line to a vertical through the wind cross shows the cross wind component on the RW in this case to be 16 kn blowing from S to P

Reading down from the top of the squared grid to a horizontal through the wind cross shows the head wind component on the RW to be 18 kn in this case

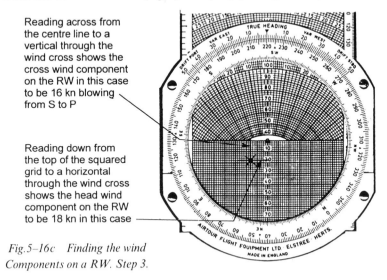

Fig.5–16c   Finding the wind Components on a RW. Step 3.

If a surface WV is marked on using the squared grid and the RW direction set results in the wind cross appearing above the squared grid (on the drift lines and speed circles) it means that there is a tail-wind on that particular

67

RW direction. The drift and speed circle readings in such a case have no validity and a more suitable RW giving a head-wind should be selected.

MAXIMUM ACCEPTABLE SURFACE WV ON A RUNWAY

5.18 Questions are sometimes set asking what is the maximum surface wind speed that could be blowing from a given direction without exceeding the given crosswind limits on a particular RW

To answer this type of question start as before by positioning the top line of the grid under the centre dot and rotating the disc to align the wind direction with the **TRUE HEADING** index.

Draw a vertical line down from the centre dot to the edge of the disc and then rotate the disc to align the RW direction with the **TRUE HEADING** index.

Horizontally across the top line of the grid mark off the crosswind limit from the centre dot on the side where the drawn wind direction line now lies. Draw a line vertically down from this mark to cut the wind direction line making a wind cross.

Rotating the disc to put the wind cross on the centre line below the centre dot enables the value of the maximum acceptable wind speed to be read off the grid.

Example:

RW 07, maximum allowable crosswind 18 kn. What is the maximum acceptable surface wind speed from a direction of 030 (M)?

Answer:

With the top line of the grid under the centre dot and the wind direction of 030 opposite the **TRUE HEADING** index draw the vertical down from the centre dot (see Fig. 5–17a).

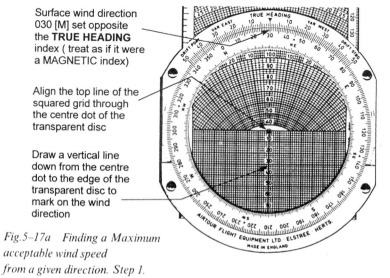

Surface wind direction 030 [M] set opposite the **TRUE HEADING** index (treat as if it were a MAGNETIC index)

Align the top line of the squared grid through the centre dot of the transparent disc

Draw a vertical line down from the centre dot to the edge of the transparent disc to mark on the wind direction

Fig.5–17a Finding a Maximum acceptable wind speed from a given direction. Step 1.

Rotate the disc to align the RW direction of 070 under the **TRUE HEADING** index which, in this case, puts the wind line to the right of the centre line (see Fig. 5–17b).

RW direction 070 [M]
set opposite the **TRUE
HEADING** index
(treat as if it were a
MAGNETIC index)

The surface wind
direction is now
displaced to the
right side of the
centre line

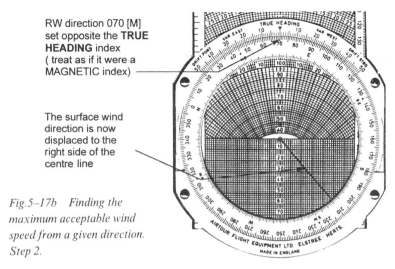

*Fig.5–17b   Finding the
maximum acceptable wind
speed from a given direction.
Step 2.*

Measure the 18 kn cross-wind limit horizontally to the right from the centre dot and draw a vertical down to cut the wind direction line forming the wind cross (see Fig. 5–17c).

Measure the maximum
acceptable cross wind
component, 18 kn in
this case, horizontally
from the centre line to
the side where the wind
direction line lies

Draw a line vertically
down from this point
to cut the wind direction
line making a wind
cross

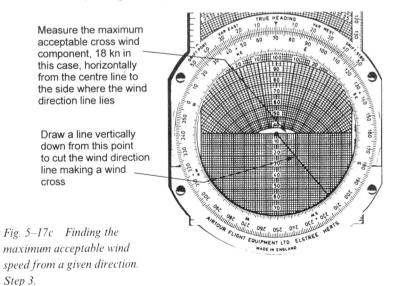

*Fig. 5–17c   Finding the
maximum acceptable wind
speed from a given direction.
Step 3.*

Rotating the disc to place the wind cross on the centre line below the centre dot enables the value of the maximum acceptable wind speed from 030 (M) to be read off as **28 kn** (see Fig. 5–17d).

Reset the surface wind direction 030 [M] opposite the **TRUE HEADING** index

Measure the maximum acceptable wind speed vertically down from the centre dot to the wind cross, in this case 28 kn

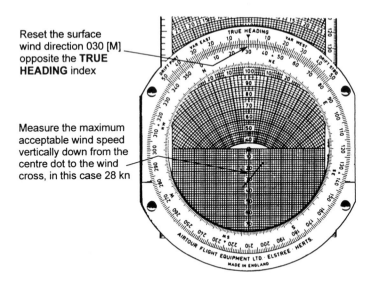

Fig. 5–17d   Finding the maximum acceptable wind speed from a given direction. Step 4.

CHAPTER 6

FUEL

6.1 Calculation of the fuel requirements for any flight and the monitoring of fuel consumption in flight are paramount to flight safety. At all times pilots must ensure that sufficient fuel is uplifted to cover the planned flight plus contingency fuel for possible air traffic delays or diversions. Detailed fuel planning for commercial flights is covered in the Flight Planning syllabus, the Navigation syllabus being restricted to dealing with the various different ways of measuring the volume and/or weight of fuel and the solution of basic fuel problems.

STANDARD UNITS OF VOLUME AND WEIGHT USED IN AVIATION

6.2 **Imperial Gallons and Pounds**. As the previous paragraph implied there is more than one standard used in aviation for the measurement of fuel volumes and weights. One system, which stems from the same Royal Statute that gave rise to the st m, has the **Imperial Gallon (Imp Gal)** as its measure for volume and the **Pound (lb)** as its measure for weight. 1 Imp Gal of water weighs 10 lb, or at least that was the original idea; the later adoption of more precise conditions of temperature and pressure under which such comparisons are carried out has modified this to a minute fraction over 10 lb of water to the Imp Gal (for practical problems in navigation the use of '1 Imp Gal of water weighs 10 lb' is an accurate enough starting point for calculating the weight of various fuel and oil loads).

6.3 **United States (US) Gallons**. The American system uses the same lb as in the Imperial system, the **US Gallon (US Gal)** however is smaller than the Imp Gal there being 1·2 US Gal to the Imp Gal.

6.4 **Litres and Kilogram**. As might be expected the third system in use is metric based, the unit of volume is the **Litre (lt)** which is 1000 cubic centimetres (cc) or 0·001 cubic metre. The weight of 1 lt of water giving rise to the metric unit of the **Kilogram (kg).**

CONVERSION FACTORS

6.5 In commercial aviation there is a definite trend towards standardisation onto the metric system of volumes and weights. However general aviation manufacturers in some countries seem loath to change to this common standard. Add to this the fact that there are still many aircraft of earlier vintages around with gauges and load sheets in gals (either Imp or US) and lbs means that pilots may be faced with the need to convert from one system to another. The conversion relationships are listed below:

1 Imp Gal = 1·2 US Gal = 4·546 lt
1 US Gal = 0·833 Imp Gal = 3·78833 lt
1 lt = 0·22 Imp Gal = 0·1833 US Gal
1 Imp Gal of water weighs 10 lb
1 US Gal of water weighs 8·33 lb
1 lt of water weighs 1 kg
1 kg = 2·205 lb
1 lb = 0·4546 kg

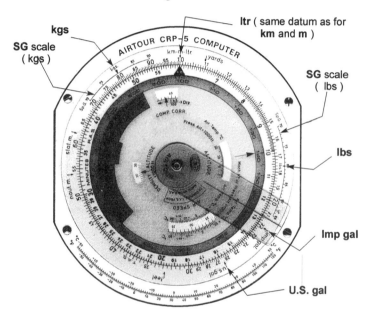

Fig. 6–1   The CRP–5 circular slide rule showing the fuel weight, volume and SG Datums.

The relationships are further complicated by the fact that aviation fuels and oils weigh less than water volume for volume, the amount varying from fuel to fuel and oil to oil. For a given volume the ratio of the weight of a fuel/oil to the weight of water is termed its **Specific Gravity (SG)** (referred to as 'relative density' in some physics text books). For instance if an Imp Gal of fuel weighed 7·4 lb as against 10 lb for an Imp Gal of water, the fuel would be said to have an SG of 0·74 (the ratio of 7·4 lb to 10 lb). In general terms the aviation fuels used in piston engines have an SG in the region of

0·72, gas turbine fuels have an SG in the region of 0·74 and most engine oils have an SG of around 0·8. Actual values for a specific fuel or oil are obtainable from the fuel suppliers. The SG of a fuel may be amended if large ambient temperature and pressure changes occur since this could affect the overall weight of fuel on board an aircraft possibly influencing its weight and balance calculations.

6.6 The circular slide rule of most navigation computers has index marks for carrying out all the conversions for fuel volumes and weights. The circular slide rule of the AIRTOUR CRP-5 is particularly well laid out, for once the known factors are correctly set on, all the possibly required answers can be read off from the one set-up. Fig. 6–1 shows the CRP-5 slide rule and its various fuel related indexes. Fig. 6–2 illustrates the various rough check calculations that should *always* be carried out *before* setting up the computer to solve fuel problems. Without such checks it is very easy to get the decimal point in the wrong place, especially when very large fuel loads are involved.

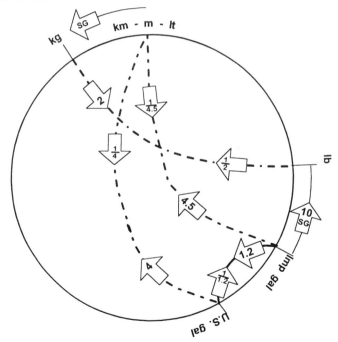

Fig. 6–2   Rough check fuel conversion factors.

6.7 Problems vary in that the fuel values may be given in Imp Gal, US Gal, lt, kg (with SG) or lb (with SG) and the solution may be required in any of the other forms:

Example:
2750 Imp Gal of fuel has an SG of 0·72, what is its volume in US Gal and lt and its weight in kg and lb?
Answer:
Rough checks. Round up to 2800 Imp Gal and call SG 0·7.
2800 Imp Gal × 4·5 = Approximately 12 600 lt
2800 Imp Gal × 1·2 = Approximately 3360 US Gal
2800 Imp Gal × SG 0·7 × 10 lb = Approximately 19,600 lb
12,600 lt × SG 0·7 × 1 kg = Approximately 8820 kg
Or 19,600 lb / 2 = Approximately 9800 kg
Setting the given value of 2750 Imp Gal on the inner scale opposite the **Imp Gal** index mark on the outer scale read off (on the inner scale):
12(5) opposite the **lt** index, rough check was 12,600 lt so the correct answer is **12,500 lt.**
33 opposite the **US Gal** index, rough check was 3360 US Gal so the correct answer is **3300 US Gal**.
19(82) opposite 0·72 on the **Sp.G** scale by the **lb** index, rough check was 19600 lb so the correct answer is **19,820 lb.**
9 opposite 0·72 on the **Sp.G** scale by the **lt** index, rough check was 8820 to 9800 kg so the correct answer is **9000 kg.** (see Fig. 6–3).

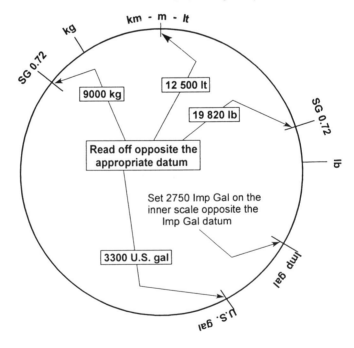

Fig. 6–3 2750 Imp Gal of fuel with SG of 0·72.

Example:

A volume of fuel with an SG of 0·74 weighs 24,600 kg. What is its weight in lb and its volume in lt, Imp Gal and US Gal?

Answer:

Rough checks. Round up to 25,000 kg and call SG 0·75

25,000 kg × 2 = Approximately 50,000 lb

25,000 kg / 0·75 = Approximately 33,000 lt

33,000 lt / 4·5 = Approximately 7000 Imp Gal

33,000 lt / 4 = Approximately 8000 US Gal

Setting the given value of 24,600 kg on the inner scale opposite 0·74 of the **Sp.G** scale by the kg index on the outer scale read off (on the inner scale) 54(4) opposite 0·74 on the **Sp.G** scale by the **lb** index, rough check was 50,000 lb so the correct answer is **54,400 lb**.

33(25) opposite the **lt** index, rough check 33,000 lt, so the correct answer is **33,250 lt**.

73(25) opposite the **Imp Gal** index, rough check was 7000 Imp Gal so the correct answer is **7325 Imp Gal**.

87(9) opposite the **US Gal** index, rough check was 8000 US Gal so the correct answer is **8790 US Gal**. (see Fig. 6–4).

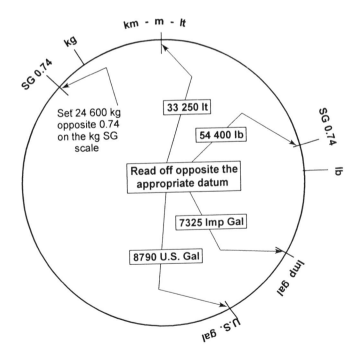

Fig. 6–4   24,600 kg of fuel with SG of 0·74.

FUEL FLOW AND FUEL CONSUMPTION

6.8 The fuel required for any flight depends on how long the flight is planned to last (this to include time on route plus diversion and holding time) and the rate of fuel consumption of the aircraft known as its fuel flow. Fuel flow can vary with changes in altitude, COAT, MNO/RAS and decreasing all-up-weight as fuel is burned off. Calculation of the fuel flow taking these factors into account does not form part of the Navigation syllabus but will be needed by candidates sitting the Flight Planning examinations. Flight Planning text books explain how to use the appropriate data sheets and graphs to extract the correct fuel flow for each situation. The *basic* rules of fuel calculation are common to all types of aircraft and are very similar to the GS/distance/time problems (see Chapter 4, paragraphs 4.11 to 4.14) in their solution. Substitution of fuel flow for GS and fuel for distance gives the ratio:

$$\frac{\text{fuel flow}}{60} = \frac{\text{fuel required (or used)}}{\text{time (mins)}}$$

The fuel units must of course be in the same units as the fuel flow (do not mix lb with kg, or Imp Gal with US Gal or lt in the same equation). In the same way as with the GS/distance/time problems if any two of the three variables are known the third can be solved on the circular slide rule of the navigation computer:

Example:
Flight time for a leg of a flight is 43 mins. If the fuel flow on the leg is 2350 kg / hr how much fuel will be consumed flying the leg?
Answer:
Rough check. Calling it 45 mins and 2400 kg / hr gives a rough answer of 1800 kg.
Rotate the inner scale to align the **60** (mins) datum with the fuel flow of

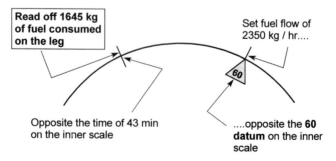

Fig. 6–5 Computer set up to solve for fuel consumed.

2350 kg on the outer scale. Locate the time of 43 mins on the inner scale
and read off 16(85) opposite it on the outer scale. The rough check put the
answer in the region of 1800 kg therefore the correct answer is **1685 kg** (see
Fig. 6–5).

Example:

An aircraft consumes 73 US Gal in 107 mins, calculate its fuel flow in US
Gal/hr.

Answer:

Rough check. Calling it 70 US Gal in 110 mins gives a rough answer of 40
US Gal in 60 mins.

Rotate the inner scale to align the time of 107 mins on the inner scale with
the 73 US Gal of fuel consumed on the outer scale. Opposite the **60** (mins)
datum on the inner scale read off 40(9). The rough check put the answer in
the region of 40 US Gal therefore the correct answer is **40·9 US Gal/hr** (see
Fig. 6–6).

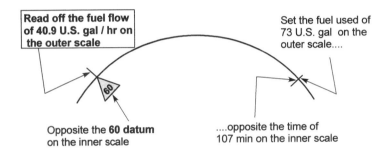

Fig. 6–6 *Computer set up to solve for fuel flow.*

Example:

An aircraft has 9700 Imp Gal of usable fuel in its tanks. How many mins
could it fly until its tanks were down to 800 Imp Gal of usable fuel if its
mean fuel flow is 1450 Imp Gal/hr?

Answer:

Available fuel 9700 – 800 = 8900 Imp Gal. Rough check. Calling it
9000 Imp Gal and 1500 Imp Gal/hr gives a rough answer of 6 hr or 360
mins.

Rotate the inner scale to align the **60** (mins) datum on the inner scale with
the fuel flow of 1450 Imp Gal/hr on the outer scale. Locate the 8900 Imp
Gal of fuel available on the outer scale and read off 36(8) opposite it on the
inner scale. The rough check put the answer in the region of 360 mins, therefore the correct answer is **368 mins** (see Fig.6–7).

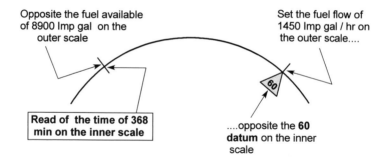

Opposite the fuel available
of 8900 Imp gal on the
outer scale

Set the fuel flow of
1450 Imp gal / hr on
the outer scale....

Read of the time of 368
min on the inner scale

....opposite the **60**
datum on the inner
scale

Fig. 6–7   Computer set up to solve for endurance.

SELECTING THE MOST ECONOMICAL CRUISING LEVEL

6.9 If the GS on a leg is divided into the fuel flow it will give the fuel required per unit of ground distance flown. If a choice of altitudes is available to the pilot this ratio can be used to select the most economical altitude for a particular flight. At different altitudes:
A given MNo or RAS will give a different TAS.
The WV will probably be different.
The fuel flow may be different.

It does not always follow that the level having the lowest fuel flow will be the most economical, changes in the TAS and WV may be such that the GS plays the most significant part in the calculation:

Example:
Select the most economical altitude to fly at from the following:
13,000 ft, -13 C, RAS 297 kn, WV 250 / 40, trk 012 (T), fuel flow 1250 kg / hr.
17,000 ft, -22 C, RAS 297 kn, WV 280 / 55, trk 012 (T), fuel flow 1170 kg / hr.
21,000 ft, -38 C, RAS 297 kn, WV 320 / 80, trk 012 (T), fuel flow 1090 kg / hr.
Answer:
13,000 ft, -13 C and RAS 297 kn gives a TAS of 356 kn.
TAS 356 kn, WV 250 / 40 and trk 012 (T) gives a GS of 382 kn.
GS 382 kn and fuel flow 1250 kg / hr gives **3.27 kg / gnm**.
17,000 ft, -22 C and RAS 297 kn gives a TAS of 377 kn.
TAS 377 kn, WV 280 / 55 and trk 012 (T) gives a GS of 372 kn.
GS 372 kn and fuel flow 1170 kg / hr gives **3.15 kg / gnm**.
21,000 ft, -38 C and RAS 297 kn gives a TAS of 395 kn.
TAS 395 kn, WV 320 / 80 and trk 012 (T) gives a GS of 340 kn.
GS 340 kn and fuel flow 1090 kg / hr gives **3.20 kg / gnm**.

Comparing the results at each level show that, in this example, the most economical level to fly at would be **17,000 ft** since it has the lowest fuel requirement for each gnm to be covered. Note: Detailed workings for the above example have deliberately not been given but readers may care to check them out for themselves. Each level has three steps:

RAS to TAS (in this case TAS > 300 kn) ... (see Chapter 4, paragraph 4.7).
Finding hdg to steer and GS (only GS is applicable to the fuel problem) . . . (see Chapter 5, paragraph 5.15).
Dividing fuel flow / hr by GS (gnm/hr) to give fuel used / gnm.

6.10 In the example above the fuel was given in kg and the distance in gnm, the consumption being in *fuel used per unit of distance*. Fuel consumption can also be quoted in terms of *distance covered per unit of fuel* in which case the greatest distance covered per unit of fuel will be the most economical. As well as ground distance (relating to GS) the distance may be given in air distance (relating to TAS). Similarly the fuel units may be given by either weight or volume. This may sound rather daunting but the golden rule is the old one of:

'Do not mix units within a calculation.'

If confronted with a problem containing a mixture of units such as Imp Gal, US Gal, lt, lb and kg make converting them all into a common base unit the first task and work from that. The same applies to distances which may be a mix of nm, st m, km, air distance or ground distance. Which common unit to work with in each case is a matter of personal preference and may well be dictated by the way the problem presents itself.

CHAPTER 7

PILOT NAVIGATION

7.1 Pilot navigation is airborne navigation carried out mainly in the pilot's head. To be successful it requires practice in the estimation of both distances and direction on a chart and the ability to work out simple ratios without the aid of a navigation computer. Another secret of good pilot navigation is careful preparation and study of the chart(s) during pre-flight planning. The main application of pilot navigation is in cross country flying by visual map reading techniques but, as will be demonstrated, aspects of pilot navigation can be used when flying on airways.

7.2 A pilot sets out to fly an aircraft along a desired trk by maintaining the pre-planned altitude, hdg and RAS. Provided the forecast WV was accurate, the aircraft should stay on trk and arrive at the far end of the trk at the planned **Estimated Time of Arrival (ETA)**. Any change in the WV from that forecast, or slight errors in hdg or RAS, will result in deviation from the planned trk or a change in the arrival time, or more likely both. Because WV is such a variable factor it means that deviations from the planned route are a common occurrence. The object of pilot navigation is to assess any such deviations and calculate hdg changes to reach the destination and revise the ETA if necessary. Calculation of hdg change will be dealt with before considering the revision of ETA.

THE 1 IN 60 RULE

7.3 At the heart of pilot navigation is what is known as the 1 in 60 rule, a method of estimating angles which gives answers that are close enough for practical navigation purposes provided the angles involved are not too large. The rule is based on the premise that if a right angle triangle has a base line 60 units long the value in degrees of the smaller enclosed angle is

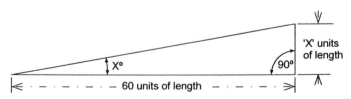

Fig. 7–1   The 1 in 60 rule for estimating angles.

80

the same as the number of units in the shorter side of the triangle (see Fig. 7–1).

A comparison of the result given by this rule against the actual value of the angle being assessed shows errors of less that half a degree for angles from 1° to 9° and only one degree of error at 16°. By 20° the error is one and a half degrees but increases rapidly as angles get larger. In pilot navigation the 1 in 60 rule is considered to be acceptably accurate for estimating angles up to 20°. Since most practical problems involve angles smaller than 20° the errors incurred are less than the accuracy to which most pilots can manually fly a hdg.

TRACK MADE GOOD AND TRACK ERROR

7.4   Once it is established (by whatever means) that the aircraft is not flying along the desired trk, the obvious conclusion is that if the present hdg is maintained the aircraft will continue along its present incorrect trk taking it further and further from the desired trk and its destination (see Fig. 7–2).

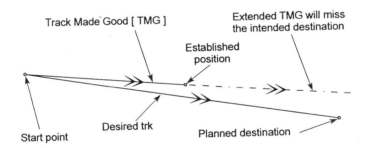

Fig. 7–2   Track Made Good (TMG).

The trk that the aircraft is actually flying along is known as the **Track Made Good (TMG)**. The angle between the desired trk and the TMG is known as **Track Error (TE)** and is measured *from* desired trk *to* TMG (see Fig. 7–3).

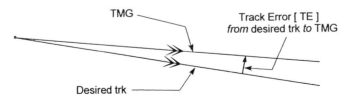

Fig. 7–3   Track Error (TE).

81

TE *is not the same as drift* and care must be taken not to mix these two up. For example Fig. 7–4 shows an aircraft being flown on a hdg of 074 (T) which was calculated to fly the aircraft along a desired trk of 077 (T) but is actually achieving a TMG of 079 (T).

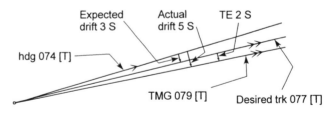

Fig. 7–4   Track Error (TE), from desired trk to TMG.

In this case:-
The TE (*from* desired trk *to* TMG) is **2S**.
The original expected drift (*from* hdg *to* desired trk) was **3S**.
The actual drift experienced (*from* hdg *to* TMG) is **5S**.

PARALLELING THE TRACK

7.5   If the hdg of the aircraft is altered towards the desired trk by the amount of TE this will alter the TMG by the same amount. The new TMG will have the same direction as the desired trk but will be parallel to it. This is known as **Paralleling the trk** (see Fig. 7–5).

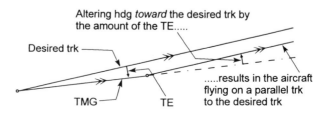

Fig. 7–5   Paralleling trk.

Paralleling the trk is used in some navigation situations to prevent the aircraft getting further off the desired trk while more fixing information is being sought. Paralleling the trk is seldom used in pilot navigation. In pilot navigation the aim, when a TE has been detected, is either to alter hdg to intercept the desired trk and then make a further hdg change to fly along it, or to alter hdg directly for the destination point at the end of the desired trk.

REGAINING DESIRED TRACK

7.6 The Double Track Error method   There are two methods of intercepting the desired trk. The one that is frequently included in the written examinations will be dealt with first. This first method can only be carried out provided the aircraft has *not* passed the half way point along the leg being flown. It requires the value of the TE to be resolved before applying a simple set of rules.

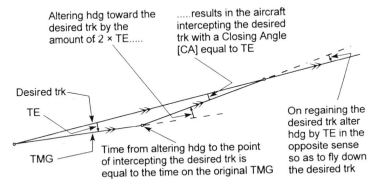

Fig. 7–6   Regaining the desired trk by the Double TE method.

From Fig. 7–6 it can be seen that by altering hdg towards the desired trk by 2 × TE the new TMG will converge onto the desired trk with a **Closing Angle (CE)** having the same value as the TE. At the point where the new TMG intercepts the desired trk a second alteration of hdg, equal to TE but in the opposite sense to the first alteration of hdg, is required to fly the aircraft down the regained desired trk. Since the TE and CA are identical, the distance from the start of the leg to the point of first altering hdg is the same as from there to the point of regaining the desired trk and the time to fly each will be the same. The drill for this technique, known as 'Regaining trk by the **Double Track Error** method' is:

Establish TE (calculation of TE is dealt with later in this Chapter).
Note the time elapsed from the start of the leg and alter towards the desired trk by
    2 × TE.
Hold this new hdg for the same amount of time as the elapsed time observed at
    moment of altering hdg.
When the time is up, alter hdg by TE in the opposite sense to the first alteration of
    hdg. The aircraft should be back on, and flying down, the desired trk.

Example:
Fig. 7–7 shows a situation where an aircraft has departed from 'A' at 1015 on a hdg of 117 (T) intending to fly down the desired trk of 120 (T) to point 'B'.

At 1024 the position of the aircraft is established at point 'x' showing that the actual TMG is 123 (T). The TE from desired trk 120 (T) to the TMG of 123 (T) is **3S** and the elapse time from point 'A' is **9 mins**.
At 1024 hdg is altered to intercept the desired trk by 2 × TE.
New hdg = 117 (T) – (2 × 3) = 117 (T) – 6 = **111 (T)**.
9 minutes later at **1033** the aircraft has intercepted the desired trk from 'A' to 'B' and hdg is altered by TE to S so as to maintain the desired trk. **At 1033 new hdg** = 111(T) + 3 = **114 (T)**.

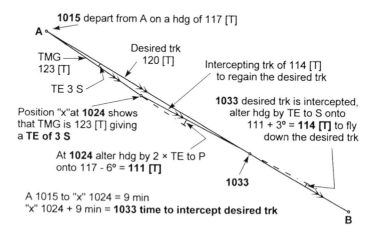

Fig. 7–7   Demonstration of Double TE method of regaining trk.

7.7 Standard Closing Angle method   The second method of regaining the desired trk is known as the Standard Closing Angle method, which is used by high speed low-flying aircraft and is of particular use when flying over areas with few navigational features. From this it can be gathered that it has more military than civilian application and as such does not at the time of writing feature in the CAA examination syllabus. However the method is based on the 1 in 60 rule and is worth looking at for its interest value. With this method for every GS there is a Standard CA which is equal to

$$\frac{60}{\text{The number of nm covered / min}}$$

From this a simple table – presented in graphical form in Fig. 7–8 – can be drawn up:-

GS 180 kn = 3 nm / min Gives Standard CA of 20°
GS 240 kn = 4 nm / min Gives Standard CA of 15°
GS 300 kn = 5 nm / min Gives Standard CA of 12°

GS 360 kn = 6 nm / min Gives Standard CA of 10°
GS 400 kn = 6·66nm / min Gives Standard CA of 9°
GS 600 kn = 10 nm / min Gives Standard CA of 6°

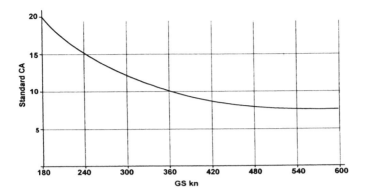

Fig. 7–8   The Standard CA graph.

During the pre-flight planning stage the GS for each leg is computed. The Standard CA for each leg is extracted from the table or graph and noted on the pilot's cockpit flight plan. In flight if position is fixed showing the aircraft to be off the desired trk the hdg is altered towards the desired trk by the Standard CA for the leg being flown. This new hdg is held for a number of minutes equal to the number of nm the fix had shown the aircraft to be displaced from the desired trk. At the end of this time the desired trk will be intercepted and hdg altered for destination at the end of the desired trk, this hdg will be the original hdg for the leg corrected for TE (which has to be calculated by the 1 in 60 rule during the closing manoeuvre).

Example:
At 1147 a pilot sets out to fly an aircraft from 'P' to 'Q' at a GS of 355 kn on an initial hdg of 067 (T). At 1155 a fix shows the aircraft to be 3 nm S of the desired trk 46 nm from the 'P'.
What is the hdg to intercept the desired trk?
At what time will the desired trk be intercepted?
What is the TE?
What is the hdg to be flown on regaining the desired trk?
Answer:
For GS 355 kn the Standard CA is 10°, so at 1155 the hdg to steer to intercept the desired trk is 067 – 10° = **057 (T)** (the 10° alteration being made to P to correct for being off trk to S).
3 nm off trk so hold hdg 057 (T) for 3 min. Desired trk will be intercepted at 1155 + 3 = **1158**.
3 nm off trk in 46 nm along = 4 nm off in 60 nm so TE = **4°**.

85

Hdg to steer on regaining the desired trk = initial hdg of 067 (T) corrected for TE of 4°, = 067 (T) – 4 = **063 (T)** (see Fig. 7–9).

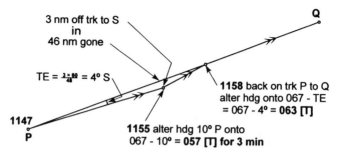

Fig. 7–9   Demonstration of the use of the standard CA.

ALTERING HEADING DIRECTLY FOR DESTINATION

7.8   This pilot navigation technique requires the assessment of both the TE (from desired trk to TMG) and the CA (between the desired trk and the direct trk required to close destination) to be carried by the pilot. From Fig. 7-10 it can be seen that an alteration of hdg towards the desired trk by the amount of TE would only cause the aircraft to fly parallel to the desired trk. To fly down the direct trk to the destination point at the end of the leg requires a further hdg change equal to the CA. The total alteration of hdg to fly directly to destination is **TE + CA.**

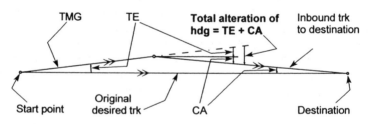

Fig. 7–10   Altering hdg directly for destination.

This method can, in theory, be carried out at any point along a leg but for practical reasons should not be left too late. The later a correction is left, the closer to destination, and the necessary corrections become larger (even for quite small distances off trk). A large hdg change often results in a change of drift angle which simple pilot navigation techniques cannot take into account. Pilots should try and detect any deviation from the desired trk during the first part of the trk before the corrections needed become too large.

7.9   Assessment of TE and CA by the 1 in 60 rule is based on ratios. For instance if an aircraft is found to be 2 nm P off the desired trk at 30 nm along trk, then:

2 nm off in 30 nm = 4 nm off in 60 nm = **4P TE** (see Fig. 7–11).

In the same way the CA can be assessed from the distance off trk and the distance to go to destination. In Fig. 7.11 this is 2 nm off the desired trk with 20 nm to go:

2 nm off in 20 nm = 6 nm off in 60 nm = **6P CA**.

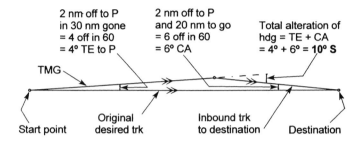

Fig. 7–11   *Demonstration TE + CA method of altering hdg directly for destination.*

So in Fig. 7–11 the alteration of hdg from the fix directly to destination is TE + CA = 4 + 6 = **10 S** (correcting for being off trk to P). Real situations seldom give rise to such straightforward figures and some rounding up or down of distances is common practice in pilot navigation. Bearing in mind the small inaccuracies of most compasses and the degree of accuracy to which the average pilot can fly a hdg manually, answers to within 2° are acceptable when carrying out pilot navigation. It is of course possible to get the answers within 1° by working the ratios out on the circular slide rule of the navigation computer. However in flight a pilot (particularly if flying solo) may have his or her hands full in which case all calculations will have to be carried out in the head. Only study and a lot of practice will achieve the necessary degree of skill needed.

Example:
An aircraft is being flown from 'A' to 'B' a distance of 136 nm. After 43 nm the aircraft's position is found to be 2·75 nm to the right of the desired trk. What is the TE?
What is the CA?
By how many degrees and in which direction should the pilot alter hdg to fly direct to 'B'?
Answer:
TE. 2·75 nm S in 43 nm gone, say 3 in 45 = 4 in 60 = **4S.**

CA. 2·75 nm S with 136 – 43 = 93 nm to go, say 3 in 90 = 2 in 60 = **2S.**
Alter hdg by TE + CA = 4° + 2° = **6° to P** (see Fig. 7–12).

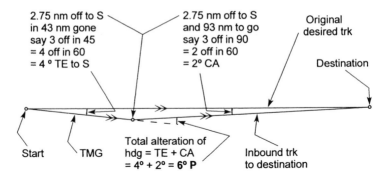

2.75 nm off to S
in 43 nm gone
say 3 off in 45
= 4 off in 60
= 4 ° TE to S

2.75 nm off to S
and 93 nm to go
say 3 off in 90
= 2 off in 60
= 2° CA

Original
desired trk

Destination

Start   TMG

Total alteration of
hdg = TE + CA
= 4° + 2° = **6° P**

Inbound trk
to destination

Fig. 7–12   Rounding figures up and down.

Checking the TE on the navigation computer the ratio of 2·75 in 43 gives
a ratio of 3.·83 in 60 = **TE of 3·83°** S. Similarly the CA ratio of 2·75 in 93
gives a ratio of 1·77 in 60 = **CA of 1·77°** S. Total alteration of hdg = TE +
CA = 3·83° + 1·77° = **5.6° to P**, indicating that the 1 in 60 rule approxima-
tion is well within acceptable limits. This method of pilot navigation
frequently appears in examination papers and candidates should be
familiar with it. When doing practice questions, *ab initio* students in particular should test their ability to carry out estimations in their head by cross
checking their answers on the navigation computer.

ESTIMATING TRACK ANGLES ON A CHART

7.10 The 1 in 60 rule can also be applied to the estimation of track angles
on a chart. This is not a skill that is formally examined but all pilots should
aim to become proficient at estimating angles to a fairly high degree of
accuracy. Such an ability can save precious time in the event of an airborne
emergency requiring a rapid unplanned diversion. The Cardinal Points
were introduced in Chapter 2, these being N 000°/360°, E 090°, S 180° and
W 270° (see Fig. 7–13). Half way between each Cardinal Point are the 45°
lines of NE 045°, SE 135°, SW 225° and NW 315°. Most people can estimate these 45° steps by eye, for anyone having trouble remember that a 45°
right angle triangle has 1 × 1 sides (see Fig. 7–14). Estimation of 15° either
side of these eight major compass points will add a further sixteen directions to the compass rose (based on the 1 in 60 rule 15° gives 15 across for
60 along, or a triangle with right angle sides of 1 to 4) (see Fig. 7–15). From
the twenty-four 15° radials the 1 in 60 rule can be used to assess intermediate angles.

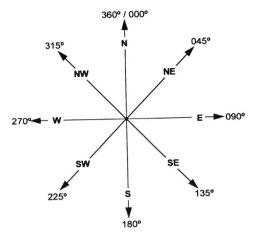

Fig. 7–13   Estimating direction, the 45° steps of the compass.

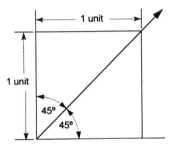

Fig. 7–14   Estimating 45°, 1:1 ratio.

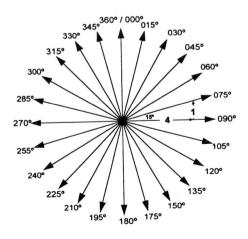

Fig. 7–15   Estimating direction, the 15° steps of the compass.

Example:
Estimate the direction of the trk in Fig. 7–16 below.

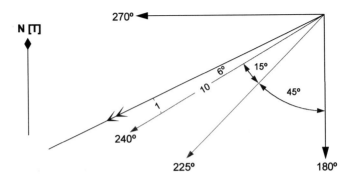

Fig 7–16   Estimation of trk direction.

Answer:
Using 1:1 and 1: 4 ratios puts the direction between 240 (T) and 255 (T). The direction is 1 across to 10 along (6 in 60) or 6° beyond 240 (T) = 246 (T). Protractor measurement gives the actual direction as being 245 (T) showing the estimate to only be 1° out.

Like all skills the estimation of direction can only be achieved with practice. A way to enhance this skill is always to estimate the trks drawn on a chart before measuring them with a protractor. Drawing straight lines at random on an old chart will provide more practice if required. Most people find they quickly reach a level of accuracy of within 5° (or less) and after a while can get the same degree of accuracy by eye alone, without recourse to the 1 in 60 rule.

AMENDING THE ESTIMATED TIME OF ARRIVAL (ETA)

7.11 Amending the ETA can be solved by:
Either Working out a revised GS and using this GS to calculate the time needed to fly the remainder of the leg.
Or Using one of the ratio methods employing time checks at pre-selected check points along the route.

CALCULATION OF REVISED GS AND ETA

7.12 **Revising GS.** Use of the navigation computer to solve the GS from distance covered in time gone was covered in Chapter 4. In pilot navigation the aim is to carry out the calculations in one's head. Consider the case where 30 nm has been covered in 11 min, applying the navigation computer ratio this would be:

$$\frac{30\,nm}{11\,min} = \frac{GS}{60\,min}$$

Transposed this becomes:

$$\frac{30 \times 60}{11} = \frac{1800}{11} = \textbf{164 kn GS}$$

Or

$$\frac{\text{Distance gone} \times 60}{\text{Time gone}} = \textbf{GS}$$

From this the pilot navigation rule for the calculation of GS is:

'multiply the distance gone by 60 and divide by the time gone in mins'.

7.13 Revising ETA. Having revised the GS the time to go for the remainder of the leg can be solved using the same basic ratios:

$$\frac{GS}{60\,min} = \frac{\text{Distance to go}}{\text{Time to go}}$$

Transposed this becomes:

$$\frac{\text{Distance to go} \times 60}{GS} = \textbf{Time to go}$$

Suppose that in the example in paragraph 7.12 that there were 54 nm to go to the end of the leg. This would give:

$$\frac{54 \times 60}{164} = \text{Time to go}$$

Working this out in one's head, say 54 goes into 164 three times (ignore the 2 over as not being significant) and 3 goes into 60 twenty times. Time to go to the end of the leg is 20 min. In the above example the solution on the navigation computer gives a GS of 163·75 kn and a time to go of 19·8 min. Rounded to the nearest whole number these are the same as the pilot navigation answers. It is often the case that the GS as such is not needed, only the time to go being required. The 'time to go' can be solved in one step by substituting the 'GS formula' in the 'time to go formula'. The 60s cancel out and the formula tidies up to give:

$$\frac{\text{Distance to go} \times \text{Time gone}}{\text{Distance gone}} = \textbf{Time to go}$$

This is a far simpler ratio to deal with in one's head, as substitution of the figures already used shows:

$$\frac{54 \text{ nm to go} \times 11 \text{ min gone}}{30 \text{ min gone}} = \frac{594}{30} \text{ say } \frac{600}{30} = \textbf{20 min to go}$$

MARKING UP CHECK POINTS ON THE CHART

7.14 Amending the ETA can also be done by other ratio methods which use pre-planned check points along a leg. These methods require the chart to be marked up during the pre-flight planning stage, there being several different options available to pilots. Which to use at any one time will depend on circumstances and, in some cases, personal preference
7.15 The marking up options are:

Distance marks, say every 10 nm for a slow aircraft and increasingly larger intervals (preferably in 10 nm increments) for faster aircraft. Whatever intervals are used each should be clearly annotated but at the same time care must be taken not to obscure features on the chart. Such marks are useful for assessing distances to use in the formulae discussed in paragraphs 7.12 and 7.13. For a route that is being flown regularly these marks will not need changing from one flight to the next (see Fig. 7–17).

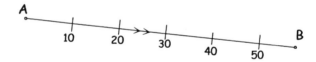

The actual marking of the distances is
a personal choice. However care should be taken
not to write over map details that may be needed in flight

Fig.7–17   Regular distance marks.

Fraction or Ratio marks. These are marks along the leg indicating the fraction of the leg travelled from the start of the leg. The most common fraction markings are at the quarter, half and three-quarter points of a leg. In some cases marking

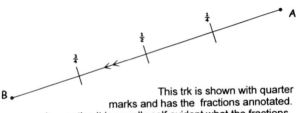

This trk is shown with quarter
marks and has the fractions annotated.
In practice it is usually self evident what the fractions
are and there is no need to write them in beside the marks.

Fig. 7–18   Fraction Marking of a trk.

the leg into thirds or even fifths may be more suitable so as to tie up with navigation features on the ground. Like the distance marks these fraction marks will not need changing for a route that is being flown regularly (see Fig. 7–18).

Regular Time marks. These are marked in after the flight plan has been worked out and the GS for each leg calculated. The GS so deduced is known as the **Deduced Reckoning (DR) GS** (also known as **Dead Reckoning**). The DR GS is used to calculate the distance the aircraft is expected to travel in a particular time interval. This distance is then stepped off down the leg each mark being annotated with its expected elapsed time from the start of the leg. This method has the drawback that the marks are good for just the one flight and only then provided it is flown during the valid period of the winds and temperatures used in preparing the flight plan (see Fig. 7–19).

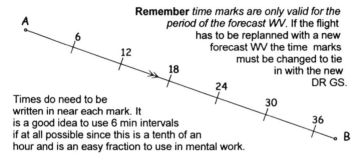

Remember *time marks are only valid for the period of the forecast WV.* If the flight has to be replanned with a new forecast WV the time marks must be changed to tie in with the new DR GS.

Times do need to be written in near each mark. It is a good idea to use 6 min intervals if at all possible since this is a tenth of an hour and is an easy fraction to use in mental work.

Fig. 7–19   Time Marking of a trk.

Time marks at prominent navigation features. These are used when flying a route that has few prominent navigation features none of which tie in with any of the above marking systems. The time to reach each feature from the start of the leg is calculated using the DR GS for the leg. These DR times are then noted on the chart beside the appropriate feature. Like the regular time marks these time marks are only valid for the one flight and the period of the forecast winds and temperatures (see Fig. 7–20).

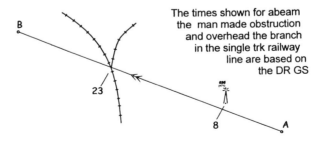

The times shown for abeam the man made obstruction and overhead the branch in the single trk railway line are based on the DR GS

Fig. 7–20   Time Marks at Prominent navigation features.

USE OF FRACTION MARKS TO REVISE ETA

7.16 Fraction marks are not normally encountered in examination questions. However their use in actual flight conditions is very popular with pilots because of the way they help simplify pilot navigation problems. For example if the elapsed time to a fraction mark is multiplied by the inverted fraction gone it will give the 'total flight time' for the leg (Note that it does not give 'time to go'). Fig. 7–21 illustrates this type of calculation for different fraction marks along a leg.

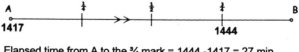

Elapsed time from A to the ¾ mark = 1444 -1417 = 27 min

Revised time for the whole leg = 27 × $\frac{4}{3}$ = **36 min**

Fig. 7–21   Revising the total time for a leg using fraction marks.

An alternative way of using fraction marks is to use the DR GS to calculate the expected time to reach each fraction mark and annotate them accordingly. The actual time taken to reach a fraction mark is noted and compared with the DR time written on the chart. If they agree the original flight plan ETA is confirmed. If they do not agree the amount of time 'early' or 'late' on the DR time is multiplied by the inverted fraction gone to give the total amendment to be applied to the original flight plan ETA. Fig. 7–22 shows a leg marked in fifths with the DR time at each fifth marked in.

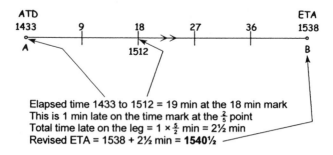

Elapsed time 1433 to 1512 = 19 min at the 18 min mark
This is 1 min late on the time mark at the $\frac{2}{5}$ point
Total time late on the leg = 1 × $\frac{5}{2}$ min = 2½ min
Revised ETA = 1538 + 2½ min = **1540½**

Fig. 7–22   Amending ETA by the time early / late at fraction marks.

If the **Actual Time of Departure (ATD)** is 1433 then the ETA would be 1433 + 45 min = 1538.

If the second mark were actually reached at 1512 this would be an elapsed time of 19 min instead of the DR time of 18 min.

This is 1 min late in $^2/_5$ so the total time late on the flight plan ETA will be:

$$1 \times {}^5/_2 = \textbf{2·5 min}$$

Revised ETA = Flight plan ETA + time late = 1538 + 2·5 min. = **1540·5**

USE OF TIME MARKS TO REVISE ETA

7.17 Regular time marks are used to amend the ETA by time 'early' or 'late' at a mark multiplied by the ratio:

DR time for the whole leg: DR time to the mark.

Fig. 7–23 shows a leg with 6 min time marks and a total DR time for the leg of 32 min.

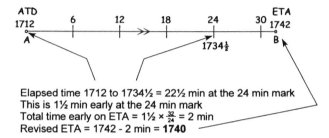

Elapsed time 1712 to 1734½ = 22½ min at the 24 min mark
This is 1½ min early at the 24 min mark
Total time early on ETA = 1½ × $\frac{32}{24}$ = 2 min
Revised ETA = 1742 - 2 min = **1740**

Fig.7–23   Amending ETA by the time early / late at time marks.

If ATD is 1712 then the ETA would be 1712 + 32 min = 1742.
If the fourth (24 min) mark is reached at 1734·5 this would give an elapsed time of 22·5 min instead of the DR time 24 min.
This is 1·5 min early at the 24 min time mark.
Total time early will be:

$$1·5 \times {}^{32}/_{24} = \textbf{2 min.}$$

Revised ETA = Flight plan ETA – time early.
1742 – 2 min. = **1740**

7.18 Time marks at prominent navigation features are used to amend the ETA in exactly the same way as regular time marks. Where unique navigation features are sparse along a leg it makes sense to mark the DR times against those features most likely to be identified even though it may make for more awkward pilot navigation calculations in some cases.

SOME PRACTICAL PILOT NAVIGATION TECHNIQUES

7.19 Some of the more practical forms of pilot navigation do not lend themselves to written examination. By their very nature written examinations usually place more emphasis on the theoretical aspects and as a result pilot navigation questions about hdg changes and ETA revision usually require candidates to employ the formulae given in paragraphs 7.12 and 7.13. The remainder of this chapter deals with some pilot navigation techniques of a more practical nature which (apart from the use of radio aids on an airway which sometimes feature in plotting) are unlikely to appear on question papers.

FRACTION GONE AND CLOSING ANGLE LINES

7.20 Fractional marking of a leg and the use of the inverted fraction gone is generally accepted as being the simplest and most practical method for revision of the ETA. The calculation of the hdg change direct to the end of a leg is also greatly simplified by fraction marks and what are known as **Closing Angle Lines**. Fig. 7–24 illustrates the pre-flight markings that prepare a topographical chart for this method of pilot navigation.

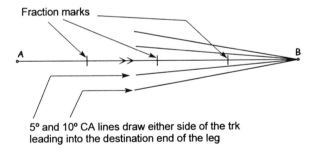

Fig. 7–24   *Fraction marks and 5° and 10° CA lines.*

The leg is divided into fractions and is marked accordingly (quarters are shown but other fractions could be used). At the destination end of the leg 5° and 10° closing angle lines are drawn extending back either side of the leg to about the half way point. If the aircraft's position is established as being off the desired trk the calculation of the hdg change required to fly direct to the destination end of the leg is as follows:

Use the 5° and 10° closing angle lines to estimate (by eye) the CA from the aircraft's position to the end of the leg. At the same time note the fraction gone along the trk.

Multiply the CA by the inverted fraction gone to give the total hdg change required.

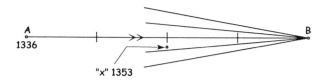

Estimated CA 4° S, fraction gone ½
Alter hdg by 4 × $\frac{2}{1}$ = **8° P**

Time gone 1353 - 1336 = 17 min at ½ fraction mark
Revised time for the whole leg = 17 × $\frac{2}{1}$ = **34 min**

Fig.7–25   Demonstation of the use of fraction marks and 5° and 10° CA lines.

Example:

In Fig. 7–25 the aircraft left 'A' at 1336 and was fixed as being off the desired trk at position 'x' at 1353.

Time gone is 17 min, fraction gone is ½ and from the closing angle lines the CA can be estimated by eye as 4° S.

Hdg change	= CA × inverted fraction gone.
	= 4° × $^2/_1$
	= **8° P** (correcting for being S of desired trk).
Total time for leg	= time gone × inverted fraction gone.
	= 17 min × $^2/_1$
	= **34 min**.
Revised ETA	= ATD + total time for leg.
	= 1336 + 34 min.
	= **1410**.

This was a simple example since at the half way point the TE and CA will be the same, and TE + CA = 2 × CA.

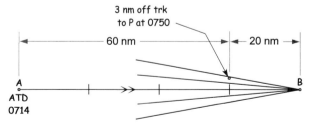

See the text for the comparative methods of working out the hdg
change and ETA for the above situation

*Fig.7–26   Solution of hdg change and ETA revision. Comparison between the 1 in
60 method and the fraction marks and CA lines method.*

97

7.21 Fig. 7–26 illustrates a situation of an aircraft off trk to P at the ¾ fraction mark. Some distances have been included on the diagram to enable the closing angle line method to be compared with the basic 1 in 60 method.

From the 1 in 60 rules:
TE = 3 nm off in 60 nm gone = 3°
CA = 3 nm off with 20 nm to go = 9°
Total alteration of hdg = TE + CA = 3° + 9° = **12° S**
From ATD 'A' to the fix is 36 min.

$$\text{Time to go} = \frac{\text{Distance to go} \times \text{time gone}}{\text{Distance gone}}$$

$$= \frac{20 \text{ nm} \times 36 \text{ min}}{60 \text{ nm}} = \textbf{12 min.}$$

Revised ETA = Fix time + time to go.
= 0750 + 12 min.
= **0802.**

From the closing angle lines:
Estimated CA (by eye) = 9°
Alteration of hdg = CA × inverted fraction gone.
= 9° × ⁴⁄₃
= **12° S.**

From ATD to the fix is 36 min
Total time for the leg = Time gone 5 inverted fraction gone.
= 36 × ⁴⁄₃
= **48 min.**
Revised ETA = ATD + total time for leg.
= 0714 + 48 min.
= **0802.**

7.22 When using pilot navigation techniques *always make the hdg change calculations first.* The revision of the ETA can be carried out at a more leisurely tempo once the hdg change has been implemented. Things can be speeded up in some cases. For instance, if the aircraft can be seen to be off the desired trk and on a TMG that will carry it over an identifiable feature the required change of hdg can be worked out before reaching the feature. On altering hdg when over the feature, a note of the time should be taken for revision of the ETA.

7.23 A pilot navigation calculation that is not often used these days is one for estimating drift and GS. Its particular use is in carrying out an un-scheduled diversion, enabling a reasonably accurate hdg and ETA to be calculated from TAS, forecast WV and estimated trk and distance to point of diversion. In paragraph 5.3 it was shown how the GS could never be less than (TAS – Windspeed) or greater than (TAS + Windspeed) and that in these limit cases the drift would be 0°. Equally it can be said that if the WV is at 90° or 270° to trk GS = TAS and the drift angle will be maximum. Fig. 7–27 shows these limits of GS and drift.

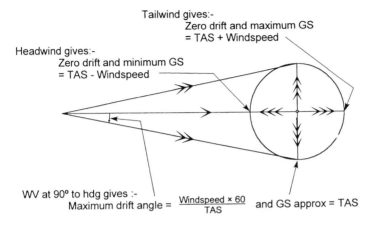

Tailwind gives:-
Zero drift and maximum GS
= TAS + Windspeed

Headwind gives:-
Zero drift and minimum GS
= TAS - Windspeed

WV at 90° to hdg gives :-
Maximum drift angle = $\dfrac{\text{Windspeed} \times 60}{\text{TAS}}$ and GS approx = TAS

Fig. 7–27   The limits of GS and drift.

The 1 in 60 rule can be used to work out the maximum drift angle: treating the TAS as distance gone and the Windspeed as distance off gives:

$$\text{Maximum drift angle} \quad = \frac{\text{Windspeed} \times 60}{\text{TAS}}$$

Fig. 7–28 shows the effect on GS and drift for WVs at 30° , 45° and 60° to trk. In all cases the effect on wind components and drift is to reduce them from their maximum values by rule of thumb factors of 0·5, 0·7 or 0·9 depending on the angle of the WV to the trk.

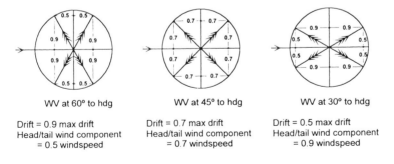

WV at 60° to hdg

Drift = 0.9 max drift
Head/tail wind component
= 0.5 windspeed

WV at 45° to hdg

Drift = 0.7 max drift
Head/tail wind component
= 0.7 windspeed

WV at 30° to hdg

Drift = 0.5 max drift
Head/tail wind component
= 0.9 windspeed

Fig. 7–28   Effect of WV at an angle to hdg.

It may seem a lot of extra information to carry in one's head but it could pay to keep in mind what the maximum possible drift and GSs are for the speeds that are flown on a day to day basis. For instance a pilot who regularly flies at 240 kn the maximum drift is 1° for every 4 kn of Windspeed and GS limits are 240 kn + or – Windspeed.

PILOT NAVIGATION ON AIRWAYS

7.24 Although pilot navigation is associated in many pilot's minds with visual map reading and topographical charts the principles are equally applicable to Airways flying using radio navigation aids. For instance, most overland Airways legs are designated between ground based radio aids from which brgs and/or ranges are obtainable on the appropriate (mandatory) radio receivers carried on board commercial aircraft. Flying along such an Airway and tuned to receive brgs from radio aids at either end of the leg in effect gives a pictorial presentation of TMG and the required inbound trk when shown on a multi-pointer display such as a **Radio Magnetic Indicator (RMI).** The information is displayed as follows:

If the aircraft is flying down the centre line of the Airway the two brgs will be in line (see Fig. 7–29a). Any drift being experienced will show on the RMI as an offset of the forward needle from the aircraft (M) hdg index at the top of the display.

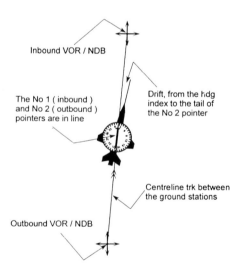

Fig. 7–29a   Use of the RMI for pilot navigation between VOR/NDB ground stations. On the Centreline.

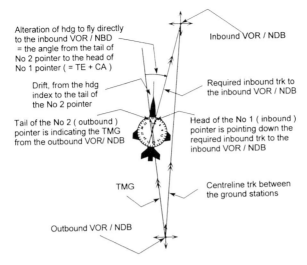

Fig.7–29b   Use of the RMI for pilot navigation between VOR/NDB ground stations. P of the centreline.

If the aircraft is going off the Airway centreline the two needles will form a shallow V, one needle pointing back down the TMG and the other forward along the inbound trk needed to reach the radio aid at the end of the leg. Fig. 7–29b shows an RMI display where an aircraft is tracking to Port of the Airway

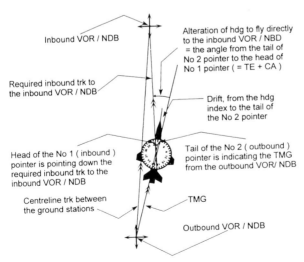

Fig. 7–29c   Use of the RMI for pilot navigation between VOR/NDB ground stations. S of the centreline.

centreline. The extended 'tail' of the back brg needle is indicating the TMG and the pointer of the other needle is indicating the required inbound trk. The total hdg change to fly down the required inbound trk (equal to TE + CA) can be read off from the 'tail' of the back brg needle to the pointer of the inbound needle, the direction from 'tail' to pointer being the required direction of the hdg change (Starboard in this case). For an aircraft tracking to Starboard of an Airway centreline the display would look something like Fig. 7–29c.

It can be seen that such a display is in effect giving a plan view of the TMG and the required inbound trk, with the aircraft at the centre of the dial. A single hdg change to reach the end of the leg being a simple reading from the 'tail' of the back brg needle to the pointer of the other needle. In the case of an aircraft that has not tracked down the centreline of the Airway drift assessment is from the present hdg to the current TMG. Along Airways, amendment of the ETA is simplified by obtaining ranges from **Distance Measuring Equipment (DME)** located at the ends of a leg or using pre-planned brgs from off-trk radio aids to check the rate of progress at fraction marks along each leg.

ESTIMATION OF DISTANCES

7.25 The ability to estimate distance on any chart is a skill all pilots should try to acquire. Since the scale of charts (see Section 3) can vary according to their intended use, pilots should always make certain that they are aware of the scale of the charts they are currently using. Estimation of distance can be carried out with a simple rule (such as a pencil with notches cut to match distance on the chart). The trouble with such a device is that it can never be found when most wanted. A good tip for all pilots is to know the chart distances covered by their handspan and top joint of their thumb. Like the estimation of direction, the estimation of distance on a chart is a matter of practice, so when pre-flight planning try estimating trk lengths before carrying out an accurate measurement.

SECTION 3

AERONAUTICAL MAPS AND CHARTS

The origin of the use of pictorial representation of features on the surface of the earth as an aid to travellers is lost in the distant past. Primitive man probably used simple directions scratched on the ground to indicate to his companions where a source of food or shelter could be found. He would have used symbols such as wiggly lines to show rivers and inverted 'V's for tops of prominent hills to help his explanation.

As man began to extend his field of exploration the pictures of the earth he produced became more detailed. With the invention of more sophisticated ways of measuring distances, direction and time the information portrayed on maps and charts improved until today the majority of the earth's surface has been surveyed and plotted to a degree of accuracy that is more than adequate for aeronautical purposes.

This section deals with the basic principles of producing maps and charts and also an in depth look at the specific projections that are currently used in air navigation

CHAPTER 8

CHART REQUIREMENTS AND SCALE

CHART REQUIREMENTS

8.1 A chart is a pictorial representation on a flat piece of paper of the earth's surface. Since the earth is for all practical purposes a sphere, it follows that in translating its surface onto a flat sheet of paper some distortions are bound to occur. It is physically impossible to produce a flat chart upon which *all* features on the earth's spherical surface are correctly reproduced at the same time.

8.2 Different methods of projection can produce charts for specific tasks. Such charts accurately represent selected earth features whilst allowing other earth features to become distorted. It is a matter of considering what earth features *must* be accurately displayed that decides whether a particular projection is suitable for navigation purposes or not. The main features on the surface of the earth are:

> Direction (between places)
> Distance (between places)
> Shape (of land masses)
> Area (of land masses)

*For navigation it is essential to be able to measure **direction** and **distance** between places and these two features have to take precedence on any navigation chart.*

ORTHOMORPHISM

8.3 The chart property of correctly showing direction is known as **Orthomorphism** or **Conformality** and is a prerequisite for any aeronautical navigation chart. The measurement of distance varies depending on the chart projection and the area of its coverage. Some charts can be considered as having a constant scale (the ratio of chart length to distance on the earth) and on such charts distances are easily measured by means of a suitably graduated straight-edge. Other charts have varying scale and distances and

105

these have to be measured using the scale at the mid lat of each leg. How, and at what point, direction and distance are measured on different chart projections is discussed later.

8.4 In achieving orthomorphism, shapes and areas get distorted by varying amounts. Whilst area is not important for navigation purposes shape can be, particularly for map reading. Fortunately distortions in shape are gradual and relative to one another so that the overall shapes of the small area visible beneath an aircraft will not appear to be distorted when map reading in flight. Shape distortions are most noticeable when large areas of chart are compared with the same areas on a globe of the world.

SCALE

8.5 Direction has already been covered in Chapter 2, along with convergency (conv) which also has to be considered when looking at various chart projections. Another factor of any chart is its **Scale**, this was mentioned briefly in paragraph 8.3 and needs to be explained in more detail before looking at the various aeronautical charts.

Scale is the ratio of chart length to the distance it represents on the earth's surface.

Scale of a chart can be given in different ways:

As a ratio such as 1 : 250 000, meaning that 1 unit of measurement on the chart represents 250,000 of the *same* unit of measurement on the earth's surface. i.e. 1 cm on the chart = 250,000 cm (2·5 km) on the earth.

As a graduated scale, Fig. 8–1 shows a typical triple scale covering the three universal units of measurement often found on constant scale charts. When using such a scale pilots must take care to use the correct scale for the units in which they are working and it is a good idea to cross out the unwanted scales to prevent their inadvertent use.

Fig. 8–1   A triple graduated Scale.

As a statement such as '1 inch equals 4 nm', such a statement is self explanatory. Such statements are no longer common on aeronautical charts.

On charts that do not have a constant scale the scale is quoted for a specified lat. To find the scale at any other lat it is necessary to know how the scale varies on the particular projection and this is one of the aspects that will be discussed later.

8.6 Different scales of charts are used for different purposes. A so-called 'large scale chart' is one that covers a relatively small area in considerable detail. This sort of chart might be used for low-level visual map reading from a helicopter or light aircraft, it would be of little use for high level map reading as most of the detail on the chart would not be discernible and if the flight was of any length, dozens of charts would be required. 'Large scale charts' used in aeronautics range from aerodrome plates with scales in the region of 1 : 40,000 up to the 1 : 250,000 UK Topographical series which is for use when map reading *below* 5000 ft.

8.7 'Small scale charts' are the exact opposite, covering much larger areas per chart but with far less detail shown. The range of 'small scale charts' could be considered as starting with the 1 : 500,000 Topographical charts (where an area approximately 280 nm × 210 nm appears on each chart) up to scales of around 1 : 6,000,000 used for oceanic or trans-continental flights.

8.8 Note that the larger the figure to the right in the scale ratio, the smaller the scale and vice versa. Anyone who has difficulty with this concept should think about scale model aircraft. An aircraft having a length of 36 ft (10.58 m) and a wingspan of 48 ft (14.11 m) modelled to a scale of $1/24$ would produce a model of 18 inches (45.72 cm) length and 24 inches (60.96 cm) span. The same aircraft modelled to a scale of $1/72$ would come out at 6 inches (15.24 cm) long and 8 inches (20.32 cm) span. A box 18 inches × 24 inches could hold only one model of $1/24$ scale but it could hold nine of the $1/72$ scale models. By virtue of its size it is obvious that the larger $1/24$ scale model can show much more detail than its smaller $1/72$ scale equivalent.

THE REDUCED EARTH

8.9 The basis of all chart projections is what is termed the **Reduced Earth (RE)**. This is a hypothetical transparent model of the earth made to the required scale for the chart. This RE is assumed to have a latitude and longitude grid on its surface and a light source at its centre or, alternatively, at one of the poles. The light source is assumed to project the graticule onto a sheet of paper which, depending on the navigation projection required, may be in the form of a cylinder wrapped around the RE in contact with its surface, a cone with its apex above one of the poles or a flat sheet of paper tangential to one of the poles. Once the graticule has been projected onto the sheet, and after any mathematical correction needed to achieve orthomorphism, geographical and man-made features are added as deemed necessary for the intended use of the chart.

CHAPTER 9

MERCATOR'S PROJECTION

9.1 This projection is based on a cylinder wrapped around the RE (see Chapter 8, paragraph 8.9) with its point of contact along the equator and the imaginary light source at the centre of the RE. The scale at the equator will be that of the RE but as Fig. 9–1 shows, the scale expands increasingly with movement N or S from the equator and neither pole can be shown on this projection. Another point to note is that the parallels of lat, which on the earth are small circles progressively reducing in diameter towards the poles, are all projected as being the same size as the equator.

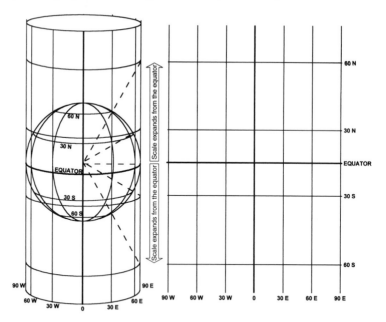

Fig. 9–1   The Basis of Mercator's projection, a cylinder wrapped around the RE along the equator.

9.2   To achieve orthomorphism on a chart it is essential that at any point on the chart the scale changes N/S and E/W are identical . Figs. 9–2 (a), (b) and c illustrate this requirement and show how direction is distorted if scale changes N/S and E/W are different.

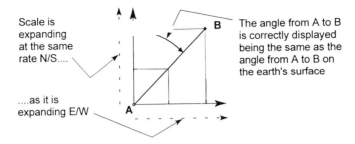

Scale is expanding at the same rate N/S....

....as it is expanding E/W

The angle from A to B is correctly displayed being the same as the angle from A to B on the earth's surface

Fig. 9–2a   Orthomorphic Chart.

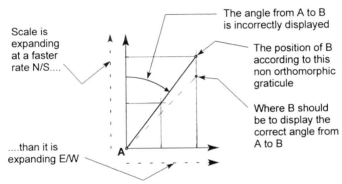

Scale is expanding at a faster rate N/S....

....than it is expanding E/W

The angle from A to B is incorrectly displayed

The position of B according to this non orthomorphic graticule

Where B should be to display the correct angle from A to B

Fig. 9–2b   Non Orthomorphic Chart.

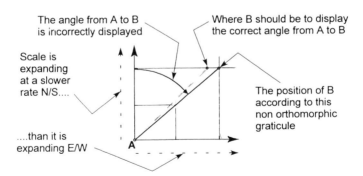

The angle from A to B is incorrectly displayed

Where B should be to display the correct angle from A to B

Scale is expanding at a slower rate N/S....

....than it is expanding E/W

The position of B according to this non orthomorphic graticule

Fig. 9–2c   Non Orthomorphic Chart.

Unfortunately the straight projection from the RE onto the cylinder as shown in Fig. 9–1 produces a different rate of scale change N/S to that E/W and a small mathematical correction has to be incorporated to make the projection orthomorphic. It is interesting to note that this projection was perfected by Gerhardus Kramer (1512–94) a Flemish mathematician and cartographer who used the *nom de plume* 'Mercator' (hence the title of the projection) and to date none of his original calculations have come to light. It seems trade secrets and industrial espionage are nothing new and 'Mercator' protected his corner of the chart-making market very efficiently.

9.3 When the mathematically corrected cylinder is cut along one of the meridians and flattened out the projection appears as in Fig. 9–3 with meridians appearing as equally spaced N/S parallel lines and the parallels of lat as parallel E/W lines increasing in spacing with increase in latitude.

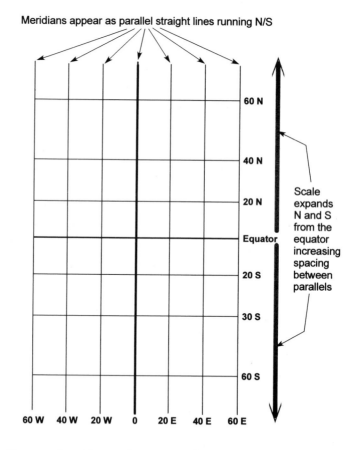

Fig. 9–3 The opened out Mercator's projection showing the appearance of the meridians and parallels.

110

SCALE ON MERCATOR'S PROJECTION

9.4 As just stated the parallels of lat are shown as parallel straight lines running E/W but because of the expanding scale away from the equator the chart spacing gets larger with increasing lat. The scale on Mercator's projection actually expands from the equator by the Secant (sec) of the latitude, thus:

Scale at latitude 'x' = Scale at the equator × sec 'x'

Since sec = 1/cosine (cos) it is more convenient to use 1/cos if required to convert from scale at the equator to scale at some other lat, this amends the formula to read:

Scale at lat 'x' = Scale at the equator × 1/cos 'x'

Example:
On a Mercator chart scale at the equator is 1 : 2 000 000, what is the scale at 60° N?
Answer:
Scale at 60° N = Scale at equator × 1/ cos 60°

$$\frac{1}{2,000,000} \quad \times \quad \frac{1}{0.5} \quad = \quad \frac{1}{1,000,000}$$

Scale at 60° N = **1 : 1,000,000** (see Fig. 9–4).

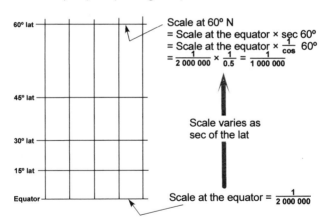

Fig. 9–4   Converting scale at the equator to scale at a lat.

9.5 Similarly if the scale is known at a particular lat the scale at the equator can be found by multiplying by the cos of that lat. Since cos = 1/sec the formula for finding the scale at the equator is:

Scale at the equator = Scale at lat 'y' × 1/sec 'y'

Example:

On a Mercator chart the scale is given as 1 : 500 000 at 44° 30'N. What is the scale at the equator on this chart?

Answer:

Scale at the equator = Scale at 44° 30' × 1/sec 44° 30'

$$\frac{1}{500\ 000} \qquad \times \qquad \frac{1}{1.402} \qquad = \qquad \frac{1}{701\ 000}$$

Scale at the equator = **1 : 701,000** (see Fig. 9–5)

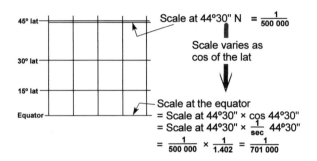

Fig. 9–5   *Converting scale at a lat to scale at the equator.*

9.6   Given the scale at one lat and asked to find the scale at a different lat on the same Mercator chart the process is to find the scale at the equator first and then use that to find the required scale. This of course can be achieved by combining the two formulae thus:

Scale at lat 'x' = Scale at lat 'y' × 1/sec 'y' × 1/cos 'x'

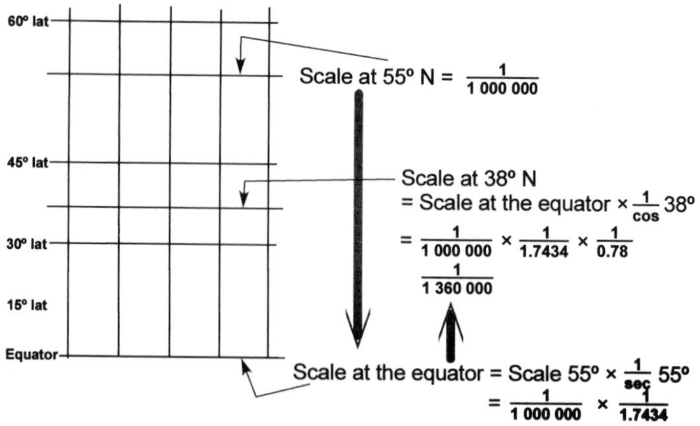

Scale at 55° N = $\frac{1}{1\ 000\ 000}$

Scale at 38° N
= Scale at the equator × $\frac{1}{\cos}$ 38°
= $\frac{1}{1\ 000\ 000}$ × $\frac{1}{1.7434}$ × $\frac{1}{0.78}$
$\frac{1}{1\ 360\ 000}$

Scale at the equator = Scale 55° × $\frac{1}{\sec}$ 55°
= $\frac{1}{1\ 000\ 000}$ × $\frac{1}{1.7434}$

Fig. 9–6   *Converting scale at one lat to scale at another lat.*

Example:

On a Mercator chart the scale is given as 1 : 1,000,000 at 55° N. What is the scale at 38° N on this chart?

Answer:

Scale at 38° N = Scale at 55° N × 1/ sec 55° × 1/cos 38°

$$= \quad \frac{1}{1,000,000} \quad \times \quad \frac{1}{1 \cdot 7434} \quad = \quad \frac{1}{0 \cdot 788}$$

$$= \quad \frac{1}{1,360,000}$$

Scale at 38 00 N = **1 : 1,360,000** (see Fig. 9–6)

CONVERGENCY ON MERCATOR'S PROJECTION

9.7 On the Mercator projection the meridians appear as parallel straight lines running N/S. This means that the value of conv is zero over the whole of this chart. On the earth the only place where conv is zero is along the equator, elsewhere conv equals d'long × sine mean lat (see Chapter 2, paragraphs 2.7 to 2.10). So on Mercator's projection the chart conv is *only* correct along the equator (which was also the point where the cylinder was in contact with the RE). With a chart conv of zero if a straight line is drawn across the chart it will cut all meridians at the same angle thus producing a RL (see Chapter 1, paragraphs 1.14 and 1.15). Apart from along the equator or up and down any meridian GCs would appear as curved lines concave to the equator. Since curvature of any GC varies with its latitude, overall direction and length, it is generally not practical to draw GCs on a Mercator chart, (see Fig. 9–7).

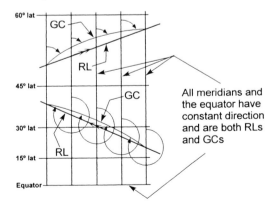

Fig. 9–7   Straight lines represents RLs on Mercator's projection. GCs are curves that vary with trk, distance and lat.

9.8 Having said that, in the vicinity of the equator earth conv is not far removed from zero and the scale expansion on this projection is small, such that in a band 600 nm either side of the equator (latitudes 10°N to 10°S) Mercator's projection can, *for all practical purposes*, be assumed to have constant scale and any straight line will approximate to a GC. Although once widely used for plotting up to latitudes as high as 70° N or S the airborne use of the Mercator chart is now confined almost exclusively to this band 600 nm either side of the equator. In this equatorial band it is used for topographical charts, radio navigation charts, plotting charts and meteorological forecast charts.

9.9 Mercator's projection is sometimes used for high lat aeronautical information charts that are not intended for use in the air. One such is the UK Danger Area Chart. Any reader who has access to this chart, or any similar high lat Mercator's chart, will easily see the effect of the expanding scale. At 60° N (where sec = 2) the parallel spacing on the chart is double the equivalent meridian spacing.

9.10 Despite the decline of the Mercator chart it is required that candidates for the UK ATPL examinations are able to demonstrate the correct basic procedures for high lat plotting on this projection. This is partly academic and partly as a back-up to cover the remote event of no other chart being available for a particular flight. The basic requirements are the measurement of direction and distance and how to convert radio bearings (which follow GCs) into their equivalent RLs for plotting as straight lines.

MEASUREMENT OF TRK DIRECTION ON MERCATOR'S PROJECTION

9.11 Since on this projection all straight lines are RLs (i.e. constant direction) the measurement of trk direction can be made from any point along the trk, however it is best to measure from a point near the start of the trk as this reduces the risk of accidentally measuring 180° out (see Fig. 9–8).

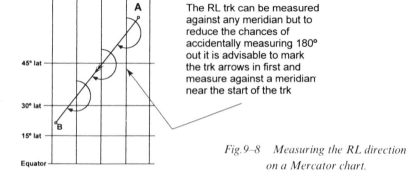

The RL trk can be measured against any meridian but to reduce the chances of accidentally measuring 180° out it is advisable to mark the trk arrows in first and measure against a meridian near the start of the trk

Fig. 9–8   Measuring the RL direction on a Mercator chart.

114

MEASUREMENT OF DISTANCES ON MERCATOR'S PROJECTION

9.12 Measurement of distances is not so straightforward. As already stated the scale expands with sec of lat, so at 48° lat the scale is almost 1·5 × the scale at the equator and at 60° lat it is 2 × the scale at the equator. Now 1° of lat = 60' of lat = 60 nm (see Chapter 3, paragraph 3.3) so, due to the expanding scale, at 60° lat the chart length equal to 60 nm will be ⅓ longer than the chart length equal to 60 nm at 48° lat on the same chart (see Fig. 9–9).

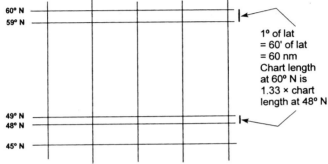

Fig. 9–9   *Difference in chart length at different lats.*

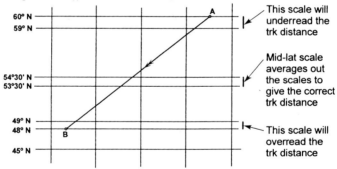

Fig. 9–10   *Measurement of distance on a Mercator chart.*

9.13 For a track as drawn in Fig. 9–10, if the chart length between 48° and 49° were used to step off 60 nm lengths along this track, the total length of the track would come out ⅓ longer than if the chart length between 59° and 60° had been used – and both answers would be wrong! The scale at the mid-lat of the trk should always be used on the Mercator projection as it cancels out the differences in the scales at the lower and higher lats so giving the correct distance overall. In the example in Fig. 9–10 the mid-lat point is at 54° and the chart length up the meridian from 53° 30' to 54° 30' will give the average length of 60 nm for this particular track.

9.14 In Chapter 2, paragraphs 2.7 to 2.10 conv was introduced and it was shown how the directional change of a GC equalled the conv between the meridians against which the bearings were being measured. Consider Fig. 9–11 which shows the RL route from New York to Paris as plotted on Mercator's projection. This RL trk is an easy to plot straight line. The appearance of the GC trk has also been sketched in although, as mentioned in paragraph 9.7, due to variations in the curvature at different lats and values of d'long this is totally impractical for accurate plotting purposes and is only shown here for academic reasons.

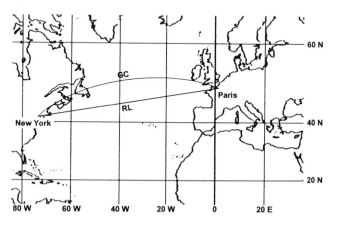

Fig. 9–11   RL from New York to Paris on a Mercator projection.

9.15 Compare the appearance of these trks with the same routes as shown in Chapter 1, Fig. 1–8. The same change of direction of the GC is obvious as is the constant direction of the RL but on Mercator's projection the RL *appears* to be shorter than the GC! This illusion is brought about by the expanding scale on Mercator's projection. The distance along the RL trk should be measured using the scale at the mid-lat of the RL trk which is, in this case, at around 45° 30' N whereas the distance along the GC trk should be measured using the scale at the mid-point of the GC trk, in this case, at about 51° 30' N. This means that a unit of chart length equal to 100 nm along the RL track only equals 88·8 nm along the GC trk, resulting in the RL earth distance coming out greater than the GC earth distance even though the RL *chart length* is shorter. The ratio of 100 nm to 88·8 nm can be verified by comparing the departure at 51° 30' N against departure for the same d'long at 45° 30' N, which due to the parallel line presentation of meridians on Mercator's projection will have a common chart length (see Fig. 9–12).

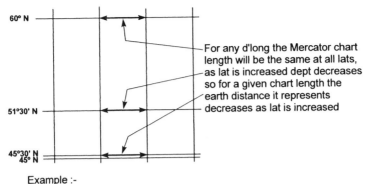

60° N

For any d'long the Mercator chart
length will be the same at all lats,
as lat is increased dept decreases
so for a given chart length the
earth distance it represents
decreases as lat is increased

51°30' N

45°30' N
45° N

Example :-

For a d'long of 143' at 45°30' N and 51°30' N the depts are :-

Dept at 45°30'	Dept at 51°30'
= d'lat ' × cos 45°30'	= d'lat ' × cos 51°30'
= 143 × 0.70091	= 143 × 0.62252
= 100 nm	= 88.8 nm

Fig. 9–12   Change of dept with lat for a given Mercator chart length.

PLOTTING RADIO BRGS ON MERCATOR'S PROJECTION

9.16 Brgs obtained from any radio aid to navigation will be GC brgs since radio waves always follow the shortest path from transmitter to receiver. Apart from the 600 nm band either side of the equator and brgs due N/S (which are also RLs) GC brgs cannot be plotted directly onto Mercator's projection and have to be converted to RL equivalents. Fig. 9–13 shows a ground-based radio station and the position of an aircraft at 1743 hrs. If at 1743 hrs the ground station took a brg on a transmission from the aircraft which measured 271 (T) at the station, by the time this radio brg was tracked back to the aircraft along the GC it would have changed its (T) direction by the amount of conv on the earth between the aircraft and the ground station.

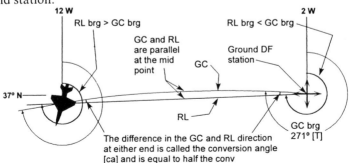

12 W

RL brg > GC brg

GC and RL
are parallel
at the mid
point

GC

Ground DF
station

RL brg < GC brg

2 W

37° N

RL

GC brg
271° [T]

The difference in the GC and RL direction
at either end is called the conversion angle
[ca] and is equal to half the conv

Fig. 9–13   Difference between GC and RL brgs on a
Mercator chart (N Hemisphere).

9.17 In this example the aircraft and ground station are in the N hemisphere with the aircraft to the W of the ground station, the straight RL is drawn in from ground station to aircraft and if this is compared to the GC which has also been sketched in (concave to the equator) it can be seen that the RL brg at the ground station is *less* than the GC brg of 271 (T) but *more* than the direction of the GC as it passes through the aircraft. Further inspection of the two lines shows the RL and GC to have the same direction at a point mid-way between the ground station and the aircraft. Since the RL direction is constant and the GC direction changes with conv it follows that the direction of the GC at the mid-way must have changed by:

½ × Conv between the ground station and the aircraft.

= ½ × d'long (in degrees) × sine mean lat.

This is also the angular difference between the RL and the GC directions at both the ground station and the aircraft and is known as the **conversion angle (ca).**

9.18 To plot the brg from the ground station on a Mercator chart it is first essential to convert the GC radio brg into a RL brg which can be plotted with a straight edge. This will require the ca to be calculated and then applied *in the correct sense* to the GC brg *at the measuring station.* Calculation of ca will need knowledge of the estimated, or DR, position of the aircraft for the time of the brg to enable d'long and mean lat between the ground station and the aircraft to be established. In the example in Fig. 9–13 the d'long is 10° and the mean lat is 37° N. This gives:

$$ca = ½ × 10° × \text{sine } 37°$$
$$= ½ × 10° × 0·6018$$
$$= 3·009°$$
$$= 3° \text{ in practical terms.}$$

In the example the RL direction from the ground station is less than the GC direction by the amount of the ca so the straight line (RL) to be plotted from the ground station is:

$$GC – ca = 271 \text{ (T)} – 3° = \textbf{268 (T)}$$

9.19 The above example showed a N hemisphere case with the aircraft W of the ground station with the ground station taking a brg of a radio transmission by the aircraft.

From Fig. 9–14 it can be seen that had it been the aircraft that was taking a brg on a transmission from the ground station (i.e. a **Non Directional Beacon (NDB)** it would have registered a brg of 085 (T) along the GC transmission *at the aircraft's longitude.* It will also be obvious that in this particular case the ca would have to be added to the GC brg to find the RL brg *from* the aircraft *to* the ground station. Since the object is to calculate

118

the RL brg to be plotted *from* the known position of the ground station 180° must now be applied to the RL brg at the aircraft.

GC brg aircraft to ground station	= 085 (T)
ca	= + 3°
RL brg aircraft to ground station	= 088 (T)
+ or – 180°	= 180°
RL brg ground station to aircraft	= **268 (T)** Plot

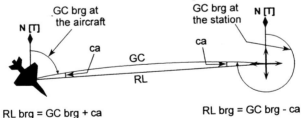

Fig. 9–14   *Calculation of RL brg to plot from a GC brg taken from an aircraft West of an NDB (N hemisphere).*

9.20 This confirms that, in the example given, the RL brg to plot from the ground station (the position of which can be found from charts or published lists) is the same whether the brg is measured at the ground station or at the aircraft. Application of the ca in the correct sense and the need to apply + or – 180° to the RL brg in the case of brgs taken by the aircraft are the points to watch. Also remember that the value of the ca will have to be recalculated with each change in d'long or mean lat.

9.21 Figs. 9–15a, b, c and d illustrate the four possible variations.

Fig.9–15a   *Converting GC brgs to RL brgs. Aircraft West of the ground radio station in the Northern hemisphere.*

In Fig.9–15a is repeated the situation used in the last example with the aircraft W of the ground station in the N hemisphere, where the RL to plot from the ground station:

= GC brg at ground station – ca **or** GC brg at aircraft + ca + or – 180°

119

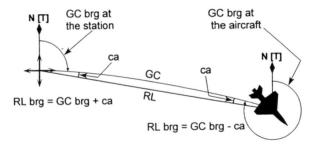

Fig. 9–15b   Converting GC brgs to RL brgs. Aircraft East of the ground radio station in the Northern hemisphere.

In Fig. 9–15b the aircraft is E of the ground station in the N hemisphere. Inspection of the figure shows that in this situation the RL to plot from the ground station:

= GC brg at ground station + ca *or* GC brg at aircraft – ca + or – 180°

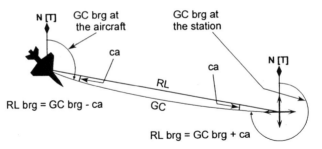

Fig.9–15c   Converting GC brgs to RL brgs. Aircraft West of the ground radio station in the Southern hemisphere.

In Fig. 9–15c the aircraft is W of the ground station in the S hemisphere. Inspection of the figure shows that in this situation the RL to plot from the ground station:

= GC brg at ground station + ca *or* GC brg at aircraft – ca + or – 180°

In Fig. 9–15d the aircraft is E of the ground station in the S hemisphere. Inspection of the figure shows that in this situation the RL to plot from the ground station:

= GC brg at ground station – ca *or* GC brg at aircraft + ca + or – 180°

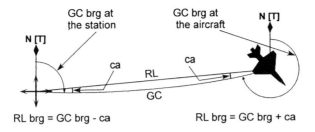

RL brg = GC brg - ca   RL brg = GC brg + ca

Fig. 9–15d   Converting GC brgs to RL brgs. Aircraft East of the ground radio station in the Southern hemisphere.

9.22 Further analysis of the above figures and application rules show that the *ca is always applied to the brg at point of measurement and always towards the equator.* Candidates for the Licence examinations confronted with a problem on plotting radio brgs on a Mercator chart may find it of help to employ a sketch of the situation given in the question:

Example:
An aircraft whose DR position is 5248N 0307W obtains a brg of 115(T) from an NDB situated at 5134N 0041E. What is the brg to be plotted from the NDB on a Mercator chart?

Answer:
First find the mean lat and the d'long between the NDB and the aircraft's DR position. Use these to calculate the ca.

5134N		00041E		
5248N	+	00307W	+	(crossing 0° meridian)
10422N / 2		00348	=	d'long
5211N = mean lat		3° 48"	=	**3·8 d'long**

$$ca = \text{d'long} \times \text{sine mean lat.}$$
$$= 3\cdot8° \times \sin 52° \ 11"$$
$$= 3\cdot8° \times 0.79$$
$$= 3\cdot002 \text{ or } \mathbf{3°} \text{ in practical terms.}$$

Now do a rough sketch marking in the known facts and indicate the RL brg to be plotted from the NDB (see Fig. 9–16).

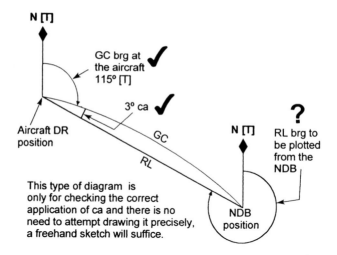

Fig. 9–16   Sketch of 'Known' and 'To be found' factors.

From the sketch it is apparent the 3° ca has to be added to the GC brg of 115 (T) at the aircraft to give the RL brg of 118 (T) at the aircraft. A further + or – 180° has to be applied to give the RL brg of **298 (T)** to be plotted from the NDB.

9.23 The use of such sketches is probably the best way of tackling one type of question related to plotting on a Mercator chart. For instance:

Question:
An aircraft and an NDB are in the same hemisphere. The aircraft takes a brg of 245 (T) on the NDB. The brg to be plotted from the NDB on a Mercator chart is 069 (T). Which hemisphere are they in and what is the value of the ca?

Answer:
From the brgs given the aircraft's position must be somewhere to the East and slightly North of the NDB. With this knowledge freehand sketches of the possible North and South hemisphere cases can be made and the known brgs at the aircraft and the NDB marked in (see Fig. 9–17a and b). It is then a matter of inspection and simple calculation to resolve which is the only feasible case and the value of the ca.

In both cases the reciprocal of the RL brg from the NDB is 069 (T) + or – 180° = 249 (T), this being the direction of the RL at the aircraft. The question gives the GC brg of the radio signal received at the aircraft as 245 (T). The ca, being the difference between the RL and GC measured at a common point, must be 4° and by inspection it can be seen that in Fig. 9–17a (N hemisphere case) the ca would have to be subtracted from the GC bearing giving a RL bearing of 241 (T) which eliminates the N hemisphere case. Inspection of the S hemisphere case, Fig. 9–17b, shows that the ca has to be added to the GC bearing giving the RL brg at the aircraft as 249 (T). Thus the correct answer is:

Southern hemisphere and the ca is 4°.

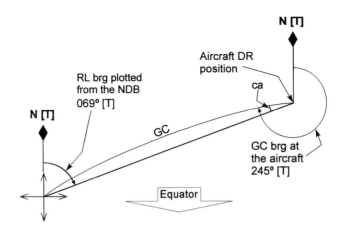

Fig. 9–17a. Sketch for assessing hemisphere and ca. Northern hemisphere situation.

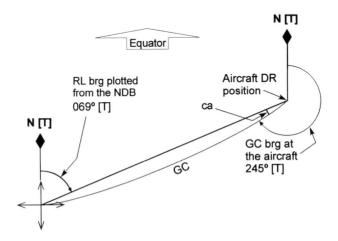

Fig. 9–17b. sketch for assessing hemisphere and ca. Southern hemisphere situation.

9.24 Summary of the properties of Mercator's projection:

Scale:

Correct (same as the RE scale) only along the equator.

Expands away from the equator as the sec of the lat.

Conv:

Only correct at the equator.

Has a constant value of zero over the chart.

Meridians:

Appear as parallel straight lines running N / S.

Parallels of lat:

Appear as parallel straight lines running E / W.

Spacing between parallels increases as scale expands with lat.

RLs:

Are straight lines (having constant direction).

GCs:

Appear as curves concave to the equator. The exceptions to this are the equator and all meridians, these are both GCs and RLs and appear as straight lines.

Uses:

Plotting, topographical and meteorology charts in a band 600 nm either side of the equator. Some aeronautical information charts at lats above 10° (i.e. UK Danger Areas Chart).

CHAPTER 10

TRANSVERSE AND OBLIQUE MERCATOR'S PROJECTIONS

TRANSVERSE MERCATOR'S

10.1 This is another cylindrical projection with the assumed light source at the centre of the RE. Instead of the cylinder being wrapped around the equator it is turned through 90° to lie along a meridian and its anti-meridian (see Fig. 10–1).

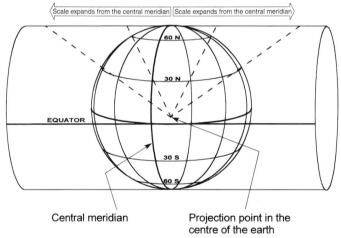

Fig. 10–1   The basis of the Transverse Mercator's projection, a cylinder wrapped around the RE along a chosen central meridian and its anti-meridian.

10.2 Like the ordinary Mercator's projection, the graticule projected has to have a small mathematical correction applied to make it orthomorphic. Furthermore since the point of contact of the cylinder with the RE passes over both poles these can be projected, but by the same token it follows that not all of the equator can be shown. The datum, or central, meridian will be chosen depending on the intended use of the chart. The scale will be correct along the central meridian and will expand with the secant of the

GC distance due E or W from this meridian, (1 nm = 1' of arc). Like the ordinary Mercator's this means that *for all practical purposes* scale can be considered constant up to 600 nm either side of the chosen central meridian.
10.3 If the cylinder is now cut at right angles to the central meridian along the two equator lines and unrolled the projection would look like Fig. 10–2, which shows one hemisphere only (the other hemisphere being identical in appearance).

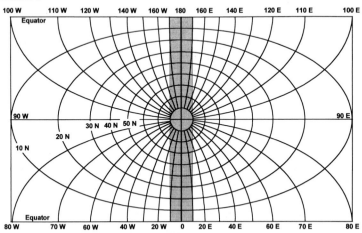

Northern hemisphere Transverse Mercator projection with the 0° Geenwich meridian shown as the central meridian of the projection. The shaded area extended 600 nm either side of the central meridian is the only part of the projection that is of practical navigation use.

Fig. 10–2   The Transverse Mercator's projection.

10.4 Inspection of the projection produced shows that the expansion of the scale at right angles to the central meridian (in Fig. 10–2 the Greenwich 0° meridian has been chosen as the central meridian) results in increasing distortion along the two meridians at 90° to the central meridian. The characteristics of this projectioin are:

Parallels of lat which are small circles on the earth's surface become portrayed as ever increasing ellipses with movement away from the pole.
The only meridians which are projected as straight lines are the central meridian, its anti-meridian and the two meridians at right angles to it. All other meridians project as curves concave to the central meridian.
The equator projects as a straight line but as stated in paragraph 10.2 not all of it can be portrayed.
From this it can be deduced that GCs are only straight lines on this projection when they are directly up or down the central meridian (or its anti-meridian) or at right angles to it. Having said that, within the band 600 nm either side of the central meridian *for all practical purposes* GCs can be considered to be straight lines.

10.5 Since the only part of this projection that is not grossly distorted is the band 600 nm either side of the central meridian, its uses are restricted to within this band. Navigation in the polar regions can be achieved on this projection but at lower lats movement E/W is limited. Apart from the polar case this projection is mainly used to map areas of considerable N/S extent that do not have a large E/W extent. Unfortunately not many natural or national land masses do this.

10.6 One of the few areas that fulfil the criterion is the UK and the Ordnance Survey (OS) maps and 1 : 250,000 Topographical maps (which are based on the OS maps) of these isles are plotted out on a Transverse Mercator's projection whose central meridian is 2° W. The choice of a meridian W of the 0° Greenwich meridian is because the 0° meridian is not central enough to the land mass to be covered. The OS is based on a 10 km squared grid (aligned N/S with the 2° W central meridian) and due to conv on the earth the direction of N (T) and the OS Grid N changes with movement E/W away from the central meridian. In production of the 1 : 250,000 Topographical map costs have been kept down by leaving the OS Grid on the map and superimposeing a lat and long grid (30' × 30') over the top. This means that inside each lat and long box there are some fifteen 10 km OS squares. Along the bottom of these charts there is a warning printed to remind pilots to be sure to measure directions from N (T) and not from the OS Grid N. On the extreme E and W of the United Kingdom measuring from the wrong datum can result in errors of up to 4°. This illustrates the need for pilots to be conversant with the properties of the different maps and charts they use. The 1 : 250,000 Topographical map features in more detail in Chapter 13.

10.7 Summary of the properties of the Transverse Mercator's projection:

Scale:

Correct (same as the RE scale) along the datum (central) meridian. Expands as the sec of the GC distance E / W of the datum meridian. At 300 nm error is 0.38% and at 600 nm error is 1.54%.

Meridians:

Datum meridian and meridians at 90° to it appear as straight lines. All other meridians are complex curves.

Parallels of lat:

Appear as ellipses with their shorter axis along the datum meridian.

RLs:

Datum meridian, meridians at 90° to the datum meridian and the equator appear as straight lines. All other RLs are complex curves.

GCs:

Datum meridian, meridians at 90° to the datum meridian, the equator and all GCs at 90° to the datum meridian appear as straight lines. All other GCs are complex curves. However within a 600 nm band GCs can be assumed to be straight lines *for all practical purposes.*

Uses:

Plotting in the polar regions only (because of the curvature of both the meridians and the parallels plotting of positions at lower lats is difficult). Topographical maps of land masses with large N/S extent and small E/W extent (such as the UK).

OBLIQUE MERCATOR'S

10.8 As its name implies this projection is not aligned with the equator or a particular meridian. It is still based on a cylinder wrapped around the RE but the point of tangency is a chosen obliquely aligned GC. Choice of the alignment of the GC will depend on the use to which the particular map or chart is to be put. Long and relatively narrow land masses whose alignment precluded them from fitting onto a Transverse Mercator's projection can be fitted onto an Oblique Mercator's aligned to a GC which bisects it longer axis. Malaysia is one such country to be mapped onto an Oblique Mercator's projection. Another use of the Oblique Mercator's is in the production of strip maps for long distance flights following a GC.

10.9 Like the Mercator's and Transverse Mercator's the Oblique Mercator's projection requires a mathematical correction to make it orthomorphic. Fig. 10–3 shows just one typical example of how the lat and long grid looks for an Oblique Mercator's. The only GCs that appear as straight lines are the ones that the cylinder is touching when wrapped around the RE and the meridian at 90° away from the point where that GC crosses the equator.

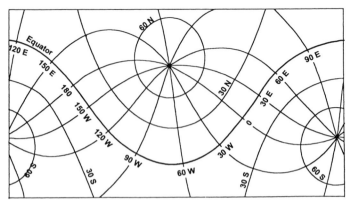

Fig. 10–3   The appearance of a typical Oblique Mercator's projection.

10.10   Use of the Oblique Mercator's is confined to the band just either side of the GC of tangency where, *for all practical purposes*, scale can be considered as constant and GCs approximate to straight lines. Because this projection is quite complex and expensive to produce plus the fact that each sheet is limited to a specific 'corridor' it is not widely used. Apart from mapping countries like Malaysia it is only used to make strip maps for long GC routes that are in regular use and therefore merit the production of special charts.

10.11   Summary of the properties of the Oblique Mercator's projection:

Scale:

Correct (same as the RE scale) along the GC of tangency. Expands as the sec of the GC distance at right angles to the GC of tangency.

Meridians and parallels:

Appear as complex curves.

RLs:

Appear as complex curves.

GCs:

The GC of tangency and all GCs at 90° to the GC of tangency appear as straight lines. All other GCs are complex curves. However within a 600 nm 'corridor' either side of the GC of tangency GCs can be assumed to be straight lines for all practical purposes (most Oblique Mercator charts do not extend to anything like 600 nm either side of the GC of tangency).

Uses:

Topographical maps of long and narrow land masses (such as Malaysia or Italy).

Strip maps of regular used GC routes.

CHAPTER 11

LAMBERT'S CONFORMAL CONICAL PROJECTION

THE SIMPLE CONIC PROJECTION

11.1 As its name implies, Lambert's projection is based on a cone. Consider a cone, like an old fashioned dunce's cap, placed over the RE so that its apex is directly above one of the Poles and the light source at the centre of the RE (Fig 11–1a). Since the apex of the cone is directly above one of the poles it can be seen that the point of contact with the RE is along a parallel of lat. Which parallel a particular cone touches will depend on the steepness of the cone, a shallow cone will contact a high parallel of lat (Fig. 11–1b) and a steep cone a lower parallel of lat (Fig. 11–1c). On conical projections the parallel that the cone is tangential with will have the same length on the chart as length on the RE, it will therefore have correct scale along that parallel of lat. Such a parallel is given the name of **Standard Parallel (SP)**.

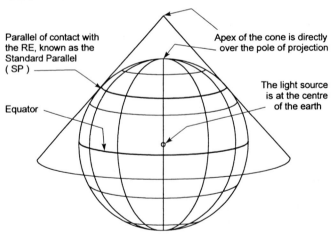

Fig. 11–1a The basis of a simple conic projection showing the Standard Parallel (SP) and light source.

130

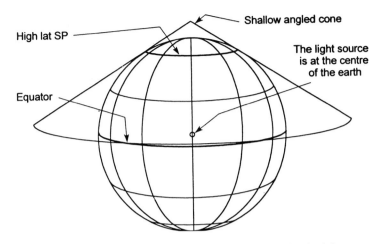

Fig. 11–1b   A shallow angled cone giving a SP with a high lat.

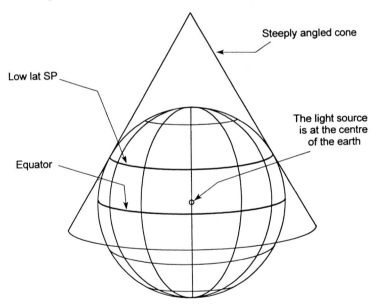

Fig. 11–1c   A steeply angled cone giving a SP with a low lat.

11.2 No matter what the angle of the cone only one Pole, the Pole it is placed over, can be projected, but the entire Equator can be projected if required. Fig. 11–2a shows the lat and long grid projected onto a cone whose SP is 55° N. If this cone is now cut along the 180° meridian and flattened out it will look like Fig.11–2b.

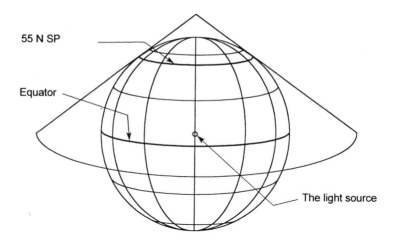

Fig. 11–2a   A Conical projection with SP at 55N.

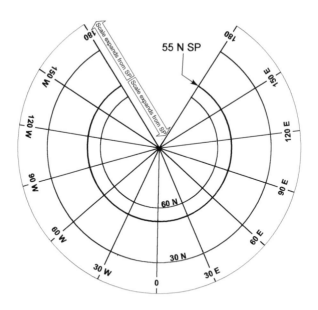

Fig. 11–2b   The Cone opened out flat to show the appearance of the graticule. The 'pie' is 360° × sine SP.

11.3 Inspection of Fig.11–2b reveals certain properties of this simple conic projection:

132

The SP is the same length on the chart as it is on the RE, therefore scale along the SP is correct. However, the flattening out of the cone results in the SP being shown as an arc of a circle instead of a full circle, the size of this arc being 360° × sine of the lat of the SP. The sine of the lat of the SP is known as the **Constant of the Cone** and is sometimes given the symbol of a lower case letter 'n'.

The other parallels and the equator also appear as arcs of 360° × 'n'.

All the meridians appear as straight lines radiating out from the Pole of projection.

Meridians and parallels cross each other at 90°.

The conv of the meridians is the same over all the chart = d'long × 'n'. The only place on the earth where conv = d'long × 'n' is along the SP. Earth conv is less towards the Equator and greater towards the Pole.

So on this projection:

Chart conv is:

Constant.

Correct along the SP.

> Earth conv between Equator and the SP.

< Earth conv between the SP and the Pole.

Scale expands N and S from the SP.

Such a simple conic chart needs mathematical adjustments to make it orthomorphic and would be limited in use to a narrow band either side of the SP.

LAMBERT'S CONICAL ORTHOMORPHIC PROJECTION

11.4 Lambert's projection is a more sophisticated mathematical treatment of this basic conic projection:

An initial SP is selected and the value of 'n' for the chart is established.

The chart scale along the initial SP is them mathematically reduced so that it no longer fits the definition of a SP and it is renamed the **parallel of origin (p/o)**.

The reduction in scale at the p/o also affects the scale either side of the p/o and works in opposition to the scale expansion that took place on either side of the initial SP. The end result is that there are now two parallels, one either side of the p/o, where scale along them is the same as on the RE, thus creating **two SPs**. Mathematical fine tuning is then carried out to ensure that the projection is orthomorphic.

11.5 The effect of all this mathematics is the same as if it had been possible to push the cone down into the RE as in Fig. 11–3a. When cut along a meridian and flattened out the Lambert's projection looks like Fig. 11–3b.

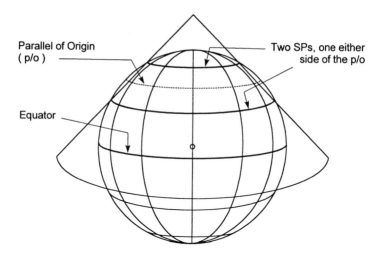

Parallel of Origin
(p/o)

Two SPs, one either
side of the p/o

Equator

Fig. 11–3a   The apparent geometry of Lambert's projection, as if the cone had been pushed into the RE.

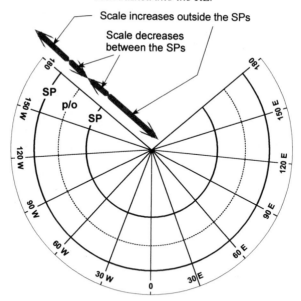

Scale increases outside the SPs

Scale decreases
between the SPs

Fig. 11–3b   The cone opened out flat to show the appearance of Lambert's graticule.

The geometry of the basis of this projection is such that the latitudes of the two SPs are not quite equally spaced either side of the p/o. This is only critical for the cartographer who has to work the mathematics out, for the practical user the p/o can be considered as lying half way between the SPs. In examination questions if the value of the p/o or 'n' is given then use these values as required, otherwise use the sine of the latitude half way between the SPs.

11.6 On Lambert's projection:

Chart conv is:

Constant over the whole chart.

Correct at the p/o.

> Earth conv between the Equator and the p/o.

< Earth conv between the p/o and the Pole.

Scale is:

Correct along both SPs.

Contracted between the SPs to become least at the p/o.

Expanded outside the two SPs.

THE ⅔ : ⅙ RULE

11.7 Provided that the chosen SPs are not too far apart (up to a maximum of just over 12° of lat) the scale within the SPs and for a distance either side of the SPs (equal to a quarter of the distance between the SPs) can be considered as constant *for all practical purposes*. This means that practical constant scale charts can be produced to cover any lat spread of up to 20° by selection of the appropriate p/o and SPs. This spread is shown in Fig. 11–4 and is sometimes referred to as the ⅔ : ⅙ **Rule.** On such a chart the maximum scale error is less than 1% at the p/o and the N and S limits.

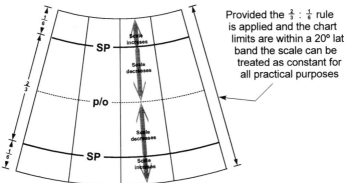

Provided the $\frac{2}{3}$: $\frac{1}{6}$ rule is applied and the chart limits are within a 20° lat band the scale can be treated as constant for all practical purposes

Fig. 11–4   The ⅔:⅙ rule for a Lambert's chart to be treated as constant scale for all practical purposes.

11.8 Some Lambert's charts cover a greater lat spread than 20° and these cannot be considered as having constant scale. Measurement of distance on such charts has to be made using a special variable scale plotted on the edge of the chart, or by use of the scale at the mid-latitude of the trk in the same way as on a Mercator chart.

APPEARANCE OF RLs AND GCs

11.9 If a straight line is drawn between two points on a Lambert chart (see Fig. 11–5) it can be seen to cross successive meridians at an angle which changes by the amount of chart conv between the meridians. A RL (which by definition has constant direction) between the same two points appears as a curve concave to the Pole of projection. It is worth noting that at the mid-point of the straight line and the RL they are running parallel to each other. This means that although curves are impractical to plot, the RL direction between two points can be ascertained by drawing a straight line trk between them and measuring the direction from the meridian at mid-point of the trk.

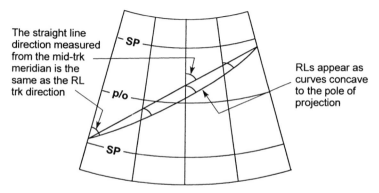

The straight line direction measured from the mid-trk meridian is the same as the RL trk direction

RLs appear as curves concave to the pole of projection

Fig. 11–5   Appearance of a RL and how to find the RL direction between points on a Lambert chart.

11.10   A straight line drawn E/W along the p/o will follow a GC since chart conv and earth conv are the same along the p/o. On the Polar side of the p/o where earth conv is greater than chart conv a straight line drawn E / W will lie closer to the p/o than the GC which appears as a curve concave to the p/o. Similarly on the Equatorial side of the p/o where earth conv is less than chart conv a straight line drawn E/W will lie closer to the p/o than the GC which appears as a curve concave to the p/o. Fig. 11–6 illustrates these cases.

11.11   For charts that fall within the ⅔ : ⅙ rule the differences between chart conv and earth conv over the chart are small and straight lines can, *for all practical purposes*, be considered as GCs. Fig. 11–7 shows the true shape of a GC drawn obliquely across such a chart compared with the straight line drawn between the same start and finish points.

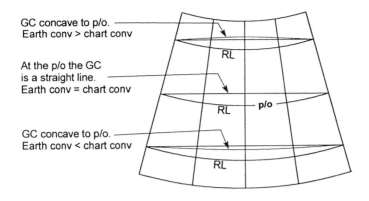

Fig. 11–6   The appearance of GCs running EW on a Lambert projection.

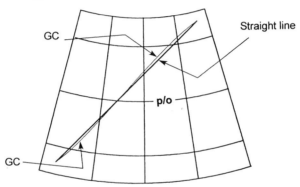

*Fig. 11–7   True appearance of a GC and an oblique straight line
joining two points either side of the p/o.*

PLOTTING BRGs ON A LAMBERT CHART

11.12   Since straight lines on the Lambert's projection can be taken to represent GCs it follows that this makes Lambert's charts ideal for plotting radio brgs be they from a VHF Omni Range (VOR), Non Directional Beacon (NDB) or a ground based Direction Finding (DF) station. The form in which information is received from each of these ground-based sources can vary but in each case the (T) brg of the GC *from* the station must be calculated before plotting it as a straight line from the station's ground position on the chart. The various ways in which the above signals are converted for plotting purposes is dealt with in detail in Chapter 17. Ground DF brgs and VOR brgs emanate at their respective ground stations and once converted into a True bearing *from* the station are plotted as straight lines from N (T) at the ground station.

11.13 In the case of an aircraft taking a brg on an NDB the brg must first be converted to a brg from N (T) at the aircraft and the reciprocal (+ or − 180°) calculated. Chart conv between the DR position of the aircraft and the ground position of the NDB must be applied (in the correct sense) to this reciprocal brg before plotting from N (T) at the NDB ground position. Fig. 11–8 illustrates what happens if chart conv is not applied to the reciprocal.

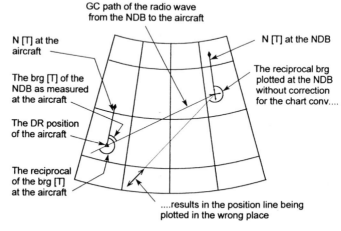

Fig. 11–8   The result of failing to apply chart conv.

11.14 In the case of plotting on a Lambert chart the calculation of the amount of chart conv to apply is found by the formula:

$$\text{chart conv} = \text{d'long} \times \text{'n' (i.e. sine of the p/o)}$$

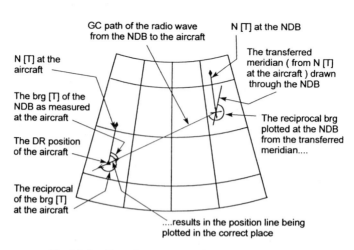

Fig. 11–9   Transferring a meridian to correct for chart conv.

This formula is more academic than practical but, since it may be needed to solve possible examination questions, candidates should commit it to memory. A more practical method can be used when plotting which does not involve calculating the value of the chart conv. Having worked out the reciprocal (T) brg at the aircraft, this is plotted from a line parallel to N (T) at the aircraft's DR position transferred to pass through the ground position of the NDB. This parallel datum is known as a **transferrred meridian** and the angle between it and the (T) meridian at the NDB is the chart conv between them. Fig. 11–9 illustrates this practical method of allowing for conv on a Lambert chart.

Example:
An aircraft takes a brg on an NDB which is positioned at 5236N 0029W. If the DR position of the aircraft is 5310N 0357W and the brg measured at the aircraft is 104 (T) what is the (T) brg to plot from N (T) at the NDB on a Lambert's chart whose p/o is 5600N ?
Answer:
d'long = 0357W – 0029W = 3° 28' = 3·467°
sine p/o (56°) = 0·829
Conv   = dlong × sine p/o
           = 3·467° × 0·829
           = 2·874143° say 3°

Brg of NDB from aircraft =   104 (T)
                    + or – 180°
Reciprocal bearing =   284 (T)
In this case Conv is +   3°
            Plot 287 (T) from NDB (see Fig. 11–10)

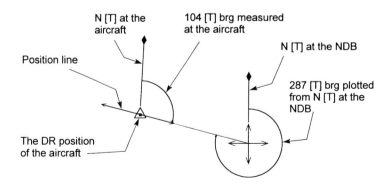

Fig. 11–10. Illustration of the mathematical worked example correcting for chart conv.

11.15   Whether conv has to be added or subtracted can be checked by means of a simple sketch. There are four possible cases:

N hemisphere, aircraft W of NDB (see Fig. 11–11a)
N hemisphere, aircraft E of NDB (see Fig. 11–11b)
S hemisphere, aircraft W of NDB (see Fig. 11–11c)
S hemisphere, aircraft E of NDB (see Fig. 11–11d)

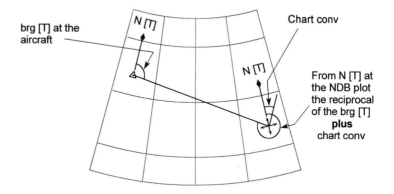

Fig. 11–11a   N Hemisphere, aircraft W of the NDB.

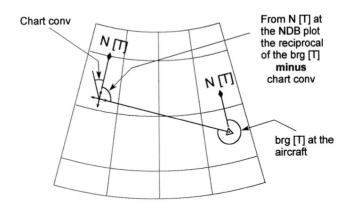

Fig. 11–11b   N Hemisphere, aircraft E of the NDB.

Figs. 11–11c and d also bring out the fact that **in the S hemisphere it is the S pole that is the pole of projection and N (T) is *away* from the pole.** Since candidates for the examinations may have to answer questions involving calculations similar to the example above Figs. 11–11a to d should be learned. Whether the cases are learned by rote or the diagrams studied for recall is a matter of personal preference.

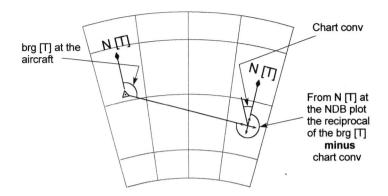

Fig. 11–11c   S hemisphere, aircraft W of the NDB.

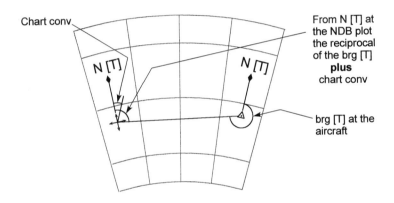

Fig. 11–11d   S hemisphere, aircraft E of the NDB.

11.16   Summary of the properties of the Lambert's projection:

Scale:

Correct (same as the RE scale) along the two SPs.

Contracts between the two SPs becoming least at the p/o.

Expands outside the two SPs.

On charts constructed to conform to the ²/₃ : ¹/₆ Rule the scale can, *for all practical purposes*, be assumed as constant.

Conv:

Constant all over the chart.

Correct at the p/o.

Greater than earth conv between the p/o and the equator.

Less than earth conv between the p/o and the pole of projection.

Meridians:

Appear as straight lines radiating from the pole of projection.

Parallels of lat:

Appear as concentric arcs (360° × sine p/o) centred on the pole of projection.

RLs:

Curves concave to the pole of projection.

GCs:

Curves concave to the p/o, except for the meridians which are straight lines. Straight lines lying E/W along the p/o are GCs. On charts constructed to conform to the ⅔ : ⅙ Rule GCs can, *for all practical purposes*, be assumed to be straight lines.

Uses:

Plotting, topographical, radio navigation and meteorology charts for lats from 10° to 80°.

CHAPTER 12

POLAR STEREOGRAPHIC PROJECTION

12.1 This projection is formed by positioning a flat sheet of paper tangential over one pole on the RE and projecting the lat and long graticule onto the sheet from a light source positioned at the other pole. Figure 12–1a illustrates the lines of projection and Fig. 12–1b shows the appearance of the resulting chart. Note how the meridians radiate out from the pole as straight lines and the parallels are concentric circles all centred on the pole. All the meridians cross the parallels at 90° exactly as they do on the earth.

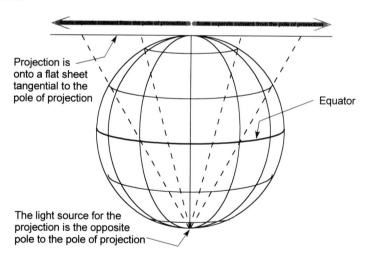

Fig. 12–1a   The Polar Stereographic method of projection.

12.2   The only point on the chart that has the same scale as the RE is at the pole of projection. The scale on the rest of the chart is expanding away from the pole. The rate of change of scale at any point is the same N/S as it is E/W so this projection is naturally orthomorphic and does not require any mathematical adjustment. The scale expands away from the

143

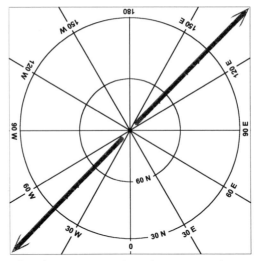

Fig 12–1b   The appearance of a Polar Stereographic projection.

pole as the **sec of ½ the co-lat** (see Fig. 12–2). The definition of the co-lat is:

90° – the lat of the parallel being projected

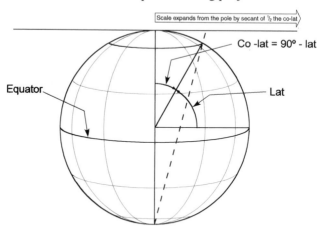

Fig. 12–2   Scale expanding by Secant of the ½ co-lat.

Example:
Scale at 80° lat = scale at the pole × sec ½ (90° – 80°)
           = scale at the pole × sec ½ (10°)
           = scale at the pole × sec 5°
           = scale at the pole × 1·0038

Which indicates that at a distance of 600 nm (10° of lat) from the pole the scale expansion on this projection is only 0·38%. Checking other latitudes shows that at 70° lat scale expansion is 1·54%, at 60° lat it is 3·53% and although the equator can be projected the scale expansion is a massive 41·42%. *For all practical purposes* the scale can be regarded as constant within 600 nm of the pole of projection. Further than 600 nm from the pole scale can no longer be considered constant and the measurement of trk distances must be carried out using the latitude scale at the mid-lat point of the trk.

12.3 Conv is constant over the whole chart and is equal to conv at the pole, that is to say it is equal to d'long, the 'n' factor for the chart being 1 (the sine of 90°). With movement away from the pole to lower lats the earth conv decreases until it becomes zero at the equator. So chart conv is only correct at the pole and is greater that earth conv at all other lats.

Example:
At 80° lat earth conv $\quad = \quad$ d'long × sine 80°
$\qquad\qquad\qquad\qquad\quad = \quad$ d'long × 0·9848

This means that at 80° lat chart conv is approximately 1·5% in error. By 70° lat the error is around 6%, at 60° lat it is 13·4% and at the equator it is 100%. In the vicinity of the pole where the error is negligible, straight lines can, *for all practical purposes*, be considered as GCs. Since RLs are lines of constant (T) brg these will appear as curves concave to the pole of projection, the parallels of lat being one example, the one exception being the meridians which appear as straight lines and qualify as both RLs and GCs. It is worth noting that if an aircraft is flown along a meridian to the pole its (T) direction will change by 180° the instant it crosses the pole and starts to fly along the anti-meridian away from the pole.

12.4 Uses of this projection are limited to the polar regions. Even a relatively short flight in the vicinity of either of the poles can involve large changes in d'long, conv and (T) direction so the use of a suitably aligned grid overlay is not uncommon (see Chapter 2, paragraphs 2.11 and 2.12).

12.5 Summary of the properties of the Polar Stereographic projection:
Scale:
   Only correct (same as the RE scale) at the pole of projection.
   Expands away from the pole of projection as the sec of ½ the co-lat.
Conv:
   Only correct at the pole of projection (equal to d'long).
   Has a constant value over the whole chart.
   Since earth conv decreases away from the poles to become zero at the equator the chart conv is greater than earth conv at all lats except the poles.

Meridians:

Appear as straight lines radiating from the pole of projection.

Parallels of lat:

Appear as concentric circles centred on the pole of projection.

RLs:

Appear as curves concave to the pole of projection, the one exception being the meridians which are straight lines and are both RLs and GCs.

GCs:

Appear as curves concave to the pole of projection, the one exception being the meridians which are straight lines and are both GCs and RLs. Within 600 nm of the pole of projection GCs can, *for all practical purposes*, be assumed to be straight lines.

Uses:

Plotting, topographical, radio aids and meteorology charts for use in the polar regions.

All the colour extracts from the 1:250000 series of charts are produced here by the kind permission of the Aeronautical Charts section of the UK CAA.

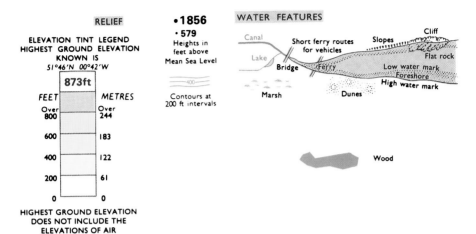

Fig. 13–1a   *Portrayal of natural features and relief on the 1:250 000 series of UK topographical charts.*

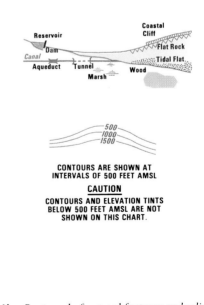

Fig. 13–1b   *Portrayal of natural features and relief on the 1: 500 000 series of UK topographical charts.*

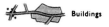

Buildings

Fig. 13–2a Portrayal of towns and built up areas on the 1:250 000 series of UK topographical charts.

BUILT-UP AREAS
City or large Town .... over 2 Sq km
Town.......................... I to 2 Sq km
Small Town, Village or Hamlet ....under I Sq km
Large-Industrial Area...............

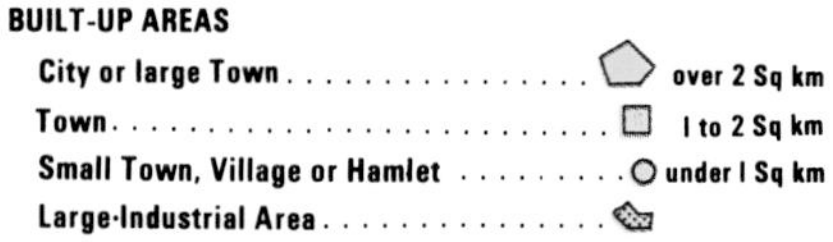

Fig 13–2b Portrayal of towns and built up areas on the 1:500 000 series of UK topographical charts.

ROADS
M1
Motorway with service area, service area (limited access) and junction with junction number
M40
Motorway junction with limited interchange
M11
Motorway and junction under construction with proposed opening date where known
Dual carriageway
A3(T)
Trunk road
Road tunnel
B2131
Secondary road
Roundabout
Road under construction
A855
B885
Narrow road with passing places
Other tarred road
Other minor road
The representation on this map of a road is no evidence of the existence of a right of way

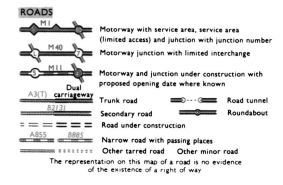

Fig. 13–3a Portrayal of roads on the 1:250 000 series of UK topographical charts.

ROADS
Motorway, with Service Area ....
M1
Dual Carriageway, with Service Area....
Multi-level Intersection.............
Primary.......................
Secondary and selected Minor ....
Under construction.................
Bridge or Viaduct, Tunnel ....

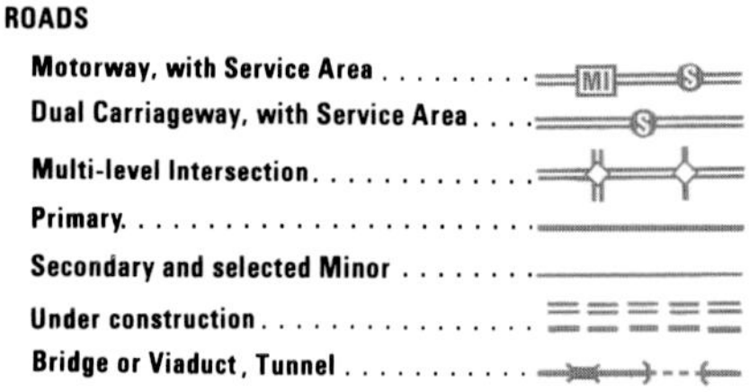

Fig. 13–3b Portrayal of roads on the 1:500 000 series of UK topographical charts.

RAILWAYS
Station
Two or more tracks
Single track
Alignment of former railway
Track removed
Narrow gauge track
Road crossing under or over
Level Crossing
Tunnel

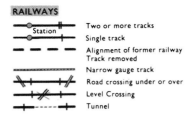

Fig. 13–4a Portrayal of railways on the 1:250 000 series of UK topographical charts.

RAILWAYS
Multiple Track
Single Track
Narrow gauge Track
Former railway, track removed (selected)
Bridge or Viaduct, Tunnel

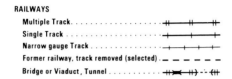

Fig. 13–4b Portrayal of railways on the 1:500 000 series of UK topographical charts.

GENERAL FEATURES
Light-vessel
Racecourse
Lighthouse
Ground mark
Windmill
Castle
Antiquity
Radio or
TV mast
Native fortress
Roman road (course of)

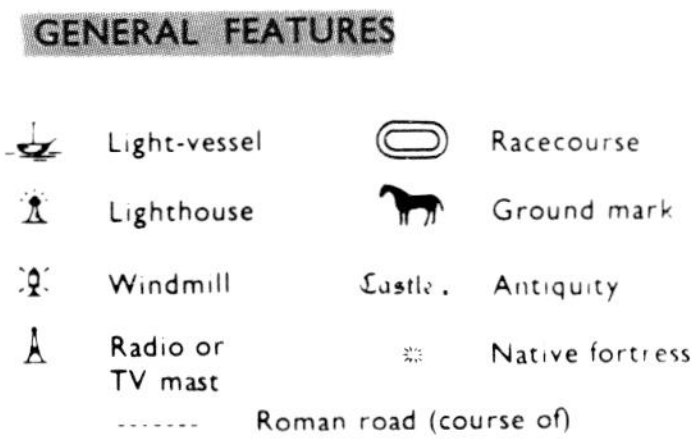

Fig. 13–5a Portrayal of other man-made features on the 1: 250 000 series of UK topographical charts.

GENERAL FEATURES
Reservoir under construction
Power Station
PS
Mine (selected)
Racecourse or Racetrack
Landmark, annotated
Hill Figure
Monument (selected)

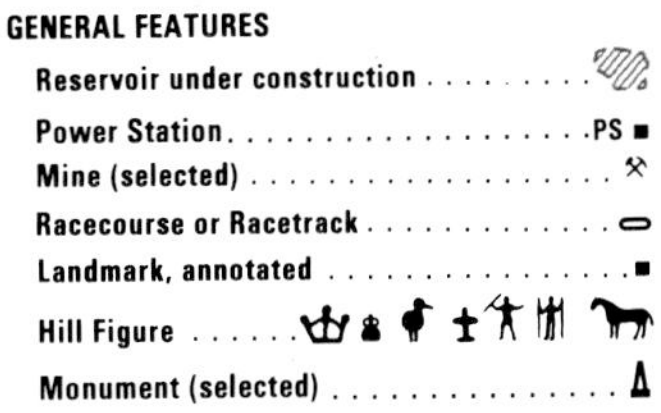

Fig. 13–5b Portrayal of other man-made features on the 1:500 000 series of UK topographical charts.

Exceptionally High Obstacle (Lighted)
Single, Multiple
1000ft or more AGL................ 1950 (1720)   1536 (1300)

Obstacle (Unlighted)................ 530 (323)

Group Obstacle (Lighted)................ 560 (425)
Numerals in italics indicate height of top of obstacle above Mean
Sea Level. Numerals in brackets indicate height of top of obstacle
above Local Ground Level.

Cables joining Obstacles, height AGL................ 310

SYMBOLS ARE NOT SHOWN ON THIS CHART FOR LAND-SITED
OBSTACLES LESS THAN 300FT ABOVE LOCAL GROUND LEVEL.
PERMANENT OFF-SHORE OIL AND GAS INSTALLATIONS ARE
SHOWN REGARDLESS OF HEIGHT CATEGORY.

Aeronautical Light................ ☆ FIR

Power transmission line................

Power transmission line over 200ft AGL................
Powerline information is not necessarily complete.

Visual Reporting Point (VRP)................ASHFORD VRP

Special Access Lane Entry/Exit................
(Arrow indicates centre of lane, see UK AIP
for conditions of use)

Altimeter Setting Region................ CHATHAM ASR   PORTLAND ASR

Bird Sanctuary................
Areas shown with name/effective altitude (in thousands of feet AMSL)

High Intensity Radio Transmission Area (See UK AIP RAC 5-1-5)................
Areas shown with name/effective altitude (thousands of feet AMSL)

AERODROMES

Field limits with hard runway pattern................ Howes 168 (M)

Howes—Name 168-Elevation (M)-Military, (C)-Civil, (J)-Joint

Aerodrome Traffic Zone (ATZ)................
Circle 2·0 or 2·5 NM radius (See UK AIP RAC 3-9-2-1)

Minor aerodromes with runway pattern unknown................
or not portrayable.

Disused or abandoned aerodromes................

Heliports (M)-Military, (C)-Civil, (J)-Joint................ (H)

Customs Aerodromes are distinguished by a pecked line
around the name of the aerodrome................ Manston

Glider Launching Site (See UK AIP RAC 5-1-4)

   a. Primary activity at locations................ Ⓖ

   b. Additional activity at locations................

Winch Launch Activity

   a. Primary activity at locations................Cables

   b. Additional activity at locations................Cables

Foot Launch Activity................

Free-fall Parachuting Site, DZ circle 1·5NM radius................ Ⓜ

Site of Intensive Microlight Flying................
(Intensive Microlight activity also takes place at certain Licenced
and Unlicenced Aerodromes. See UK AIP RAC 5-1-5).

Class A Airspace................ CTR Ⓐ SFC-2500'ALT

Class D Airspace................ CTA Ⓓ 2500'ALT-FL245

Class E Airspace................ CTR Ⓔ SFC-FL60

Class F Airspace................ W3D Ⓕ 2500'ALT-FL235
(Advisory routes. Centre line only is shown)

Class G Airspace................
(FIR Bdys shown)

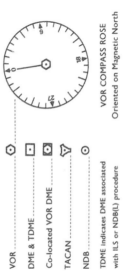

NO AIRSPACE CLASSIFIED AS [B] OR [C] EXISTS WITHIN THE COVERAGE OF THIS CHART SERIES.

Low Level Corridor or Special Route.............. 500'–4500'ALT

Military Aerodrome Traffic Zone (MATZ)....... MATZ
and Honington Military CTR.
MATZs have the following vertical limits: SFC to 3000ft AAL within circle and 1000ft AAL to 3000ft AAL within stub. Controlling Aerodromes are marked with an asterisk within a circle thus

Radar Advisory Service Zone
or Area..................

Area of Intense Aerial Activity (AIAA)...

Mandatory Radio Area.............

Instrument Approach Procedure (IAP)............
(Outside Controlled Airspace, the existence of an IAP is indicated by the symbol aligned to the **Main** Instrument Rwy. Other IAPs may also exist. See UK AIP RAC 3-9-1-7).

VOR ....

DME & TDME ....

Co-located VOR DME ....

TACAN ....

NDB ....

TDME indicates DME associated
with ILS or NDB(L) procedure

High Intensity Radio Transmission Area (See UK AIP RAC 5-I-5)........
Areas shown with name/effective altitude (thousands of feet AMSL)

Gas Venting Station (See UK AIP RAC 5-I-6)........
Areas are shown with effective altitude (in thousands of feet AMSL).

Airspace Restrictions........ D308/II

Prohibited 'P', Restricted 'R', and Danger Areas 'D', are shown with identification number/vertical limits in thousands of feet AMSL.
Areas activated by NOTAM are shown with a broken boundary line.
For those Scheduled Danger Areas whose upper limit changes at specified times, only the higher of the upper limits is shown on the chart.
Danger Areas whose identification numbers are prefixed with an asterisk* contain airspace subject to Byelaws which prohibit entry during the period of Danger Area Activity. See UK AIP RAC 5-I-I.

VOR COMPASS ROSE
Oriented on Magnetic North

Fig. 13–6a Portrayal of aeronautical information on the 1:250 000 series of UK topographical charts.

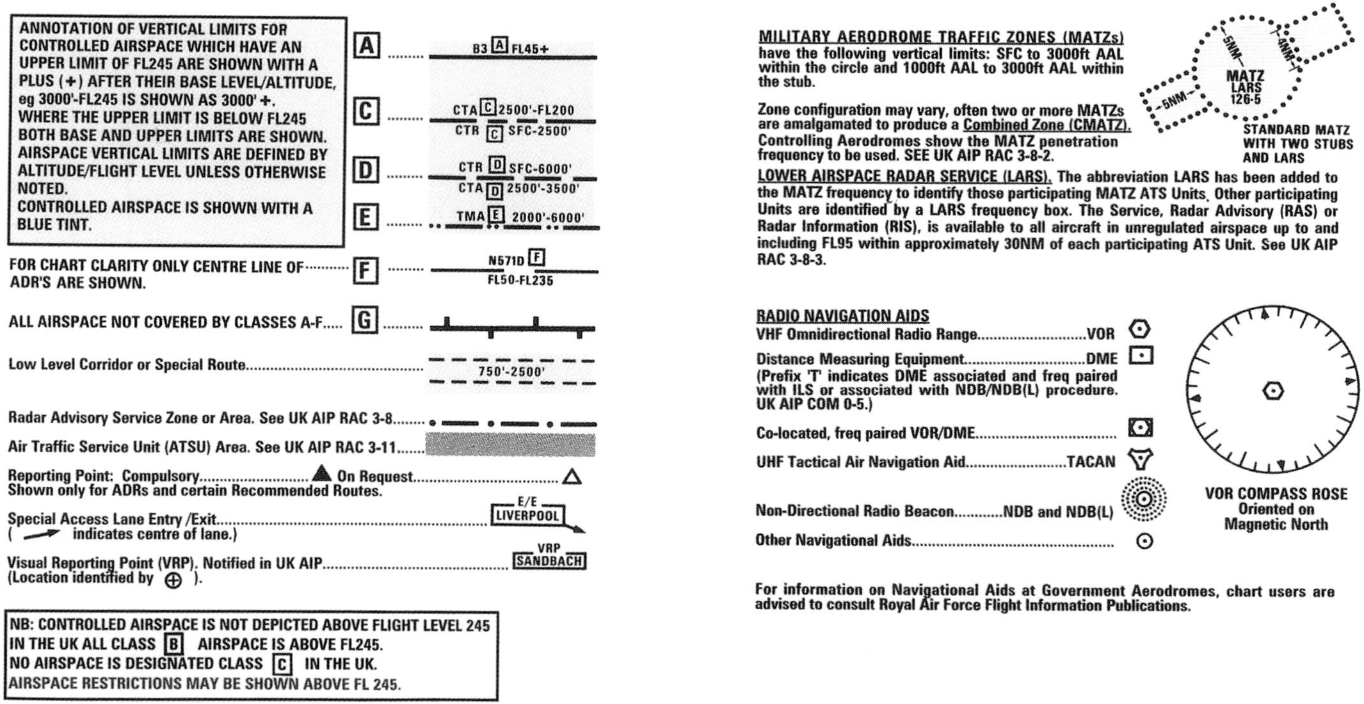

Fig. 13–6b   Portrayal of aeronautical information on the 1: 500 000 series of UK topographical charts.

Aerodrome symbols

Aerodrome - Civil..

Aerodrome - Civil, limited or no facilities......................

Heliport - Civil..

Aerodrome - Government, available for Civil use. See UK AIP AGA 0-5......

Aerodrome - Government...

Heliport - Government..

Aerodrome - Disused or Abandoned. Shown for navigational
landmark purposes only. See AIC 46/91...........................

AERODROME ELEVATION. Numerals adjacent to aerodrome indicate elevation
of aerodrome in feet above Mean Sea Level........................ 250   250

CUSTOMS AERODROMES are distinguished by a pecked line around
the name of the aerodrome.. [MANCHESTER]

Aerodrome Light Beacon... ☆FIG : . - .`   ☆FIR : . - . ·

Site of Intensive Microlight Flying..............................
Intensive Microlight Activity also takes place at certain Licensed and Unlicensed
Aerodromes.See UK AIP RAC 5-1.

FOR CURRENT STATUS, AVAILABILITY, RESTRICTIONS AND WARNINGS APPLICABLE
TO AERODROMES SHOWN ON THIS CHART CONSULT AIR INFORMATION PUBLICATIONS
AND AERODROME OPERATORS OR OWNERS. PORTRAYAL DOES NOT IMPLY ANY RIGHT
TO USE AN UNLICENSED AERODROME WITHOUT PERMISSION.

FREE-FALL PARACHUTING SITE. UK AIP RAC 5-1.
Parachutists may be expected within the airspace contained
in a circle radius 1·5NM or 2NM of the DZ up to FL150. Night
parachuting may take place at any of the sites shown on this chart.

Marine Light....................... ● Fl(3)30-9secs Lightship................ ⚓ FlWR 12-0secs
(Normally shown if visibility range is not less than 15NM).

MAGNETIC VARIATION

LINES OF EQUAL MAGNETIC VARIATION
(ISOGONALS) ARE SHOWN FOR JUNE 1995.   6¹⁄₂°W
ANNUAL CHANGE 9' (decreasing)

GLIDER LAUNCHING SITES. UK AIP RAC 5-1.

a. Primary activity at locations.................................... Ⓖ cables.....   Ⓖ cables

b. Additional activity at locations................................ ⊞ cables.....   ⊞ cables

cables indicate winch launch

HANG/PARA GLIDING

FOOT LAUNCH ACTIVITY. UK AIP RAC 5-1-4.

Foot Launch Site..............(Most commonly used)................

CABLE LAUNCH ACTIVITY. UK AIP RAC 5-1.

a. Primary activity at locations.................................... ➤ cables.....   ➤ cables

b. Additional activity at locations................................ ▼ cables.....   ▼ cables

cables indicate winch launch

Notified sites where activity exceeds 500ft AGL are shown with elevations. It should
be noted that at some sites, cables may be carried above 2000ft AGL. These can be
identified on the chart by the Hazard altitude, (in thousands of feet AGL) shown after
the annotation 'cables' eg cables/3. Ascending paragliders may be encountered within
the airspace contained in a circle radius 1·5NM of the notified position of the site.

AIR NAVIGATION OBSTACLES

Exceptionally High Obstacle (Lighted)   1978   2297
1000ft or more AGL. Single, Multiple.   (1031)   (1050)

                                                          825   1614
                                                         (360)   (605)

Single Obstacle (Unlighted)......................................
Multiple Obstacle (Lighted)......................................
Cable joining Obstacles..   ⚡⚡⚡ cables
Numerals in italics indicate elevation of top of obstacle above Mean Sea Level.
Numerals in brackets indicate height of top of obstacle above local Ground Level.
Obstacles annotated 'flarestack' burn off high pressure gas. The flame, which may not
be visible in bright sunlight, can extend up to 600ft above the installation.

KNOWN LAND SITED OBSTACLES ABOVE 300ft AGL ARE SHOWN ON THIS CHART.
A SMALL NUMBER OF OBSTACLES BELOW 300ft AGL ARE SHOWN FOR LANDMARK
PURPOSES. PERMANENT OFF-SHORE OBSTACLES ARE SHOWN REGARDLESS OF
HEIGHT CATEGORY. See UK AIP RAC 5-1.

MAXIMUM ELEVATION FIGURES (MEF)

3² Maximum Elevation Figures are shown in quadrangles
bounded by graticule lines for every half degree
of latitude and longitude. MEFs are represented
in thousands and hundreds of feet above mean
sea level. Each MEF is based on information available concerning
the highest known feature in each quadrangle, including terrain
and obstacles and allowing for unknown features.
NB THIS IS NOT A SAFETY HEIGHT

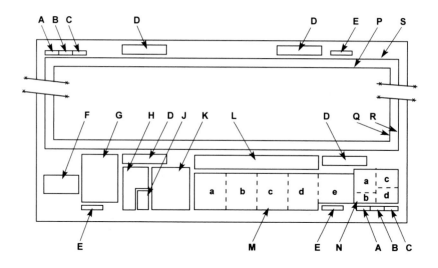

Fig. 13–7   Information panels around the borders of a typical 1 : 250 000 series UK topographical map.

(For legend – see pages 151–152)

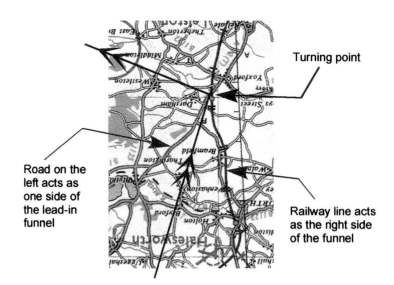

Turning point

Road on the left acts as one side of the lead-in funnel

Railway line acts as the right side of the funnel

Fig. 13–8   Example of funnel features.

CHAPTER 13

TOPOGRAPHICAL MAPS

13.1   The function of an aeronautical topographical map (or chart) is to provide a formalised pictorial representation of ground features that will help a pilot to plan and execute a flight that is to be carried out wholly, or partly, within visual contact of the ground. Map reading from the air is frequently referred to as an art and in a sense this is an appropriate statement since any topographical map is, in its own way, a work of art. In the case of topographical maps designed for aeronautical use, the starting point would be one of the projections discussed in the previous chapters. Which projection is used depends on what particular part of the earth's surface is to be portrayed. In general terms Mercator's projection is used in equatorial regions, Lambert's projection (with appropriate SPs) for mid-latitude regions and the Polar stereographic for polar regions. Transverse and Oblique Mercator's projections are used for some special cases (i.e. long narrow land masses or strip maps). Ground features are then applied, in their correct geographical position, on to the latitude and longitude graticule. Aeronautical information is then added as appropriate to complete the overall picture.

13.2   One of the first questions that arises in the production of a topographical map is 'how much and just what detail is to be shown?' To decide on the degree of detail to be shown, reference must be made back to 'scale' (see Chapter 8, paragraphs 8.5 to 8.8). The 'larger' the scale of a map the smaller the area it can portray within a given sheet size and the more detail can be fitted in. Conversely the 'smaller' the scale of a map the larger the area it can portray within a given sheet size but far less detail can be shown on it. The UK is currently covered on two different scales of topographical maps. The 1 : 500,000 series, printed on Lambert's projection, covers England, Scotland, Wales and Northern Ireland on three sheets and the 1 : 250,000 series, printed on a Transverse Mercator's projection (central meridian 2W) requiring 17 sheets to cover the same geographical region. It follows that much more detail can be given on the 1 : 250,000 series than on the 1 : 500,000 series.

13.3   Details shown on the map must be things that a pilot can identify from his or her cruising level on a clear day. The 1 : 250,000 UK series is primarily intended for low level, relatively slow speed, cross-country navigation purposes. Like all maps designed for use in the air the 1 : 250,000 series also carries aeronautical information of a non-topographical nature (such as Controlled Airspace) restricted to those items applicable to *below 5000 ft above mean sea level (amsl)* and this series of maps should not be used above 5000 ft amsl without a 1 : 500,000 series map (all of which have full aeronautical information coverage up to 40,000 ft) as a back-up. From around 3000 ft amsl the field of view is quite good and it is possible to identify many features on the ground quite clearly. As a result it has been possible to utilise the excellent UK OS maps as the basis for the 1 : 250,000 series of aeronautical topographical maps. This gives more detail than is necessary for air work but is not a serious disadvantage. The only slight problem is the retention of the OS 10 km Grid which is aligned with the 2W meridian and has been known to catch out the unwary when measuring direction (see Chapter 10, paragraph 10.6).

13.4 In the case of the 1 : 500,000 series the intended use is for map reading at higher levels and higher speeds of flight. At high levels greater distances can be seen on a clear day but the amount of detail that can be identified on the ground will be reduced. High features such as hills become flattened to the pilot's view and most roads, other than motorways and trunk roads, become difficult to discern. Only large features like cities, coastlines and major rivers can be identified clearly and the reduced amount of detail shown on the 1 : 500,000 series reflects this changed situation. Map reading at high altitudes may be further complicated by the fact that the flight deck can restrict the view of a large area of the ground directly beneath the aircraft and for some miles around.

13.5 The information that is displayed on any aeronautical topographical map falls into one of three categories:

Natural features, i.e., coastlines, rivers, mountains etc.

Man-made features, i.e., towns, roads, railway lines, bridges etc.

Aeronautical information, i.e., boundaries and heights of areas of restricted airspace, geographic positions of ground based radio aid such as NDBs with their callsigns and frequencies, sites of special air activity such as gliding, etc.

How these features are portrayed follow fairly standard patterns. There are however some variations in presentation of man-made items on the different scale maps and these are discussed later in paragraph 13.7.

13.6 The main natural features are portrayed in fairly obvious colours, blue for water features and green for wooded areas. These rather idealistic colours are all very well but are not necessarily what the pilot will see. With changing seasons and weather the natural colours may change. The shapes of woods will remain pretty constant (even after felling) but flooding can alter the shape of water features for short periods of time and the colour may well be more like brown than blue at times. Relief, or height of the ground amsl, is shown by contour lines. These are lines joining places having a common height amsl and colours are used to shade the various contour layers to produce what is known as 'layer tinting'. The lowest layer is white and progressive layers are coloured with deepening amber tints, the darker the tint the higher the ground. By this method high ground is pictorially indicated and this is reinforced by individual high points being marked with a black dot and the height amsl printed in black beside it. In the UK heights are given in *feet* but maps produced in some countries use similar methods for indicating high ground but, and it is a big 'but', heights may be indicated in *metres*! Never take height readings on an unfamiliar map for granted – always check before using. For example, high ground shown as 700 m amsl is actully 2300 ft amsl. You have been warned! (Figs. 13–1a and 13–1b on the colour plates show the way natural features and relief are portrayed on these two UK topographical charts.)

13.7 Man-made features vary in their colouring depending on the materials used and the fashions at the time they were constructed. Furthermore colours can be changed, what is red today may be repainted yellow tomorrow. To cater for such variables, a set of conventions to cover all cases has been evolved for use on UK topographical charts:

Towns. These are portrayed in grey on the 1 : 250,000 series maps and in yellow on the 1 : 500,000 series maps. On the 1 : 250,000 series the shapes of quite modest built-up areas are given and in remote places individual buildings are shown. By contrast the 1 : 500,000 series only gives the shapes of the major cities, other towns merit small squares or dots depending on the size of the town and many small villages are not portrayed at all (see Figs 13–2 a and 31–2 b on the colour plates).

Roads. On the 1 : 250,000 series roads are outlined by parallel thin black lines and coloured according to designation. Motorways are in blue and trunk/main roads are in a brick red, secondary roads in a lighter shade of brick red and other tarred roads in white. For the aviator the lesser distinctions are of no real value. On the 1 : 500,000 series all roads are in red with no outlines. The line styles vary to signify Motorways, dual carriageways and lesser roads (see Figs. 13–3a and b on the colour plates).

Railway tracks. These are shown as solid black lines. Tracks have a small black slash across them at regular intervals, a single slash denoting a single track line and a double slash indicating two or more tracks. Where a track has been removed but the line of the original track bed is still visible from the air it is shown as a series of black dashes. Other symbols indicate features such as tunnels, bridges and level crossings (see Figs 13–4a and 13–4b on the colour plates).

Other man-made features may be visible from the air depending on the height of the aircraft above the ground. Some, such as giant figures or animals carved in chalk, can be seen from considerable altitudes and feature on both series of topographical maps; no matter what the natural colour of such ground marks they are portrayed, by shape, in solid black. Features such a lighthouses, windmills, radio masts, TV masts and racecourses which are far too diverse in shape and colour to be individually portrayed are given standardised symbols. Whilst all such features are marked in on the 1 : 250,000 series only the large features, like racecourses, are shown on the 1 : 500,000 series (see Figs 13–5a and 13–5b on the colour plates).

Aeronautical information is printed in purple on the 1 : 250,000 series of maps and in purple (for Civil items) or blue (for Government items) on the 1 : 500,000 series of maps. Apart from aerodromes, high obstructions (i.e. TV transmitter masts) and power transmission lines most of these items are not visible to the naked eye. Regulated airspace such as controlled, restricted and prohibited areas are designated by coded boundary lines along with information on the vertical extent of each designated area and the controlling authority. The geographical positions of ground based radio aids to navigation (such as NDBs) are given by means of standardised symbols along with their operating frequency and identifying callsign. Other symbols are used to signify sites of special aeronautical activities, such as gliding and parachuting (see Figs. 13–6a and 13–6b on the colour plates).

13.8 It is an examination requirement that candidates have a comprehensive knowledge of all of the above standard symbols. Although most have been given above, by far the best way to learn them is to study the information panels found on the edge of all topographical charts. One of each scale will be needed because as noted earlier in this chapter there are slight differences in the presentation of some features. It goes without saying that only current editions should be referred to as small changes do occur from time to time (usually with aeronautical information) and pilots are required to be up-to-date at all times.

13.9 At the time of writing the format of the information displayed around the edge of the 1 : 250,000 series is as shown in Fig. 13–7. This layout has changed very little over many years and unless there is a major rethink it seems unlikely there will be much significant change in the foreseeable future.

The current layout decodes as follows. At the top left and repeated at the bottom right of the sheet is:-

A – SHEET Number.
B – NAME of area covered.
C – Edition number.

Example: **SHEET 14 EAST ANGLIA Edition 12.**

Twice on the top and twice on the bottom of the sheet is:

D A **Special Note,** reminding users that regulated airspace is only shown up to 5000 ft amsl and that above 5000 ft amsl the 1 : 500,000 series chart should be used for regulated information.

Top right and bottom left and right is:

E A reminder that (on these charts) Elevations are in ft amsl.

Along the bottom are to be found:

F A **Caution** about the date of currency of the air information given, plus a reminder that users should always check NOTAMS, UK AIPs and current UK Airspace Restriction charts for any update of information. There is also a note about aerodrome use and UK Military Low Flying Systems.

G Specific notes about activities and procedures that apply *to that particular chart's area.*

H **Relief** information. This shows the contour line intervals and the layer tinting used. It also shows how spot heights are displayed.

J Orientation. Showing the differences between True, Magnetic and the OS 10 km overlay Grid North *on that particular sheet.*

K A diagram showing the adjoining sheets and the amount of overlap with these sheets. There is also a note on how to use the National Grid. This is not essential reading for aviators since the National Grid is not used in aviation, however it may be of use for anyone who wishes to use their maps for walking or motor rallying as well as flying.

L A statement that the chart **Scale** is **1 : 250,000** on a **Transverse Mercator Projection** plus three graduated scales in **Kilometres, Nautical Miles** and **Statute Miles** respectively.

M Aeronautical information, which is printed in purple and is laid out in five main groups:

　(a) *Aerodromes.* Type, name, elevation, layout (where known), present usage and any special activities.

　(b) *Obstructions.* Land sited obstructions are only shown if they are 300 ft or more **above the local ground level (AGL)**. Different symbols are used to differentiate between those obstructions which are less than 1000 ft AGL and those that are more than 1000 ft AGL. The symbol is doubled to indicate a group of obstructions (such as a collection of tall factory chimneys) as opposed to a single obstruction (like a TV transmitter mast). The dot at the base of the symbol indicates the geographical position of the obstruction. Two numbers by each symbol give the height of the top of the obstruction amsl in ***bold italics*** and AGL (*light* *italics in brackets*). A small ray symbol at the top of the obstruction symbol indicates that it carries obstruction lighting. Symbols for cables joining obstructions, power lines and aeronautical lights also appear in this block.

    (c) *Symbols used to outline areas of regulated airspace*, the different line types identifying the function of the enclosed area. The controlling authority and vertical extent of an area will also be given, either along a boundary line or within the area itself.

    (d) *Miscellaneous symbols* covering items from Visual Reporting Points (VRPs) to Airspace Restrictions including notes on Danger / Restricted / Prohibited Areas.

    (e) *Symbols used to indicate the presence and type of ground based radio aids*. Note that where these appear on the chart they have the identification callsign and frequency beside the symbol and where a **VOR** compass rose is shown it is always aligned with local N(M).

N   Symbols covering:

    (a) *Roads.*

    (b) *Water features.*

    (c) *Railways.*

    (d) *General features.*

Here the 1 : 250,000 series reveals its origins in the OS series of maps. Some of the features in this block are of no practical use to aviators as they are not discernible from the air. Retention of such features is purely to keep the cost of production down, the removal of items like the telephone call box and battle site symbols from the master plates would be an expensive exercise.

Along the top and bottom inner frame of the map:
P **OS Eastings Grid**. Each number is at a 10 km interval from its neighbour.

Along the left and right inner frame of the map:
Q **OS Northings Grid**. Each number is at a 10 km interval from its neighbour.

Along the left and right outer frame of the map:
R **The lat scale**. Whole degrees and every 10' are numbered and each two minutes marked by alternate black and white segments.
Along the top and bottom outer frame of the map:
S **The long scale**. Whole degrees and every 10' are numbered and each two minutes marked by alternate black and white segments. The spacing of this long scale is approximately half the spacing of the lat scale. Reference to Chapter 3, paragraph 3.11 and the departure formula confirms this is what

one should expect since the UK lies roughly between 50N (cos = 0·6428) and 60N (cos = 0·5).

13.10   A look around the borders of a 1 : 500,000 series map will reveal a different layout but similar information. Some symbols have been deleted and others modified to suit the reduced details a pilot can expect to see when flying at greater altitudes. Likewise the Restricted Airspace details are now shown up to Flight Level 40 (FL 40 or 40,000 ft above the 1013 mb Standard Datum setting. See the Instrument and Meteorology syllabi for altimeter setting procedures). Two items that appear only on the 1 : 500,000 series are:

Minimum Elevation Figures (MEF). The MEF is shown in each 30' × 30' box that contains any land mass. It gives the Thousands and Hundreds of ft of the highest terrain or known obstructions in the box. **It is not a safety height** (the reasoning behind, and calculation of, safety height is covered in depth in the altimetry sections of both the Instruments and Meteorology syllabi).

UK ATS Airspace Classifications chart. This gives, in pictorial form, all the do's and don'ts for **Instrument Flight Rules (IFR)** and **Visual flight Rules (VFR)** flying within the different types of Classified Airspace.

13.11   Pilots should be totally familiar with the symbols on the topographical maps that they use. As explained above, full details are available around the borders of topographical maps for reference at any time, but in a busy cockpit/flightdeck environment space to spread out a map, and time to do so, may be limited. Like so many aspects of navigation, time spent in study and preparation on the ground can save precious time in the air. Some people find trying to memorise columns of symbols extremely boring. Learning symbols can be made easier by making a game of it. Cut a hole of about 4 inches (10 cm) diameter in a piece of card, drop the card on the map and try to decode the items visible inside the hole. Look up any that do not come quickly to mind. Keep repeating the exercise on different parts of the map until decoding becomes second nature.

13.12   There are some basic rules about the best way to use topographical maps during pre-flight study and when map reading in the air:

Pre-flight:

Various ways of marking up a map for use with pilot navigation techniques were given in Chapter 7. In the preliminary stages of pre-flight planning study of the topographical details along a route will help in deciding which marking method is best suited to that particular route.

During the planning stages look for features that are unique along the route and are likely to be easily identified. In particular look out for combinations of different features that together form distinct pictures which are unlikely to be confused with anything else.

Look for what are termed 'funnel' features. These are ribbon features

153

such as roads, rivers or railway lines that can act as a funnel into a turning point or destination. Such features may not be present at the end of every leg but when they are they can be as good as a signpost (see Fig. 13–8 on the colour plates).

It also pays to bear in mind the meteorological conditions that the flight is to be flown in. Under certain haze conditions visibility into sun may be poor and the only thing likely to be seen up sun will be reflections off water features. If such a situation is forecast concentrate most planning effort on features along the route that are down sun.

Try to get a clear picture how the beginning of each leg should look once the hdg has been set up. This is an insurance against a wrong compass hdg being set at the beginning of a leg. Suppose 352° (C) was set on in error for 325° (C), the expected view would be skewed off by almost 30°, an anomaly that should alert the prepared pilot to something being amiss.

In the air:

Map reading in the air is made easier if the map is orientated so that the trk on the map is pointing in the direction of the trk over the ground. This may require careful folding of the map prior to flight, especially if it is to be used in a cramped cockpit.

When map reading from a known position the technique is to read from map to ground. Look on the map to see what features should be coming into view ahead and to left and right, then look out in the relevant directions to verify those features on the ground. On the map mark places with the time as they are pinpointed, this will keep the progress of the flight up to date and help to make pilot navigation calculations easier.

When for any reason a pilot is uncertain of position the procedure for map reading is reversed (i.e. read from ground to map):

In a simple case of uncertainty, such as low cloud obscuring the ground for a period of time, once the ground becomes visible again it is a straightforward task to estimate the DR position on the map. Provided the planned elements of the flight plan have been adhered to since the last known position the map features in the vicinity of the DR position should match the features now visible on the ground.

Sometimes the situation can develop from being 'uncertain of position' to being 'lost'. If this occurs a definite plan of action known as **'lost procedure'** is needed. Certain questions should be asked and appropriate action taken if the answers call for it:

What is the Safety Height? Climb up if below it.

Does the route go near any Controlled Airspace? If so try and contact the Controlling Authority on RT for fixing assistance and guidance away from any Controlled area.

When and where was the last known position of the aircraft?

Have all the planned elements of the flight plan been adhered to since that time?

Are the compasses functioning correctly? Is the Directional Gyro Compass Indicator (DGI) correctly synchronised? Are there any magnetic items placed near the magnetic compass? If something is wrong correct the mistake and note the amount of hdg error that has to be allowed for in working out a DR positon.

Do not keep changing hdg in the hope of identifying some feature on the ground, such activity usually only serves to make matters worse by losing a record of the DR trks and GSs. By sticking to a steady hdg (even if it is found to be in error) it is possible to work out a DR position from which to start comparing the map features with the observed ground features.

13.13   It has been said that the secret of good navigation is not to get lost, something that cannot always be guaranteed. By careful pre-flight planning, route study, sticking to the flight plan, accurate flying, regular compass checks in flight and continual practise of pilot navigation techniques a pilot can greatly reduce the chances of getting lost on a map reading exercise. It is a true saying of most things in aviation, 'Time spent in preparation and continual practise makes for safe and enjoyable flying'. In the author's view if an hour spent in preparation on the ground can save a minute of hassle in the air then it is an hour well spent.

SECTION 4

MISCELLANEOUS PROCEDURES

This section covers those aspects of navigation that have a direct bearing on flight safety, planning and airborne procedures.

The practicality of the flight safety aspects is fairly obvious and in the case of collision avoidance explains the rationale behind the Aviation Law rules for the rapid assessment of collision risk (i.e. an aircraft observed to be on a constant relative brg).

The chapter on Time and Time Conversions has considerable significance for commercial pilots whose work can take them to almost any quarter of the world and have them passing through time zones and crossing the International Date Line.

With the availability of so many automatic navigation devices on the flightdeck of commercial aircraft, the subject of plotting may seem obsolete. Nonetheless to get the maximum benefit from such aids requires a pilot to have a knowledge of the underlying principles behind them, hence the licence requirement for plotting.

In places there are references to earlier chapters and paragraphs. These are for the guidance of any reader who wishes to recap on a basic point before continuing with the main text.

CHAPTER 14

RELATIVE VELOCITY

14.1 Velocity is, as already defined, the movement of an object in terms of direction and speed in relation to a specified datum. Thus the TAS of an aircraft is its velocity in relation to the surrounding air whereas its GS is its velocity in relation to the earth's surface below it. The term **Relative Velocity** is used to define the direction and speed of one moving object in relation to another moving object. The relative velocity between two aircraft can be used to work out separation along airways, adjusting speed to achieve a specified overhead time at a reporting point or the assessment of possible collision risk. Furthermore the assessment of collision risk introduces the concept of a **Line of Constant Bearing (LCB)** which is also used in the calculation of the **Point of No Alternate (PNA)** (see later in Chapter 15).

CALCULATION OF THE RELATIVE VELOCITY BETWEEN TWO AIRCRAFT

14.2 The calculation of relative velocities is achieved by plotting vectors. The individual velocity vectors for the two aircraft are plotted from a common datum for a common period of time and the ends of the vectors are then joined up to give a vector of the relative velocity. The direction of the relative velocity will of course depend on which aircraft the relative movement is being observed from.

14.3 Fig. 14–1a shows the velocity vectors for two aircraft, 'A' on a trk of

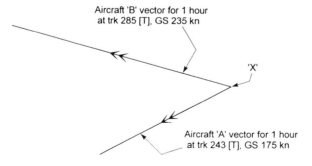

Aircraft 'B' vector for 1 hour
at trk 285 [T], GS 235 kn

'X'

Aircraft 'A' vector for 1 hour
at trk 243 [T], GS 175 kn

Fig. 14–1a   One hour vectors for two aircraft departing from a common datum point 'X'.

159

243(T) at GS 175 kn and 'B' on a trk of 285(T) at GS 235 kn plotted from a common datum 'X' for one hour. Figure 14–1b shows the relative velocity vector drawn in, the arrows on this vector indicating the relative movement of aircraft 'B' as seen from aircraft 'A' **(333(T) at 156 kn)**. In Fig. 14–1c the arrows are reversed indicating the relative movement of aircraft 'A' as seen from aircraft 'B' **(153(T) at 156 kn)**.

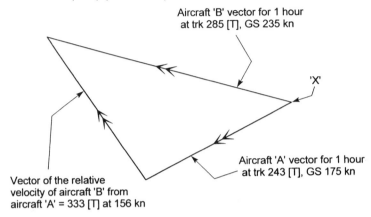

Fig. 14–1b   Vector of relative velocity of aircraft 'B' from aircraft 'A'.

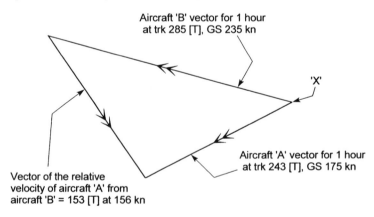

Fig. 14–1c   Vector of relative velocity of aircraft 'A' from aircraft 'B'

USES OF RELATIVE VELOCITY

14.4   Overtaking. The most basic case of the use of relative velocity is in the assessment of the position and time at which a fast moving aircraft will overtake a slower aircraft that is ahead of it on the same trk. The vector method for calculating the relative velocity mentioned in paragraph 14.2 works for *all* cases but is not necessary in this case where both aircraft are moving in the same direction and the only difference is their speeds. Fig. 14–2 shows two aircraft on a common trk, with aircraft 'D' (GS 275 kn) 48 nm ahead of aircraft 'E' (GS 335 kn) at 1100.

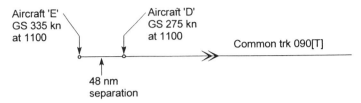

Aircraft 'E'
GS 335 kn
at 1100

Aircraft 'D'
GS 275 kn
at 1100

Common trk 090[T]

48 nm
separation

Fig. 14–2   Overtaking on a common trk.

The relative velocity of 'E' as seen from 'D' is in the direction of the trk at the difference in their GSs (**090(T) at 60 kn**).

With 'E' overtaking 'D' at 60 kn it will close up the 48 nm gap in 48 min.

By plotting either aircraft forward for 48 min at its GS the overtaking point can be found.

In this case it is some 220 nm ahead of 'D's position at 1100 hrs, or some 268 nm ahead of 'E's position at 1100, (see Fig. 14–3).

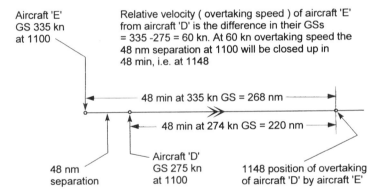

Aircraft 'E'
GS 335 kn
at 1100

Relative velocity (overtaking speed) of aircraft 'E' from aircraft 'D' is the difference in their GSs = 335 -275 = 60 kn. At 60 kn overtaking speed the 48 nm separation at 1100 will be closed up in 48 min, i.e. at 1148

48 min at 335 kn GS = 268 nm

48 min at 274 kn GS = 220 nm

48 nm
separation

Aircraft 'D'
GS 275 kn
at 1100

1148 position of overtaking of aircraft 'D' by aircraft 'E'

Fig. 14–3   Calculation of the point of overtaking.

14.5   Adjusting speed to achieve a revised ETA. For Air Traffic Control reasons a pilot may be requested to meet a revised (delayed) ETA by reducing the TAS of the aircraft to a specified value, this to be done at the latest time possible for achievement of the new ETA.

Example:
An aircraft is on a trk of 152 (T), TAS 390 kn and WV 230 / 55 with an ETA of 1024 at the next reporting point. At 0940 the pilot is instructed to reduce TAS to 350 kn so as to arrive over the reporting point at 1027. At

what time should the TAS be changed from 390 kn to 350 kn? (see Fig. 14–4.)

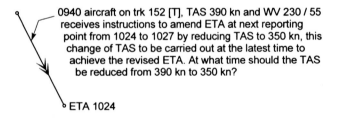

0940 aircraft on trk 152 [T], TAS 390 kn and WV 230 / 55 receives instructions to amend ETA at next reporting point from 1024 to 1027 by reducing TAS to 350 kn, this change of TAS to be carried out at the latest time to achieve the revised ETA. At what time should the TAS be reduced from 390 kn to 350 kn?

ETA 1024

Fig. 14–4   Reducing TAS to revise ETA, the scenario.

Solution:

The first step is to calculate the GSs the two TASs give (in some examination questions the GSs are quoted instead of TASs, thus making calculations easier for the candidate).

In this case a TAS of 390 kn will give a GS of 376 kn and a TAS of 350 kn a GS of 335 kn.

The original ETA was 1024 and the distance to run at 0940 is 44 min at GS 376 kn = 276 nm.

If, at 1940, the TAS was immediately reduced to 350 kn the amended ETA at the reporting point would be 1940 + (276 nm at GS 335 kn) = 1940 + 49·4 min = 1029·4 a loss of 5·4 minutes on the original ETA.

The revised ETA called for is 1027, a delay of only 3 minutes. Since 276 nm at the reduced TAS lost 5·4 minutes a simple ratio will solve for the distance required to lose 3 minutes:-

$$\frac{\text{Time lost (min)}}{\text{Distance (to reporting point)}} \quad \frac{5\cdot4}{276} \quad = \quad \frac{3}{\text{'d'}}$$

Where 'd' is the distance, *measured back from the reporting point*, at which the reduced TAS must be started.

Rough check. Since 3 is just over ½ of 5·4 then 'd' must be just over ½ of 276, say about 150.

The circular slide rule readout gives **158 nm** as the distance to run at the reduced TAS.

At 0940 the distance to run was 276 nm so before reducing the TAS there is still (276 – 158) = 118 nm to fly at the original TAS which in this case was giving a GS of 376 kn. The time to reduce the TAS is:

$$0940 + (118 \text{ nm at } 375 \text{ kn})$$
$$= \quad 0940 + 18\cdot8 \text{ min.}$$
$$= \quad \textbf{0958·8.} \text{(see Fig. 14–5)}$$

162

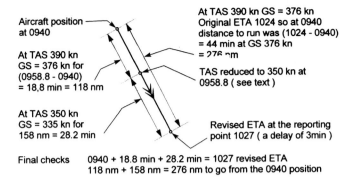

Aircraft position at 0940

At TAS 390 kn
GS = 376 kn for
(0958.8 - 0940)
= 18,8 min = 118 nm

At TAS 350 kn
GS = 335 kn for
158 nm = 28.2 min

At TAS 390 kn GS = 376 kn
Original ETA 1024 so at 0940
distance to run was (1024 - 0940)
= 44 min at GS 376 kn
= 276 nm

TAS reduced to 350 kn at
0958.8 (see text)

Revised ETA at the reporting
point 1027 (a delay of 3min)

Final checks   0940 + 18.8 min + 28.2 min = 1027 revised ETA
118 nm + 158 nm = 276 nm to go from the 0940 position

Fig. 14–5   Reducing TAS to revise ETA, the solution.

A final cross check can be made to confirm the answer. At 0958·8 there are 158 nm to go at the reduced GS of 335 kn = 28·2 min giving the revised ETA of 1027 as requested.

14.6   Calculation of collision risk. In Fig. 14–1 the establishment of the relative velocity between two aircraft that were diverging from a common starting point and time was demonstrated. Their individual positions after 60 min were joined by a line whose direction and length vectorially represented the relative velocity between the two aircraft for one hour. Had their positions after 30 min been plotted and then joined by a line, this line would be seen to be parallel to the line joining the 60 min positions. The same holds good for lines joining the 15 min positions, 45 min positions, in fact for any common time positions. Since the bearing is the same for all times it is known as a **Line of Constant Bearing(LCB)**. A pair of arrow-heads, pointing in towards each other, are used to denote that a line is a LCB (see Fig. 14–6).

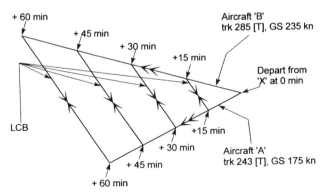

Fig. 14–6   Line of Constant Bearing (LCB).

163

14.7 By running the above diagram backwards using the same GSs the two aircraft would meet back at the starting point having maintained a steadily shortening LCB between them throughout the return journey (see Fig. 14–7). If they were at the same altitude a collision risk would exist at the point where the trks meet.

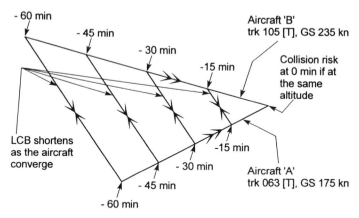

Fig. 14–7   Collision risk with aircraft converging whilst maintaining a LCB.

14.8 Consider the same two aircraft flying down the same trks at the same GSs as in Fig. 14–7 but with one of them starting some 30 nm further away from the point where the trks cross. Plotting common time positions and joining them with straight lines does not produce a LCB. (see Fig. 14–8) The two aircraft will not arrive at the crossing point of the trks at the same time and a collision risk does not exist.

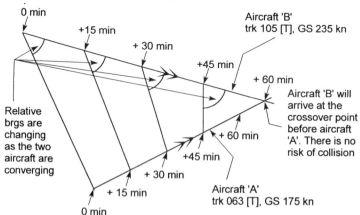

Fig. 14–8   Relative brgs that do not make a LCB signify no collision risk exists.

164

14.9 Only if a LCB exists between two converging aircraft flying at the same altitude is there a collision risk. If the bearing from one aircraft changes relative to another aircraft flying at the same altitude then a collision risk does not exist between them. These two statements give rise to some possible examination questions:

For two aircraft flying on converging trks at the same altitude calculate if a collision risk exists.

If a collision risk exists between two aircraft flying on converging trks at the same altitude calculate the position and time of the point of collision risk.

If a collision risk does not exist between two aircraft flying on converging trks at the same altitude calculate which aircraft will pass ahead of the other and by how many nm.

In examinations it is common practice to issue candidates with graph paper for solving any of the above type of questions. Trk, GS and the position of both aircraft *for a common time* are needed. These parameters may be given in the question or the candidate may have to work them out from other given information.

14.10   The decision whether a collision risk exists or not is straightforward. Plot both aircraft for a common time and draw the bearing between them, repeat the process for a later common time and check to see if the bearing is the same or changing. If they make a LCB a collision risk exists (see Fig. 14–7); if the bearing is changing a collision risk does not exist. (see Fig. 14–8.)

Example:
At 0843 aircraft 'X' (trk 112 (T), GS 160 kn) has aircraft 'Y' (trk 088 (T), GS 140 kn) flying at the same altitude on a brg of 170 (T) range 60 nm from 'X'.
Does a collision risk exist?
If a collision risk exists at what time will the collision risk occur?
If there is no collision risk which aircraft will cross in front of the other and by how many nm?

Answer:

Plot the 'X''s trk of 112(T) and mark it with the double arrow trk symbol pointing in the direction of 112(T).
Put a pinpoint symbol (a dot with a small circle around it) near the left hand end of this trk and label it with 'X' and the time 0843.
From this pinpoint plot a brg of 170 (T) and (using a suitable constant scale) measure 60 nm from 'X' down this brg.
Put another pinpoint symbol at this 60 nm point and label it with 'Y' and the time 0843.
From the pinpoint symbol for 'Y' plot 'Y''s trk of 088 (T) so that it crosses 'X''s trk. Mark with trk arrows.

What is now plotted is the situation at 0843, with both aircraft and their respective trks shown (see Fig. 14–9).

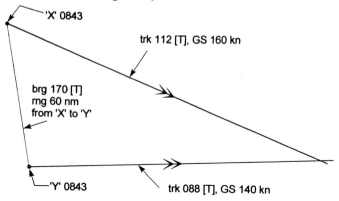

Fig. 14–9   The situation at 0843.

Plot each aircraft down its respective trk for an equal time interval. A time interval of 30 min is ideal as the movement will equal half the GS. Mark these new positions with the time to which they have been moved and join them with a line giving the brg between them. Fig. 14–10 shows the aircraft moved for 30 min down their trks, 'X' for 80 nm and 'Y' for 70 nm, both labelled with the time 0913.

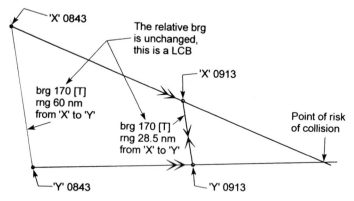

Fig. 14–10   Plotting forward to a common time and checking the new relative brg.

Measurement of the brg between 'X' and 'Y' at 0913 shows it to be the same as the brg between them at 0843. **It is a LCB and a collision risk exists.**
It is possible to measure from say 'X''s 0843 position to the point where the trks cross and using 'X''s GS calculate the time of collision. This method has the drawback that with trks that are converging at a shallow angle any

small error in plotting the trks will cause the position where the trks meet to be in error by several miles.

A far more accurate method is to use the relative closing speed. In the example the original distance apart at 0843 was 60 nm. A measurement of the LCB at 0913 shows the distance apart has shrunk to 28·5 nm. The LCB has a decreasing relative speed of:

$$(60 - 28·5) \text{ nm in 30 min.}$$
$$= 31·5 \text{ nm in 30 min.}$$
$$= 63 \text{ nm in 60 min.}$$
$$= \textbf{63 kn}$$

At 0843 the LCB was 60 nm long, it is closing up at a relative speed of 63 kn. So the 0 nm (collision point) will be reached in just under 60 min after 0843, the exact time (**t**) being found by the ratio:

$$\frac{60}{t} = \frac{63}{60}$$

The circular slide rule gives **t = 57 min**. Therefore the time of collision risk is 0843 + 57 min = **0940**.

Example:
At 1417 aircraft 'P' (trk 260 (T), GS 130 kn) has aircraft 'Q' (trk 286 (T), GS 150 kn) flying at the same altitude on a brg of 182 (T), range 70 nm. Does a collision risk exist?
If a collision risk exists, at what time will the collision risk occur?
If there is no collision risk, which aircraft will cross in front of the other and by how many nm?

Answer:
Plot the 'P''s trk of 260(T) and mark it with the double arrow trk symbol pointing in the direction of 260(T).
Put a pinpoint symbol near the right hand end of this trk and label it with 'P' and the time 1417.
From this pinpoint plot a brg of 182 (T) and (using a suitable constant scale) measure 70 nm from 'P' down this brg.
Put another pinpoint symbol at this 70 nm point and label it with 'Q' and the time 1417.
From the pinpoint symbol for 'Q' plot 'Q's trk of 286 (T) so that it crosses 'P''s trk. Mark with trk arrows.
What is now plotted is the situation at 1417, with both aircraft and their respective trks shown. (see Fig. 14–11)

Plot each aircraft down its respective trk for an equal time interval. Mark these new positions with the time to which they have been moved and join

167

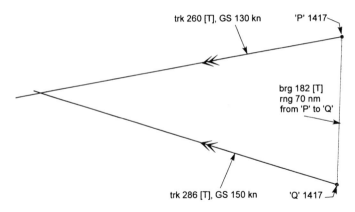

Fig. 14–11   The situation at 1417.

them with a line giving the brg between them. Figure 14–12 shows the aircraft moved for 30 min down their trks, 'P' for 65 nm and 'Q' for 75 nm, both labelled with the time 1447.

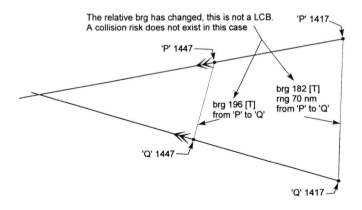

Fig. 14–12   Plotting forward to a common time and checking the new relative brg.

Measurement of the brg between 'P' and 'Q' at 1447 shows it not to be the same as the brg between them at 1417, **it is *not* a LCB therefore a collision risk does *not* exist** .

To calculate which aircraft will cross ahead of the other and by how many nm it is necessary to plot the LCB that these aircraft would have to be on for a collision risk to exist. To do this plot the aircraft from the point where the trks cross back up their trks for equal amounts of time. Joining these two points will plot the collision risk LCB. Figure 14–13 shows the positions plotted back for 30 min with the LCB plotted between them.

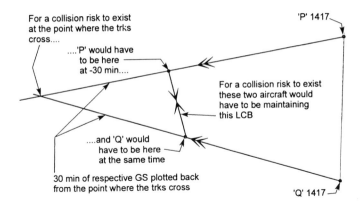

For a collision risk to exist at the point where the trks cross....

....'P' would have to be here at -30 min....

'P' 1417

For a collision risk to exist these two aircraft would have to be maintaining this LCB

....and 'Q' would have to be here at the same time

30 min of respective GS plotted back from the point where the trks cross

'Q' 1417

Fig. 14–13   Establishing the LCB that the aircraft would have to be on for a colli-sion risk to exist.

Draw lines parallel to this LCB through the two 1417 aircraft positions. In this example the LCB through the 1417 position of aircraft 'Q' cuts the trk of aircraft 'P' between the 1417 position of 'P' and the crossover point of the trks. The LCB through the 1417 position of 'P' does not cut 'Q''s trk to the crossover point. The aircraft whose LCB cuts the trk of the other aircraft is the one that will reach the crossover point first. In the example aircraft, 'Q' will reach the crossover point ahead of aircraft 'P'.

Measuring the distance from 'P''s 1417 position to where the LCB through 'Q''s 1417 position cuts 'P''s trk will give the separation between the two aircraft at the crossover point, in this example it is 21 nm. (see Fig 14–14)

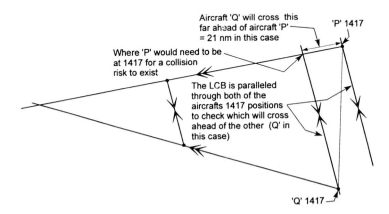

Aircraft 'Q' will cross this far ahead of aircraft 'P' = 21 nm in this case

'P' 1417

Where 'P' would need to be at 1417 for a collision risk to exist

The LCB is paralleled through both of the aircrafts 1417 positions to check which will cross ahead of the other (Q' in this case)

'Q' 1417

Fig. 14–14   Establishing which aircraft will pass in front of the other and by what distance.

CHAPTER 15

NAVIGATIONAL EMERGENCY DATA

15.1 Pilot training includes many hours of practice in handling emergencies in the air. Engine failure, asymmetric flight, forced landing, limited flight panel and many other such problems are grist to the mill for a good pilot. Preparation and practice are the pilot's insurance policy against the fortunately rare chance of being confronted with a real in-flight emergency. Some situations require navigational decisions to be taken. For instance a passenger is taken ill, is it quicker to continue to destination or return to the point of departure? This chapter deals with the various navigational emergencies and the pre-flight planning methods that provide the pilot with the answers before getting airborne.

CRITICAL POINT (CP)

15.2   The single leg case. The question posed above 'Is it quicker to go on or turn back?' gives rise to what is known as the **Critical Point (CP)** or 'equal time' point. Taking a single leg trk from 'A' to 'B' (see Fig 15–1) there must be a point along the leg where it is as quick to fly on to 'B' as it is to fly back to 'A'.

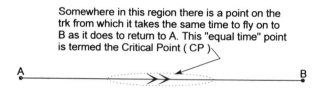

Somewhere in this region there is a point on the trk from which it takes the same time to fly on to B as it does to return to A. This "equal time" point is termed the Critical Point (CP)

A   B

Fig. 15–1   The Single leg Critical Point (CP)

If the **GS On (O)** to 'B' were the same as the return **GS Home (H)** back to 'A' then this equal time point, or CP would fall exactly half way between 'A' and 'B'. Such a situation will only occur in the rare condition of zero WV or with a WV exactly at right angles to the track. The normal effect of WV leads to different values for GS O and GS H resulting in the CP moving from the half way position on the leg, this movement always being into wind.

15.3 Fig. 15–2 shows the leg 'A' to 'B' of **total Distance (D)**. If from 'A' the **distance to the CP is called (d)** then the distance from the CP to 'B' must be **(D – d)**. The problem is to calculate **d** using the known total leg distance **D**, GS **O** and GS **H**.

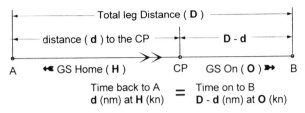

Fig. 15–2   *The basic elements of the single leg CP.*

Since the CP is an 'equal time' point the time to fly (**D – d**) (from the CP on to 'B') at GS **O** must be the same as the time to fly **d** (from the CP back to 'A') at GS **H**. The basic ratio formula:

$$\frac{\text{Distance}}{\text{Time}} = \frac{\text{GS}}{60} \quad \text{Transposes as Time} = \frac{60 \times \text{Distance}}{\text{GS}}$$

$$\text{Time from CP on to 'B'} = \frac{60 \times (D - d)}{GS\ O}$$

$$\text{Time from CP back to 'A'} = \frac{60 \times d}{GS\ H}$$

As these are equal times
$$\frac{60 \times (D - d)}{O} = \frac{60 \times d}{H}$$

The 60s cancel, leaving
$$\frac{(D - d)}{O} = \frac{d}{H}$$

Cross multiplying gives
$$H(D - d) = Od$$
$$HD - Hd = Od$$
$$HD = Od + Hd$$
$$HD = d(O + H)$$
$$\frac{HD}{O + H} = d$$

This can best be set on the circular slide rule of the navigation computer in the form of the ratio:

$$\frac{H}{O + H} = \frac{d}{D}$$

Example:
An aircraft is to be flown from 'A' to 'B' Trk 105 (T), distance 372 nm, TAS 230 kn and WV 245 / 35. Calculate the distance and time from 'A' to the CP.

Answer:

Using the **L** slide of the navigation computer speed slide gives a GS **O** of 256 kn (hdg 111 (T)) for the trk 105 (T) and a GS **H** of 202 kn (hdg 279 (T)) for the reciprocal trk of 285 (T). **O** + **H** in this case is 256 + 202 = 458.

The ratio to set up on the circular slide rule is:

$$\frac{202}{458} = \frac{d}{372}$$

Rough check. 202 is just under half of 458 so **d** must be just under half of 372, say around 170 nm.

The circular slide rule readout for **d** is **164 nm** from 'A'.

Time from 'A' to the CP is 164 nm at the GS **O** of 256 kn. Rough check. Say 150 nm at 250 kn is ⅗ of an hour or approximately 36 min.

The circular slide rule readout gives the time as **38·5 min.**

It is always possible to check the CP calculation by comparing the time to cover d at GS **H** with the time to cover **(D – d)** at GS **O**, if the CP has been correctly calculated they should be the same, give or take half a minute.

In the example above **d** of 164 nm at GS **H** of 202 kn.
Rough check. Say 150 nm at 200 kn is approximately 45 min.
The circular slide rule readout gives the time as **48·75 min.**
(D – d) = (372 – 164) = 208 nm at GS **O** of 256 kn.
Rough check. Say 200 nm at 250 kn is approximately 48 min.
The circular slide rule readout gives a time of **48·8 min** (see Fig. 15–3).

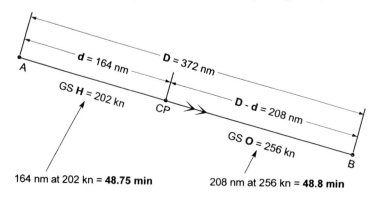

164 nm at 202 kn = **48.75 min**   208 nm at 256 kn = **48.8 min**

Fig. 15–3   Example of a single leg CP calculation.

15.4   The Multi-leg case. For reasons of safety and Air Traffic Control many flights have to be routed to their destination by circuitous means rather than in a direct line. A flight may consist of a series of legs of varying lengths and directions and solving the position of the CP requires the elimination of equal time from each end of the route to isolate that part to which the CP formula can be applied. Consider the three-legged route in Fig. 15–4 and the associated TAS and WV information.

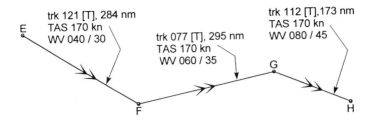

Fig. 15–4   Multi-leg CP calculation, basic scenario.

It pays to be methodical, so start by working out the flight plan along the entire route, 'E' to 'F', 'F' to 'G' and 'G' to 'H'. This will give GS **O** and time out on each leg (see Fig. 15–5).

Leg	TAS kn	WV	Trk (T)	Hdg (T)	GS kn	Dist nm	Time min
'E' to 'F'	170	040 / 30	121	111	162	284	105
'F' to 'G'	170	060 / 35	077	074	136	295	130
'G' to 'H'	170	080 / 45	112	104	130	173	80

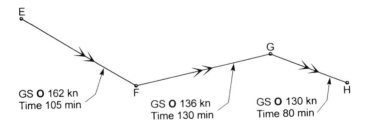

Fig. 15–5   Multi-leg CP calculation, GSs and times Out.

Now return to the first leg of the route and work out GS **H** 'F' to 'E' and the time it will take to fly from 'F' back to 'E', compare this time with the time to fly the last leg from 'G' to 'H' and note which is the longer time (see Fig. 15–6).

Leg	TAS kn	WV	Trk (T)	Hdg (T)	GS kn	Dist nm	Time min
'F' to 'E'	170	040 / 30	301	311	172	284	99

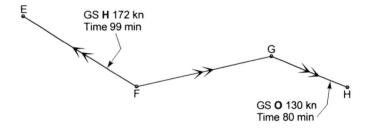

*Fig. 15–6   Multi-leg CP calculation, comparison of time Home for the first leg
with time On for last leg.*

The leg back home from 'F' to 'E' is the longer by 99 min – 80 min = 19
min. So during the time to fly back 'home' from 'F' to 'E' all of the leg 'on'
from 'G' to 'H' can be flown plus the last 19 min of the leg 'on' from 'F' to
'G'. This 19 min of leg 'F' to 'G' will be at 136 kn (the GS **O** for the leg 'F'
to 'G'):

Rough check. Say 20 min at 120 kn GS gives approximate distance of 40 nm.
The circular slide rule readout gives the distance as 43 nm.
Plotting this distance back from 'G' towards 'F' will give a point (call it 'x') on the
   leg 'F' to 'G' from which it will take as long to fly on to 'H' via 'G' as it would
   to fly from 'F' back to 'E'. This leaves part of the 'F' to 'G' leg (from 'F' to 'x')
   somewhere along which the CP must lie. (See Fig. 15–7)

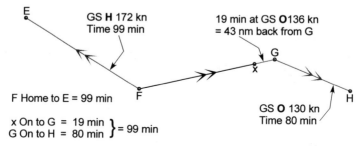

*Fig. 15–7   Multi-leg CP calculation, elimination of equal time
at each end of the route.*

The part of the leg 'F' to 'x' can now be treated as a single leg (equal time
having been eliminated from either side of these limits) for the calculation
of the CP. GS **O** of 136 kn has already been found for the leg 'F' to 'G' (see
Fig. 15–5) GS **H** for the leg 'G' back to 'F' is now calculated (see Fig. 15–8)
and the distance from 'F' to 'x' obtained from total distance 'F' to 'G'
minus the distance from 'G' to 'x' = 295 – 43 = 252 nm, this being the
distance **D** for the CP calculation.

Leg	TAS kn	WV	Trk (T)	Hdg (T)	GS kn	Dist nm	Time min
'G' to 'F'	170	060 / 35	257	260	204	-	-

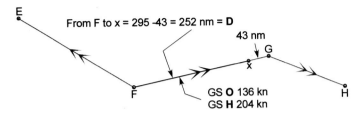

Fig 15–8   Multi-leg CP calculation the basic scenario of the leg from F to 'x'.

For 'F' to 'x':

D = 252 nm, **O** = 136 kn, **H** = 204 kn, **O** + **H** = 136 + 204 = 340

Setting up the ratio on the circular slide rule gives:

$$\frac{204}{340} \quad = \quad \frac{\mathbf{d}}{252}$$

Rough check. 204 is approximately ⅔ of 340 so **d** must be in the region of ⅔ of 252, say around 160 nm.

The circular slide rule readout for **d** is **151 nm**.

The CP is therefore 151 nm from 'F' on the leg 'F' to 'G'. The total time from 'E' to the CP will be the time for the leg 'E' to 'F' plus the time to fly the 151 nm from 'F' to the CP at the GS **O** for the leg 'F' to 'G'.

This is 105 min + 66·5 min (151 nm at GS 136 kn) = **171·5 min**.

A final check on the accuracy of the calculations gives:

From CP on to 'G' = (295 – 151) = 144 nm at GS **O** of 136 kn	= 63·6 min.
From 'G' on to 'H' = 173 nm at GS **O** of 130 kn	= 80·0 min.
Total time on	= **143·6 min**

From CP back to 'F' = 151 nm at GS **H** of 204 kn	= 44·6 min.
From 'F' back to 'E' = 284 nm at GS **H** of 172 kn	= 99·0 min.
Total time back	= **143·6 min**

With the CP plotted on the chart the decision whether to carry on or turn back is simple. If past the CP carry on, if not turn back.

15.5   The reduced TAS case. For a given route and set of WVs a change in the value of the TAS of the aircraft will alter the position of the CP. One emergency likely to require a 'carry on or turn back' decision would be failure of one engine on a multi-engined aircraft. Since such a failure would also result in a decrease of the TAS a second CP, based on the 'engine-out' TAS, is needed to cater for this possible emergency. To demonstrate this consider the route in Fig. 15–4 but with a reduced 'engine-out' TAS of 150 kn. What is required first are the reduced TAS calculations of the various reduced GS **O** and GS **H** figures. In this case the reduced GS **O** for leg 'E' to 'F' and the reduced GS **H** for leg 'H' to 'G' need not be calculated to start with. These can be calculated later in the unlikely event of the reduced TAS CP not falling on the leg 'F' to 'G'. Figure 15–9 shows the reduced TAS calculations:

Leg	TAS kn	WV	Trk (T)	Hdg (T)	GS kn	Dist nm	Time min
OUT							
'F' to 'G'	150	060 / 35	077	073	116	-	-
'G' to 'H'	150	080 / 45	112	103	109	173	95·5
HOME							
'F' to 'E'	150	040 / 30	301	312	152	284	112
'G' to 'F'	150	060 / 35	257	261	183	-	

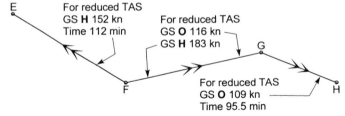

*Fig. 15–9   Multi-leg CP calculation, revised GSs **O** and **H** for a reduced TAS.*

The leg back home from 'F' to 'E' is (112 min – 95·5 min) = 16·5 min longer than the time to fly from 'G' to 'H' of 95·5 min. The equal time point 'x' is therefore 16·5 min at 116 kn (reduced GS **O** leg 'F' to 'G') = 32 nm back from 'G' towards 'F'. (See Fig. 15–10)

This leaves 295 nm – 32 nm = 263 nm, the distance **D** from 'F' to 'x' somewhere along which the CP must lie. Along this part of the route GS **O** = 116 kn and GS **H** = 183 kn giving **O** + **H** = 116 + 183 = 299. The ratio to set on the circular slide rule becomes:

$$\frac{183}{299} = \frac{d}{263}$$

Rough check. 262 is slightly less than 299 so **d** must be slightly less than

183. The computer readout gives **d** = **161 nm**. Plotting this distance on from 'F' towards 'x' gives the position of the CP for the 'engine out' reduced TAS. (See Fig 15–11)

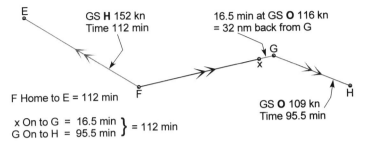

E

GS **H** 152 kn
Time 112 min

16.5 min at GS **O** 116 kn
= 32 nm back from G

G
x

H

F Home to E = 112 min   F

GS **O** 109 kn
Time 95.5 min

x On to G = 16.5 min
G On to H = 95.5 min } = 112 min

Fig. 15–10   Multi-leg CP calculation, elimination of equal time at each end of the route for the reduced TAS case.

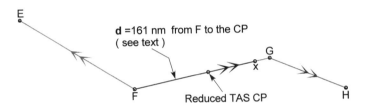

E

d =161 nm from F to the CP
(see text)

G
x

F   Reduced TAS CP   H

Fig. 15–11   Multi-leg CP calculation, position of the CP for the reduced TAS case.

A final check gives:

From CP on to 'G' = 295 nm – 161 nm = 134 nm at GS **O** of 116 kn =	69·4 min
From 'G' on to 'H' = 173 nm at GS **O** of 109 kn =	95·5 min
Total time on	= **164·9 min**
From CP back to 'F' = 161 nm at GS **H** of 183 kn =	52·8 min.
From 'F' back to 'E' = 284 nm at GS **H** of 152 kn =	112·0 min.
Total time back	= **164·8 min.**

Since the 'reduced TAS CP' is only applicable after failure of an engine the time to reach the 'reduced TAS CP' has to be calculated at the 'all engines operating' GSs. In this case using the GSs **O** 'E' to 'F' and 'F' to 'G' at a TAS of 170kn (see Fig. 15–5). These give:

Time 'E' to 'F'	= 105 min.
Time 'F' to the 'engine out' CP at the GS **O**	
'F' to 'G' (all engines) = 161 nm at 136 kn	= 71 min.
Total time from 'E' to the 'engine out' CP	= **176 min.**

Which is 4·5 min beyond the 'all engines operating TAS CP' (See Fig. 15–12).

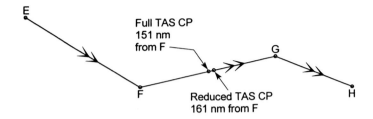

Fig. 15–12   Multi-leg CP calculation, comparison of the positions of the CP for the full and reduced TAS cases.

POINT OF NO RETURN (PNR)

15.6 The next navigational decision point is known as the **Point of No Return (PNR)**. As the name implies once the PNR has been passed it is impossible to return to the point of departure within the safe endurance of the aircraft and the pilot is committed to continuing on to the planned destination or a designated alternative airfield. From the fuel to be carried for the flight the safe **Endurance (E)** has first to be established. This is based on the available fuel and rate of fuel consumption for the planned cruising speed and altitude, (mandatory fuel carried for holding and diversion contingencies is never included when calculating the safe endurance **E**). As with the Speed/Distance/Time problems in Chapter 4 **E** is expressed in minutes for ease of use on the computer.

15.7 (PNR) Single leg case. Consider a single leg route from 'A' to 'B'. If the fuel available gives a safe endurance **E** which is insufficient to fly the round trip 'A' to 'B' and back again without landing then calculation of the PNR is essential. The formula for calculating the **Time out (To)** from 'A' to the PNR is evolved below for those who like to know how such things come about, being able to reproduce this proof is not part of the licence requirement so there is no need to commit it to memory.

Let GS out from 'A' to the PNR	=	**O**
Let GS home from the PNR back to 'A'	=	**H**
Let the distance from 'A' to the PNR	=	**d**
Let Time out from 'A' to the PNR	=	**To** (min)
Let Time home from the PNR back to 'A'	=	**Th** (min)
Let safe Endurance	=	**E** (min)

The ratio $\dfrac{d}{To} = \dfrac{O}{60}$ gives $d = \dfrac{To \times O}{60}$ 'X'

The ratio $\dfrac{d}{Th} = \dfrac{H}{60}$ gives $d = \dfrac{Th \times H}{60}$ 'Y'

'X' = 'Y' therefore $\dfrac{To \times O}{60} = \dfrac{Th \times H}{60}$

The 60s cancel out leaving $\quad To \times O = Th \times H$ 'P'

The round trip from 'A' to the PNR and back to 'A' is:-

$$To + Th = E$$

Therefore $\quad Th = E - To$ 'Q'

Substituting 'Q' for **Th** in 'P' gives:

$$To \times O = (E - To)\,H$$
$$To \times O = (E \times H) - (To \times H)$$
$$(To \times O) + (To \times H) = E \times H$$
$$To\,(O + H) = E \times H$$
$$To = \dfrac{E \times H}{O + H}$$

For solving on the circular slide rule this is rearranged as the ratio:

$$\dfrac{To}{E} = \dfrac{H}{O + H}$$

Candidates for Licence examinations should commit this ratio to memory and be able to apply it.

Example:
'A' to 'B' distance 624 nm. TAS 200 kn, Wind component + 20 kn out and – 20 kn home, safe endurance 5 hours and 20 minutes. Calculate the time and distance to PNR.

Answer:

E	=	5 hr 20 min	=	320 min.
GS **O**	=	TAS 200 kn + 20 kn	=	220 kn.
GS **H**	=	TAS 200 kn – 20 kn	=	180 kn.
O + H	=	220 + 180	=	400

The ratio to set on the circular slide rule is:

$$\dfrac{To}{320} = \dfrac{180}{400}$$

Rough check. 180 is just under half of 400 so **To** must be just under half of 320, say 140 to 150.
The circular slide rule readout makes **To = 144 min**.
Distance **d** to the PNR = 144 min at GS **O** of 220 kn.
Rough check. Approximately 2·5 hrs of GS **O**, say about 550nm.
The circular slide rule readout gives **d = 528 nm**.

A final check can now be carried out:

Th = E − To = 320 − 144 = 176 min at GS **H** of 180 kn confirms **d** as **528 nm**.

With a total distance from 'A' to 'B' of 624 nm once the aircraft has passed the PNR it cannot return to 'A' within the safe endurance and is committed to continue on to 'B'. (see Fig. 15–13)

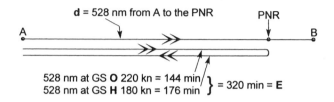

Fig. 15–13   Example of a single leg point of No Return (PNR).

15.8   (PNR) Multi-leg case. Where a multi-leg route is involved the sum of **To** and **Th** for each leg is worked out and these values are sequentially subtracted from the total safe endurance **E** until a leg is reached where **To** + **Th** for that leg is greater than the remaining endurance available at the beginning of the leg. The PNR must therefore lie on this leg and is calculated as for a normal PNR using the speeds and times for the leg and the value of the remaining endurance. Fig. 15–14 shows a route 'A' to 'E' via 'B', 'C' and 'D' with GS **O**, GS **H** and distance for each leg. The safe endurance **E** is 4 hours and 58 minutes = 298 min.

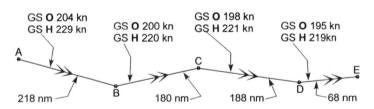

Fig. 15–14   Multi-leg PNR, a basic scenario.

For the leg   **O** =   204 kn for distance 218 nm gives **To**   =   64 min
'A' / 'B'   **H** =   229 kn for distance 218 nm gives **Th**   =   57 min
          Total time 'A' to 'B' and back to 'A'   = **121 min**
      E of 298 min − 121 min = **177 min endurance remaining**.

For the leg	O	=	200 kn for distance 180 nm gives **To**	=	54 min
'B' / 'C'	H	=	220 kn for distance 180 nm gives **Th**	=	<u>49 min</u>
			Total time 'B' to 'C' and back to 'B'	=	**103 min**

Available endurance 177 min – 103 min = **74 min endurance remaining.**

For the leg	O	=	198 kn for distance 188 nm gives **To**	=	57 min
'C' / 'D'	H	=	221 kn for distance 188 nm gives **Th**	=	<u>51 min</u>
			Total time 'C' to 'D' and back to 'C'	=	**108 min**

Available endurance remaining is 74 min, therefore the aircraft cannot fly to 'D' and return to 'C' within the safe endurance and the PNR must lie somewhere on the leg 'C' to 'D'.

Summarising for the leg 'C' to 'D':

Safe endurance **E**	=	74 min.
O	=	198 kn.
H	=	221 kn.
Giving **O + H**	=	419.

The ratio to set on the circular slide rule is:

$$\frac{\text{To}}{74} = \frac{221}{419}$$

Rough check. 221 is just over half of 419 so **To** (the time to the PNR) must be just over half of 74, say about 40 min.

The circular slide rule readout gives **To** = **39 min**.

39 min at GS **O** of 198 kn gives the distance **d** from 'C' to the PNR = **129 nm.**

Cross checking, **Th** from PNR back to 'C' = 74 min – 39 min = 35 min at GS **H** of 221 kn = 129 nm.

Total time from 'A' to the PNR

= **To** 'A' to 'B' + **To** 'B' to 'C' + **To** 'C' to PNR.

= 64 min + 54 min + 39 min.

= **157 min.**

15.9 (PNR) Alternative solution. An alternative way of solving the PNR is first to calculate GS **O** and GS **H** and then work out the total time to fly out and home over a selected distance (it is common practice to use the distance that would be covered in 60 min at GS **O**, so dispensing with one calculation). With the total time taken to fly out and home over a known distance and a known value for **E**, the distance **d** to the PNR can be solved on the circular slide rule by setting the ratio:

$$\frac{\text{d}}{\text{E}} = \frac{\text{Selected distance}}{\text{time out and home over selected distance}}$$

A rework of the last part of the previous question from 'C' to the PNR with E=74 min, O=198 kn, H=221 kn. Selecting 198 nm for the calculation distance gives:

198 nm out at **O** of 198 kn	=	60·0 min.
198 nm home at **H** of 221 kn	=	53·8 min.
Total time out and home over 198 nm	=	**113·8 min.**

The ratio to set on the circular slide rule is:

$$\frac{d}{74} = \frac{198}{133\cdot8}$$

Rough check. 198 is just over 1·5 × 113·8 so **d** must be just over 1·5 × 74 or around 120.
The circular slide rule readout gives **d = 129 nm**.

15.10 (PNR) Varying fuel flow case. A variation on the ratio method in paragraph 15.9 can be used to solve the PNR using the amount of usable fuel (excluding contingency fuel) and the fuel flow for the cruising speed and altitude. Fuel carried and fuel flow may be expressed by volume or by weight. Either can be used in this ratio method provided common units are used within each calculation. The method is to calculate the total fuel used out and back over an arbitrary distance (as before one hour's worth of distance out at GS **O** is a common figure to use since it will use one hour's worth of fuel flow, again reducing the number of steps to be calculated), with a known amount of usable fuel the ratio to be set on the circular slide rule is:

$$\frac{d}{\text{Usable fuel}} = \frac{\text{Selected distance}}{\text{Fuel used out and home over selected distance}}$$

This may seem like an unnecessary extension of the GS method of finding the PNR but in fact it is a far more accurate method when varying fuel flows are involved. On large aircraft, with fuel flows in thousands of kg/hr, as fuel is burnt off and the all-up-weight decreases, so will the fuel flow decrease. By the end of several hours flying the rate of fuel consumption will be considerably lower than at the start of the flight.

15.11 For a single track out and home route with decreasing fuel flow and insufficient fuel for a complete round trip the calculation of the PNR is a straightforward application of the formula in paragraph 15.10. Fig. 15–15 shows just such a case along with the relevant GSs, Fuel Available and Fuel Flows.

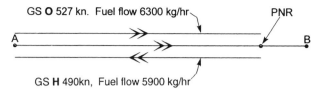

Fuel available (excluding contingency fuel) = 27 000 kg

Fig. 15–15   Single leg PNR with decreasing fuel flow, a basic scenario.

The calculation of Total fuel used out / home over this distance is:
GS **O** = 527 kn so using 527 nm as the selected distance.

Fuel used out	=	527 nm at GS **O** 527 kn.
	=	60 min at 6300 kg / hr.
	=	**6300 kg.**

Fuel used home	=	527 nm at GS **H** 490 kn.
	=	64.5 min at 5900 kg / hr.
	=	**6350 kg.**

Total Fuel Used out and home over the selected distance
= 6300 + 6350 kg.
= **12 650 kg.**

The ratio to set on the circular slide rule is:

$$\frac{d}{27\ 000} = \frac{527}{12\ 650}$$

Rough check. 27,000 is just over 2 × 12,650 so **d** must be just over 2 × 527, say in the region of 1100 nm.
The circular slide rule readout gives **d = 1127 nm.**

15.12   For a multi-leg out and home route the procedure is as follows:

Calculate the fuel required to fly the first leg out and home and subtract this amount from the total fuel available.
Repeat for the second leg subtracting the fuel required to fly out and home from the fuel remaining after the first leg calculation.
Proceed in this fashion in sequence down the route until a leg is reached where the total fuel out and home for the leg is greater than the remaining fuel available at the start of the leg.
The PNR must lie on this leg and is calculated in the same way as for a single leg route.

Fig. 15–16 shows such a multi-leg route. At this stage the GS, fuel flow and distance for each leg is given as these are the only required elements needed to illustrate the multi-leg PNR procedure. In an examination the candidate may have to work out the GSs **O** and **H** from given TAS, WV and trk before proceeding with the PNR calculation.

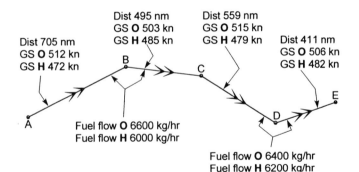

Fuel available (excluding contingency fuel) = 49 000 kg

Fig. 15–16   Multi-leg PNR with decreasing fuel flow, a basic scenario.

From/To	Distance (nm)	GS (kn)	Time (min)	Fuel flow (kg / hr)	Fuel used (kg)
Leg 1					
'A' to 'B'	705	512 (**O**)	82·5	6600 (**O**)	9 080
'B' to 'A'	705	472 (**H**)	90	6000 (**H**)	9 000
		Total fuel used 'A' to 'B' and back to 'A'			**18 080 kg.**
Leg 2 Fuel available 49 000 kg – 18 080 kg = **30 920 kg.**					
'B' to 'C'	495	503 (**O**)	59	6600 (**O**)	6 490
'C' to 'B'	495	485 (**H**)	61·2	6000 (**H**)	6 120
		Total fuel used 'B' to 'C' and back to 'B'			**12 610 kg.**
Leg 3 Fuel available 30 920 kg – 12 610 kg = **18 310 kg.**					
'C' to 'D'	559	515 (**O**)	65	6400 (**O**)	6 940
'D' to 'C'	559	479 (**H**)	70	6200 (**H**)	7 240
		Total fuel used 'C' to 'D' and back to 'C'			**14 180 kg.**
Leg 4 Fuel available 18 310 kg – 14 180 kg = **4130 kg.**					
'D' to 'E'	411	506 (**O**)	48·6	6400 (**O**)	**5200 kg.**

This is more than the 4130 kg of available fuel so the PNR must lie along the leg 'D' to 'E'. Proceed as for a single leg route:

GS **O** on leg 'D' to 'E' = 506 kn so use 506 nm as the selected distance.
Fuel used out   = 506 nm at GS **O** 506 kn.
                      = 60 min at 6400 kg / hr.
                      = **6400 kg.**
Fuel used home   = 506 nm at GS **H** 482 kn.
                      = 63 min at 6200 kg / hr.
                      = **6500 kg.**

Total fuel used out and home over the selected distance.
$$= \quad 6400 + 6500 \text{ kg}.$$
$$= \quad \mathbf{12{,}900 \text{ kg}}.$$
The ratio to set on the circular slide rule is:

$$\frac{\mathbf{d}}{4130} = \frac{506}{12\,900}$$

Rough check. 4130 is approximately ⅓ of 12 900, so **d** must be about ⅓ of 506, say in the region of 150 to 170.
The circular slide rule readout gives **d = 162 nm** from 'D' on the leg 'D' to 'E' as the position of PNR.

The answer can be verified by working out the fuel used from the start of the leg to the PNR and back to the start of the leg. The total should check out against the fuel available at the start of the leg.

In the above example fuel available at 'D'	=	4130 kg.
GS O	=	506 kn.
GS H	=	482 kn.
Distance from 'D' to the PNR calculated as	=	162 nm.

Fuel used out =   162 nm at 506 kn.
      =   19·2 min (at 6400 kg / hr)
      =   **2050 kg.**
Fuel used home =   162 nm at 482 kn.
      =   20·15 min (at 6200 kg / hr)
      =   **2080 kg.**
Total fuel used out and home from 'D' to the PNR and back
      =   2050 + 2080 kg.
      =   **4130 kg.**

This checks out with the fuel available at the start of the leg.
The total time to reach the PNR from the moment of leaving 'A' is the sum of all the outbound times. In this case:

Time 'A' to 'B'	=	82·5 min.
Time 'B' to 'C'	=	59·0 min.
Time 'C' to 'D'	=	65·0 min.
Time 'D' to PNR	=	19·2 min.
Time 'A' to PNR	=	**225·7 min.**

POINT OF NO ALTERNATE (PNA)

15.13 The Point of No Alternate (PNA) only applies where the available alternate airfield lies some way off from the planned route and is too distant from the destination airfield to be reached from overhead the destination airfield within the safe limits of the contingency fuel carried. In such a case there will be a point along the route beyond which the alternate airfield cannot be reached within the safe fuel limits and the aircraft is committed to landing at the planned destination airfield. This point is called the PNA and any decision to divert to the alternate airfield must be taken before this point is passed. In practical terms this means the conditions for the destination airfield should be checked by RT just before the PNR is reached, in case a diversion is advisable.

15.14 The PNA is found by means of a constant scale geometrical solution carried out on the plotting chart. A Line of Constant Bearing (LCB) (see Chapter 14) is used in the solution of this problem along with the concept of a 'phantom' aircraft. The DR position of the aircraft is established for a point along the route some way before the PNA is likely to occur. A point before the aircraft is abeam the diversion airfield will usually suffice. From this DR position a trk is drawn in to the diversion airfield. This trk is not actually going to be flown but will be used to establish a LCB between the trk 'on' to destination and an imaginary (or 'phantom') aircraft assumed to be flying directly from the DR position so as to arrive at the diversion airfield at the end of the safe endurance. Fig. 15–17 shows a route with the trk to destination airfield 'B' marked in:

Diversion airfield 'C' is shown some way North and West of 'B'.

A DR position prior to coming abeam 'C' has been plotted on the chart and its time noted beside it.

A trk from this DR position to 'C' is plotted for the 'phantom' aircraft to fly along.

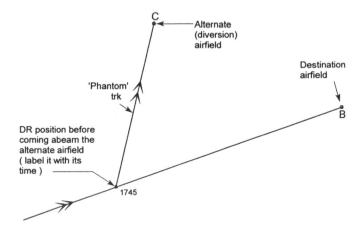

Fig. 15–17   Point of No Alternate (PNA) a basic scenario.

A LCB can now be established through:

The real aircraft's position on track to destination. and
The position of a 'phantom' aircraft flying from the DR position directly to the diversion airfield at a speed that will have it arriving at the end of the safe endurance.

To do this the GS of the 'phantom' aircraft must be calculated first. The distance of the direct trk from the DR position to the diversion airfield is measured using the appropriate scale for the plotting chart and the time (in minutes) from the DR position to the end of safe endurance ascertained. These two facts are then used to calculate the GS the 'phantom' aircraft must fly at to arrive at the diversion airfield just within safe endurance. Suppose the trk distance is found to be 297 nm and the time to run to the end of safe endurance is 115 minutes, the GS of the 'phantom' aircraft will have to be:

$$\frac{297 \text{ nm} \times 60}{115 \text{ min}} \qquad \text{or, as a ratio on the} \qquad \frac{297}{115} \qquad = \qquad \frac{GS}{60}$$
navigation computer

Rough check. 60 is just over ½ of 115 so GS must be just over ½ of 297, say about 150 kn.

Computer readout gives 155 kn as the GS of the 'phantom' aircraft.

15.15   In paragraph 15.14 it was stated that this problem is solved geometrically using a constant scale. Although it is now common practice to use Lambert's projection for most plotting purposes, there are occasions when a variable scale chart such as Mercator's may have to be used and in such cases the construction that is explained below *must* be made using the (constant) longitude scale of the chart or even a Metric or Imperial rule. During construction an arc equal to the TAS has to be drawn so select a constant scale that will enable this to be done fairly large to reduce errors. Fig. 15–18 shows the construction which is built up as follows:

To scale plot in a vector for one hour of WV blowing OUT from the DR position. From the end of this wind vector strike a circle of radius equal to one hour of TAS. Where this cuts the actual trk to destination gives the aircraft's position (P) in one hour's time *according to the constant scale.* (This will not necessarily be the actual geographical DR position for one hours time except in the case of a constant scale chart where the latitude scale is being used for the PNA construction).

To the scale being used the length of the vector from the DR position to (P) gives GS to destination and the direction from the end of the wind vector to (P) gives the required hdg.

To the same scale a distance equal to one hour's movement at the GS of the 'phantom' aircraft is marked along the trk from the DR position towards the diversion airfield. This establishes the position of the 'phantom' aircraft (Q) for the same time that the actual aircraft will be at (P).

The LCB is then drawn by plotting a straight line through (P) and (Q) and extending it to cut the TAS circle at (R).

A line from the DR position to (R) gives the trk direction into the diversion airfield from the PNA and its vector length (to the constant scale) will give the GS.

The geographical position of the PNA is found by plotting a line parallel to this trk direction through the diversion airfield so as to intersect the actual trk into the destination airfield. The point of intersection is the PNA.

At the same time a line drawn from the end of the wind vector to (R) will give the hdg from the PNA to the diversion airfield.

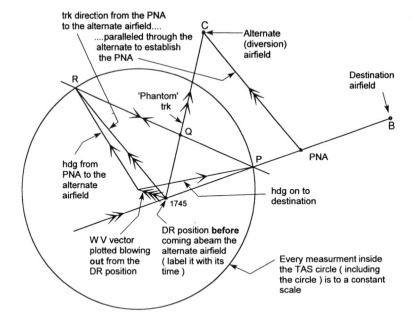

Fig. 15–18   Construction for solving the PNA.

Having found the PNA, plus hdg and GS to the diversion airfield, normal navigation techniques must be resumed and all distances must once more be measured by the appropriate scale for the chart in use.

CHAPTER 16

TIME AND TIME CONVERSIONS

INTRODUCTION

16.1 Earlier chapters in this book have shown time to be an intrinsic part of most navigational problems. So how has the measurement of time evolved? Early man would have appreciated the sequences of dark and light (one day), the complete cycle of the phases of the moon (a lunar month) and the passage of the seasons (one year). Observation showed that there were 28 days in a lunar month and there appeared to be 13 lunar months in a year. A slight error in the last observation came to light when users of this early form of calendar found that the seasons (a basis for planting and harvesting crops) were slipping in relation to their lunar based calendar by about one and a quarter days per year. The year was not 364 days long but more like 365¼ days in length.

16.2 The Julian Calendar. It was Julius Caesar (100 – 44 BC) who had the calendar modified to give the world the Julian Calendar of 365 days length for the year, the odd ¼ day being allowed for by adding one day every fourth year (a leap year). The passage of centuries once more showed the seasons slipping in relation to this calendar. The year based on the seasons was some 11¼ mins shorter than the 365¼ days assumed in the Julian Calendar so each leap year overcorrected by 45 mins. In four centuries this gave an over correction of three days and three hrs.

16.3 The Gregorian Calendar. In 1582 Pope Gregory XIII (1502–1585) had the Gregorian Calendar introduced which rectified the accrued error of the Julian Calendar and further reduced the error by making the century years leap years only if divisible by 400 (thus 1700 AD, 1800 AD and 1900 AD were not leap years but 2000 AD will be). This reduced the accrued error in each 400 years from three days and three hrs to just three hrs, or put another way, it will take 3200 years for the Gregorian Calendar to slip one day. Most of continental Europe quickly went over to the Gregorian Calendar but the UK did not change from the Julian Calendar until 1752 by which time the UK was out of step with the rest of Europe by eleven days. When the change was made there were riots in parts of the UK by people who thought that 11 days of their lives were being stolen!

16.4 Although the above paragraphs give the background to the Calendar in use today they do not explain the origins of how the length of the day is determined. For that it is necessary to mention a group of scientists who were living around the time of Pope Gregory XIII. The first of these was the Italian astronomer Galileo Galilei (1564–1642). Among his many achievements was the making of a telescope with which he observed the movements of the planets and confirmed the theory of Nicholas Copernicus (1473–1543) that the earth rotated on its axis and that earth and the other planets were in orbit about the sun. The Roman Church at the time regarded this as heretical. Galileo was made to recant his findings and as a result science in Italy was virtually brought to a standstill for decades.

16.5 In Denmark Tycho Brahe (1546–1601), another astronomer, spent years measuring and recording the movements of the planets. After the death of Tycho Brahe his brilliant one time assistant, Johann Kepler (1571–1630) spent many more years analysing the mass of figures he left behind.

KEPLER'S LAWS OF PLANETARY MOTION

16.6 The result of Kepler's endeavours with Brahe's records are known today as Kepler's Laws of Planetary Motion which state:

The planets describe elliptic orbits, of which the sun is one focus.

An imaginary line joining a planet to the sun sweeps out equal areas in equal time.

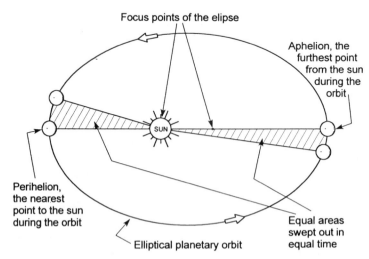

Focus points of the elipse

Aphelion, the furthest point from the sun during the orbit

Perihelion, the nearest point to the sun during the orbit

SUN

Equal areas swept out in equal time

Elliptical planetary orbit

Fig. 16–1 Planetary orbit of the Earth around the Sun.

190

The square of the period of revolution of a planet is proportional to the cube of its average distance from the sun.

The first two of these laws are pertinent to the calculation of time (see Fig. 16–1). The third law is of interest to astronomers but plays no part in the subject matter of this Chapter.

16.7 From Fig. 16–1 it can be seen that in its elliptical orbit around the sun, for an imaginary line between the earth and the sun to sweep out equal areas in equal time, the speed of movement around the sun must vary. It is fastest at the point when it is closest to the sun (known as Perihelion) and slowest when it is at the point furthest from the sun (known as Aphelion). As well as moving at a varying speed on an elliptical path around the sun, the earth is also rotating at a constant speed about its own N/S axis, the N/S spin axis being inclined at 23° 30' from the vertical to the plane of the elliptical path around the sun (see Fig.16–2). At Perihelion the N pole is at maximum tilt away from the sun (the Winter Solstice) and at Aphelion the N pole is at maximum tilt towards the sun (the Summer Solstice).

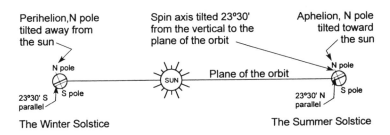

Fig. 16–2   *The tilt of the Earth's spin axis to the Plane of Orbit.*

THE SEASONS AND APPARENT MOVEMENT OF THE SUN

16.8 From Fig. 16–2 it can be seen that at Perihelion the sun will be vertically (90° to the earth's normal) overhead the parallel of 23°30'S and at Aphelion it will be vertically overhead the parallel of 23°30'N. It follows that at two points on its elliptical path the sun will be vertically over the equator. If all the vertically overhead points throughout the year are plotted on the surface of the earth a GC will be made giving the annual path of the sun over the earth known as the Ecliptic. (See Fig. 16–3) This path reaches its highest lats at the solstices and crosses the equator going Northwards at the Vernal Equinox (20 March, N hemisphere Spring) at a point known as the first point of Aries. Six months later it crosses the equator going Southwards at the Autumnal Equinox (22 or 23 September, N hemisphere Autumn) at a point known as the first point of Libra.

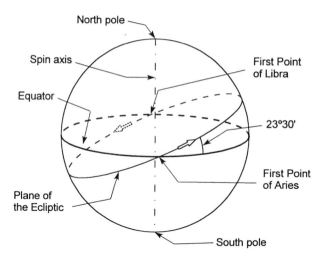

Fig. 16–3   The Plane of the Ecliptic.

If the daily path of the overhead position of the sun is plotted out it will appear to move along successive parallels of lat, changing lat by about 15' per day. The direction of rotation of the earth results in the sun appearing to move from E to W over the earth's surface. The tilt of the earth means that the length of the period of daylight will be least when the tilt is away from the sun and greatest when tilt is towards the sun, giving rise to the seasons (see Fig. 16–4).

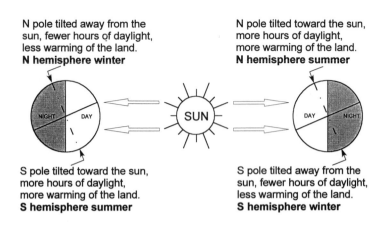

Fig. 16–4   How the tilt of the earth's spin axis varies the hours of day and night giving rise to the seasons.

DERIVATION OF TIME

16.9 The length of a day is measured by observing the interval between successive transits of a meridian by a chosen celestial body. The body chosen could be the sun, the moon, a star or even an imaginary celestial body. As already explained above, due to the rotation of the earth the sun appears to move from E to W over the earth's surface. This apparent E to W movement is also true of other celestial bodies but depending on their distance from the earth and their own movement in space the rates at which they appear to move will be different. It follows that the time interval between successive transits of an observer's meridian will be different for different celestial bodies. Most celestial bodies can be ruled out because the time taken for them to make two successive transits of a meridian does not contain a full natural cycle of daylight and darkness.

16.10   The Siderial Day. The celestial body chosen to measure the **Siderial Day** is *a fixed point in space*, such as a star at an infinite distance from the earth. Since the rotation of the earth is being measured against a fixed datum it follows that the resultant unit of time will be a true measure of the rotation of the earth through 360°. (see Fig. 16–5)

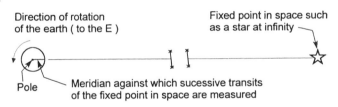

This gives the true time for the earth to rotate through 360°

Fig. 16–5   Measurement of the Siderial Day.

The Siderial Day is important in astronomy but has the major drawback that it gets out of step with the natural daily sequence of light and dark which is based on the position of the sun. From Fig. 16–1 it can be seen that at any two points on opposite sides of the earth's elliptical path around the sun for the same time of the Siderial Day one will be in daylight and the other in darkness. This will always be the case, no matter in which direction the chosen fixed point in space lies.

16.11   The Apparent Solar Day is measured between two successive transits of the *sun* across a meridian on the earth. Because the earth is moving around the sun (anti-clockwise viewed from above the N pole) it will have to rotate more than 360° between successive transits. This means the Apparent Solar Day is longer than the Siderial Day (see Fig. 16–6).

Unfortunately because the speed of the earth varies on its elliptical path around the sun (see para. 16.7) the length of the Apparent Solar Day will also vary, being longest when its orbital speed is greatest (at Perihelion) and shortest when its orbital speed is least (at Aphelion).

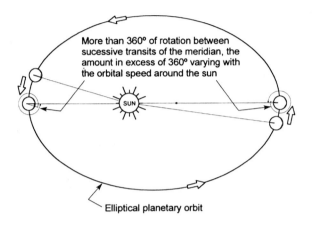

More than 360° of rotation between sucessive transits of the meridian, the amount in excess of 360° varying with the orbital speed around the sun

SUN

Elliptical planetary orbit

Fig. 16–6   The apparent Solar day.

16.12   Mean Solar Time and Civil Time. Since the Apparent Solar Day does not have a constant length it is not directly used in measuring time. An *imaginary* body called the **Astronomical Mean Sun** is assumed to orbit the earth at a constant speed, averaging out the variations in the Apparent Solar Day and giving a **Mean Solar Day** of constant length. The length of the Mean Solar Day is divided up into 24 equal hrs each containing 60 mins, each of 60 secs. Mean Solar Time is the basis of **Civil Time**. and the 24 hrs of a Mean Solar Day constitutes a **Civil Day**. The Siderial Day (see para. 16.10) has a constant length of 23 hrs and 56 mins of Civil Time.

16.13   The Siderial Year. The measurement of the time for the earth to make one elliptical orbit around the sun gives the length of a year. The **Siderial Year** is the measure of time between two successive conjunctions of the earth, sun and a *fixed point in space.* (see Fig.16–7) This is the true measure of one orbit of the earth around the sun and is approximately 365 days and 6 hours of Civil Time. The problem with the length of the Siderial Year is that the seasons gradually move in relation to any calendar based upon it (see paras. 16.4 and 16.7).

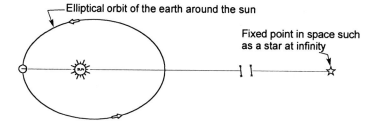

Measurement of sucessive conjunctions of earth, sun and a fixed
point in space gives the true time for the earth to orbit the sun

Fig. 16–7   Measurement of the Siderial Year.

16.14   The Tropical Year. Ideally what is required is a full cycle of the
seasons within a year and to have the seasons occurring at about the same
date(s) in each year. To obtain this it is necessary to base the length of the
year on the interval between successive passages of the sun through the first
point of Aries at the Vernal Equinox. This is some 365 days 5 hours and 48
¾ minutes of Civil Time and is known as the **Tropical Year**. It is the basis
of the Gregorian Calendar (see para. 16.3).

16.15   Local Mean Time (LMT). Relative to the Astronomical Mean Sun
the earth rotates 360° in 24 hrs of Civil Time, or in other words 15° per hr
or 1° per 4 mins. Time based on the position of the Astronomical Mean
Sun is known as **Local Mean Time (LMT)**. For an observer on the earth as

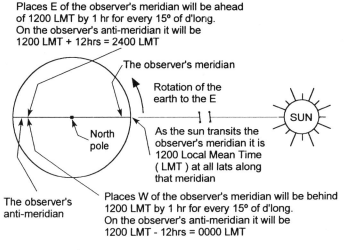

Fig. 16–8a   Local Mean Time (LMT).

195

the sun transits his or her meridian it will be midday according to the Astronomical Mean Sun, the time being 1200 hr LMT. No matter what the lat all points on the observer's meridian will have the same LMT. It follows that at the same moment on the observer's anti-meridian, the time will be different by 180° / 15° per hr = 12 hrs. With the earth rotating to the E all places to the E of the observer will have passed their midday point and have times later in the day than 1200 hr LMT, the anti-meridian time being 1200 hr LMT + 12 hr = 2400 hr LMT. To the W of the observer all places will have times earlier in the day than 1200 hr LMT, the anti-meridian time being 1200 hr LMT – 12 hr = 0000 hr LMT. This identifies the observer's anti-meridian as the point from which LMT is measured clockwise round to the meridian of the Mean Sun. (see Fig.16–8a)

Fig. 16–8b shows two observers 'A' and 'B', on different meridians, with the measurement of their LMTs from their individual anti-meridians clockwise round to the meridian of the Mean Sun. In the example shown the LMT of 'A' is 1000 hr and the LMT of 'B' is 1500 hr. There is a difference of 5 hrs which means the d'long between 'A' and 'B' must be 5 hr × 15° per hr = 75° d'long.

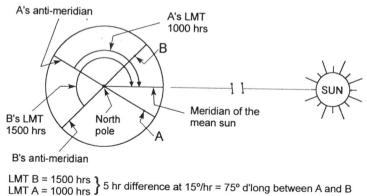

LMT B = 1500 hrs }
LMT A = 1000 hrs } 5 hr difference at 15°/hr = 75° d'long between A and B

Fig. 16–8b   Relationship of LMT and D'long.

16.16   Greenwich Mean Time (GMT)/Co-ordinated Universal Time (UTC). If LMT were used as the basis for distributing international travel information there would be chaos. Departure and arrival points around the world with their different longs each operating on the LMT applicable to the meridian on which they were situated would result in almost incomprehensible time tables. The solution to this problem is the selection of one meridian as the Prime Meridian and to use the LMT of that meridian for all international communications involving time. The meridian chosen as the Prime Meridian is the one passing through Greenwich (see Chapter 1 para. 1.8) whose LMT is known as **Greenwich Mean Time (GMT)** or, as recently retitled, **Co-ordinated Universal Time (UTC)**. Conversion of LMT to UTC (GMT) and vice versa is by 'arc to time'. The d'long between the meridian through a place and the meridian through Greenwich is first converted to the time difference ('arc to time') between their LMTs (see para. 16.15) and this time is then applied, *in the correct sense*, to make the required conversion.

For places E of Greenwich:-

LMT minus 'arc to time' difference	=	UTC (GMT)
UTC (GMT) plus 'arc to time' difference	=	LMT

For places W of Greenwich:-

LMT plus 'arc to time' difference	=	UTC (GMT)
UTC (GMT) minus 'arc to time' difference	=	LMT

In other words *add* time if *moving Eastwards* and *subtract* time if *moving Westwards*.

16.17   Conversion of 'Arc to Time' is simplified by the use of a table to be found in the **Air Almanac** an extract from which is supplied for use in the written examinations. Part of this extract is reproduced (by kind permission of the Controller, Her Majesty's Stationery Office) as an appendix to this chapter and should be referred to when studying the various worked examples of time problems to be found later in this Chapter. The full extract used in the examinations is available for purchase from Her Majesty's Stationery Office. Reference to the **Conversion of Arc to Time** table (to be found at the back of the extract) shows, from the left-hand side, six vertical columns giving conversion of whole degrees of long from 000° to 359° into hrs and mins of time. On the right-hand side a seventh column gives conversion of minutes of long to mins and secs of time. The table can be used *either* to convert d'long into time difference *or* to convert time difference into d'long.

Example:
Convert a d'long of 137°43' to time difference.
Answer:

137°	=	9 hrs 8 min	........3rd column
43'	=	2 min 52 sec	.........7th column
137°43'	=	**9 hrs 10 min 52 sec**	

Example:
Convert a time difference of 14 hrs 37 min 28 sec to d'long.
Answer:

14 hrs 36 min	=	219° d'long	..........4th column
1 min 28 sec	=	22' d'long	..........7th column
14 hrs 37 min 28 sec	=	**219°22' d'long**	

STANDARD TIME AND THE INTERNATIONAL DATE LINE

16.18   Use of LMT, as well as posing a world wide communication problem, can also complicate administration within a countries boundaries. For example two centuries ago in the UK, LMT was used throughout the country. In those days the UK was mainly an agricultural society, daily life was governed by the hours of daylight and local church clocks were set by the sun. The lack of high speed transport between places meant that the fact that LMT in London was some 20 min ahead of LMT in Bristol which was itself some 12 min ahead of LMT in Plymouth was not important. The industrial revolution brought about by the coming of the railways changed this tranquil way of life for ever. By the mid-19th century journeys that previously had taken days could be completed in hours. The preparation of railway timetables led to a need for a common **Standard Time** to be adopted for use throughout the country. The railways led the way by adopting the LMT of Greenwich (GMT) and issued its customers with an 'arc to time' table to enable them to work out the LMT of arrival and departure at stations anywhere in the country. With the speeding up of transport, countries throughout the world were all faced with similar problems and the Washington conference of 1884 (which selected the Prime meridian) also agreed on an international system of standard times. The UK adopted GMT as its Standard Time. Other countries adopted their own standard times, usually based on the LMT of a meridian close to the country's capital city which differed from GMT (UTC) by a whole number of hours or, in some cases a whole number of hours plus 30 minutes. Countries to the E of Greenwich keep standard times ahead of UTC (GMT), countries along the Greenwich meridian keep UTC (GMT) as standard time and countries W of Greenwich keep standard times behind UTC (GMT). There are some exceptions to these generalisations. For example:

If the capital city is on the extreme E or W of a country's land mass, the standard time chosen for the country may be that of a more centrally placed meridian well away from the capital city.

Some countries, such as the United States of America, Australia and Indonesia have extensive E to W territorial coverage with a d'long well in excess of 15°. In such cases more than one Time Zone, each with its own standard time, may be employed within the country's boundaries.

The land mass of Spain is almost entirely W of the Greenwich meridian but the standard time is 1 hr ahead of UTC (GMT) thus keeping Spanish clocks on the same time as their French neighbours.

Many countries, including the UK, put their clocks ahead by one hr during the summer months as a means of daylight saving.

In paragraph 16.15 it was shown that the 180° meridian could have two times 24 hrs apart, dependent on whether it was approached from the E or the W.

Crossing the 180° meridian in an Easterly direction takes one into the Western hemisphere and changes the time by minus 24 hrs (or in other words changes the date by minus one day). It follows that crossing the 180° meridian in a Westerly direction will take one into the Eastern hemisphere and add one day to the date. This gives rise to the 180° meridian being termed the **International Date Line**. As mentioned in Chapter 1 para. 1.8, one of the factors in the selection of the Greenwich Meridian as the Prime Meridian was because it's anti-meridian passed through so few land masses it could be used as the International Date Line with the minimum of modification. The few territories and island groups that do straddle the 180° meridian have the International Date Line modified by taking it away from the 180° meridian and round the affected territories so as to keep all their administrative areas on a common date. The territories that fall within the areas of the modified International Date Line can be identified by the fact that their standard time difference from UTC (GMT) is more that 12 hrs (see LIST 1 mentioned below).

There are three lists of **Standard Times** giving the Standard Time differences from UTC (GMT). The lists fill four pages of the *Air Almanac* and are to be found at the front of the reduced extract appended to this chapter:

LIST I   Places Fast on UTC (GMT) – Mainly places E of Greenwich
Add to UTC (GMT) to give Standard Time
Subtract from Standard Time to give UTC (GMT)
LIST II   Places Keeping UTC (GMT)
LIST III   Places Slow on UTC (GMT) – Places W of Greenwich
Subtract from UTC (GMT) to give Standard Time
Add to Standard Time to give UTC (GMT)

CONVERSION BETWEEN LMT, UTC (GMT) AND STANDARD TIMES

16.19   Paragraphs 16.16 and 16.17 showed how conversion between LMT and UTC (GMT) is achieved by use of the Conversion of Arc to Time tables and para.16.18 showed how conversion between UTC (GMT) and Standard Time is achieved by use of the Standard Time tables. The common factor in both cases being UTC (GMT), it follows that to convert LMT to Standard Time, or vice versa, UTC (GMT) must be solved as an intermediate step.

LMT<Arc to Time>**UTC (GMT)**<Standard Time Diff>**Standard Time**

It is advisable with time problems, particularly those involving flight times or the crossing of the 180° meridian, to convert into UTC (GMT) at the earliest possible stage and carry out all the intermediary workings in this form, only converting back to the required LMT or Standard Time as the final step in the calculations. Working in UTC (GMT) enables 'like' to be compared with 'like' and, as will be demonstrated by worked example, date changes on crossing the 180° meridian come out correctly without having to agonise about whether to add or subtract a day!

Example:

An aircraft is scheduled to depart from Tokyo (Japan) (35°30' N 134° 45' E) for a flight to Hawaii (USA) (21°20' N 158°10' W) at 0815 Standard Time on 21 November . The estimated flight time is 5 hrs and 35 mins. What is the LMT and local date of the ETA at Hawaii?

Answer:

Depart Tokyo.........................	0815 ST Japan	Nov 21
Standard Time diff (Japan)...	- 0900 (to find UTC (GMT))	
Depart Tokyo.........................	2315 UTC (GMT)	Nov 20
Flight time.........................	+ 0535	
ETA Hawaii.........................	0450 UTC (GMT)	Nov 21
Arc to time (158°10' W)......	- 1033 (to the nearest min)	
ETA Hawaii.........................	**1817 LMT**	**Nov 20**

Candidates should be aware that the rules for adding or subtracting are given at the top of each of the *Standard Time* lists and at the *bottom* of the *Conversion of Arc to Time* table. If in doubt check before proceeding. The above example highlights the chances of confusion if the calculations are not carried out in a methodical manner. Note that the time datum (LMT, UTC or ST) and the date is entered on completion of each step in the calculation, thus keeping track of the thought process.

SUNRISE AND SUNSET

16.20   Fig. 16–4 showed the tilt of the earth's spin axis to the vertical of it's elliptical path around the sun and how this varied the length of the hours of daylight. Figs. 16–9a and b illustrate in side and plan views the earth at Perihelion with the N pole tilted away from the sun.

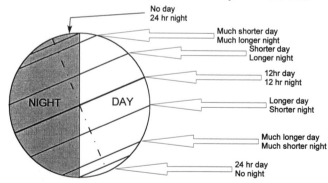

Fig. 16–9a   The Earth at Perihelion with the N Pole tilted away from the sun. The N hemisphere has fewer hours of daylight than night.

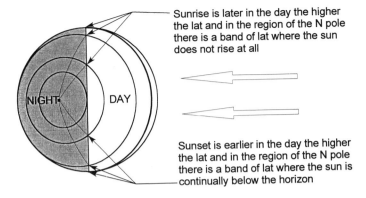

Sunrise is later in the day the higher the lat and in the region of the N pole there is a band of lat where the sun does not rise at all

Sunset is earlier in the day the higher the lat and in the region of the N pole there is a band of lat where the sun is continually below the horizon

Fig. 16–9b   The Earth at Perihelion with the N Pole tilted away from the Sun. Variations in sunrise and sunset times with lat.

Note how the periods of day and night vary along different parallels of lat, the further N of the equator a parallel is the fewer hours of daylight it receives and in the region of the N pole there is a band of lat that does not get any sunlight at all. In the S hemisphere with movement towards the S pole the parallels are progressively receiving more hours of daylight and there is a region around the S pole that is in continual daylight. Figs. 16–10a and b illustrate how this situation is reversed when the earth is at Aphelion with the N pole tilted towards the sun.

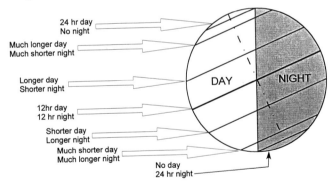

Fig. 16–10a   The Earth at Aphelion with the N pole tilted towards the sun. The N hemisphere has more hours of daylight than night.

Along any chosen parallel of lat, as the earth moves on its elliptical path around the sun, the length of daylight in a 24 hr period will vary between the Perihelion and Aphelion extremes illustrated above. The length of daylight any parallel receives in a 24 hr period is a function of Hemisphere,

Lat and Time of the Year (Calendar Date). The greatest changes throughout the year occur in the polar regions which vary from 24 hrs of continual daylight to 24 hrs of continual night. On the other hand in the region of the equator the number of hrs of daylight in any 24 hr period only vary from around 11 to 13 hrs throughout the year.

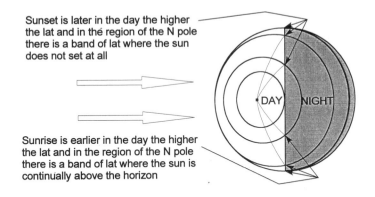

Sunset is later in the day the higher the lat and in the region of the N pole there is a band of lat where the sun does not set at all

Sunrise is earlier in the day the higher the lat and in the region of the N pole there is a band of lat where the sun is continually above the horizon

Fig. 16–10b   The Earth at Aphelion with the N Pole tilted towards the sun. Variations in sunrise and sunset times with lat.

16.21 **Sunrise** and **Sunset** are taken from the moment the centre of the sun is observed to be on the horizontal to an observer at sea level. Because the earth's atmosphere refracts light the sun is actually visible when it is approximately 1° below the true horizontal. The times of SUNRISE and SUNSET listed in the *Air Almanac* are the times the sun's centre is observed as rising or setting on the visible horizon and not on the true horizontal.

16.22 Paragraph 16.8 and Fig. 16–4 showed how, during the course of one day, the path of the sun appeared to move over the earth from E to W tracking overhead one parallel of lat. It will of course appear to be tracking E to W along all other parallels (except those in continual polar night) but not directly overhead. Along any parallel of lat the length of the hrs of daylight will be the same for all meridians along that parallel. Therefore for any particular day and parallel of lat the observed LMT of Sunrise and Sunset must be the same for all meridians along that parallel. Paragraph 16.20 explained how the length of daylight varied with hemisphere, Lat and Calendar Date and it is these variables that have to be incorporated into the SUNRISE and SUNSET tables of the *Air Almanac*. Study of these tables in the appended extract at the end of this chapter reveal how this is achieved.

16.23 SUNRISE tables occupy the top half of the left-hand page and SUNSET tables the bottom half of the same page. Along the top of each table are Month blocks with Dates (for every third day) at the head of vertical columns. Down the left-hand side are listed lats starting with N 72° at the top and going down to 0° about two thirds of the way down, then moving into the S hemisphere going down to S 60°. Inspection reveals that starting from 0° the lat spacing is every 10° as far as N 30° and S 30°, from 30° lat to 50° lat the spacing is every 5° and from 50° lat the spacing is every 2°. The reason for this difference in line spacing is that at the lower lats where conv is small and changes slowly with change of lat the Sunrise and Sunset times also change slowly with change of lat. At higher lats conv changes faster with change of lat (with the sine of the lat) causing the Sunrise and Sunset times also to change more rapidly with change of lat. The reason for the gaps in the columns and lines is really one of sensible economy. To produce a table listing the LMT of Sunrise and Sunset for every day and every degree of lat would require twelve times the area of the present tables. The layout of the tables does however mean that the user has to interpolate the times for dates and/or lats not specifically listed.

Example:
What is the LMT of Sunrise on the 63°30' N parallel on 27 July?
Answer:
The SUNRISE tables list N 62° and N 64° for July 25 and July 28. What is required in this case is ¾ of the way between N 62° and N 64°, and ⅔ of the way between July 25 and July 28. Prepare a box four by three, extract the figures from the tables and enter them into the appropriate boxes. (see Fig. 16–11a)

	July 25 h m	July 26	July 27	July 28 h m
N 64	02 44			02 54
N 63 30				
N 62	03 06			03 14

Box prepared for interpolation with figure from the Air Almanac Sunrise tables inserted (bold). The unlisted dates and required lat are also inserted (light). The target box is shaded here for demonstration purposes only

Fig. 16–11a   Interpolation of the LMT of Sunrise from the
Air Almanac tables. Step 1.

On 25 July there is 0306 LMT – 0244 LMT = 22 mins difference between N 62° and N 64°. Interpolating for N 63°30' either add ¼ of 22 mins to 0244 LMT or subtract ¾ of 22 mins from 0306 LMT, in either case the answer is 0249·5 LMT. Doing the same for 28 July (time difference 20 mins) gives the time at N 63°30' as 0259 LMT. Enter these two times into their appropriate boxes. (see Fig. 16–11b)

	July 25 h m	July 26	July 27	July 28 h m
N 64	02 44			02 54
N 63 30	02 49.5 ☞ ☞ ☞		**02 56**	☜02 59
N 62	03 06			03 14

Interpolation for lat N 63 30 on July 25 and July 28

Fig. 16–11b   Interpolation of the LMT of sunrise from the
Air Almanac tables. Step 2.

At N 63°30' the time difference between 25 July and 28 July is 0259 LMT – 0249·5 = 9·5 mins. The time of Sunrise at N 63°30' on 27 July is either 0249·5 LMT + ⅔ of 9·5 mins or 0259 LMT – ⅓ of 9·5 mins, in either case the answer, to the nearest min, is **0256 LMT**.

The solution could just as easily have been found by interpolating the Sunrise times on 27 July for N 62° and N 64° and then interpolating these time for N 63°30'. As Fig.16–11c shows the end result is the same as above.

	July 25 h m	July 26	July 27 h m	July 28 h m
N 64	02 44 ☞ ☞ ☞		02 50.66	☜02 54
N 63 30			02 56	
N 62	03 06 ☞ ☞ ☞		03 11.33	☜ 03 14

Interpolation for July 27 at N 64 and N 62 as the first step

Fig. 16–11c   Interpolation of the LMT of Sunrise from the Air Almanac Tables.
Alternative route to the solution.

Some hints of a practical nature are worth mentioning:

When extracting figures from the Air Almanac, make sure that the correct table is entered (**SUNRISE** or **SUNSET** as appropriate) for the desired **Month** and **Date(s)** and the correct **Hemisphere** and **Lat(s)**

To reduce the risk of reading figures from the wrong line it is advisable to lay a rule, or the edge of a sheet of paper, under the line from which the figures are to be extracted.

Having extracted figures which have to be interpolated, note the earliest and latest times. *Any answer obtained that falls outside these limits must be wrong* and the interpolation should be reworked taking care to add and/or subtract in the correct sense.

These may seem obvious precautions to most people but the author has seen so many extraordinary answers produced by students who have not followed these basic checks that he feels they are well worth including them in this book.

16.24 Before leaving the SUNRISE and SUNSET tables, a look at the July tables reveal a series of empty rectangular boxes in quite a few of the high lat columns. Turning to the December tables reveal solid black rectangles boxes in the same general area of the tables. The empty boxes indicate that the sun does not set on that date at that particular lat (i.e. it is above the horizon for the full 24 hrs), the solid black boxes indicate that the sun does rise on that date at that particular lat (i.e. 24 hrs of darkness). These are the zones that have periods of continual daylight or darkness around the Perihelion and Aphelion points of the earth's orbit around the sun. (See para.16.20.)

MORNING CIVIL TWILIGHT AND EVENING CIVIL TWILIGHT

16.25 Just before Sunrise and just after Sunset there is a period of time when although the sun is not visible its light is refracted by the earth's atmosphere giving a degree of light known as **Twilight**. There are three zones of twilight depending on the depression of the centre of the sun below the visible horizon (the one used in assessing the time of Sunrise and Sunset):

Up to 6° of depression.....Civil Twilight. Out of doors operations are possible without artificial lighting and only the brightest stars are visible in the sky.

From 6° to 12° of depression.....Nautical Twilight. Out of doors operations are only possible with the aid of artificial lighting, bright stars are visible in the sky and at sea the horizon can be distinguished.

From 12° to 18° of depression.....Astronomical Twilight. The horizon is not visible at sea, most stars are visible in the sky but there is not quite total darkness which is deemed to occur when the depression is greater than 18°.

Nautical Twilight and Astronomical Twilight are of importance to seamen and astronomers but do not form part of a pilot's curriculum. However

Civil Twilight is of significance to pilots, since during this period many daylight activities may be carried out in a normal and safe way without recourse to artificial lighting.

16.26   The period of Civil Twilight before Sunrise is known as **Morning Civil Twilight** and after Sunset as **Evening Civil Twilight**. The *Air Almanac* lists the LMTs of the *beginning* of **Morning Civil Twilight** and the *end* of **Evening Civil Twilight** in exactly the same format as the SUNRISE and SUNSET tables. The Twilight tables are printed on the right-hand pages facing the SUNRISE and SUNSET tables, each pair of facing pages covering the same block of Calendar Dates. The method of interpolating the TWILIGHT tables to find the times for dates and lats not specifically listed is exactly the same as that demonstrated for interpolating the SUNRISE and SUNSET tables. (See para. 16.23)

16.27   Comparison of the time of the beginning of Morning Civil Twilight and the time of Sunrise for a given Lat and Calendar Date will give the length of the period of Morning Civil Twilight for that Lat and Calendar Date. Similarly for a given Lat and Calendar Date the length of the period of Evening Civil Twilight can be found by comparing the Sunset time and the end of Evening Civil Twilight time. Because the times listed in the tables are the LMT of phenomena occurrence for all points along a given parallel of Lat on a given Calendar Date, this is one of the rare cases where it is possible to carry out comparisons of LMTs without converting into UTC (GMT) first. Some Morning Civil Twilight periods worked out from the tables for 28 June to 15 August are given below:

Sunrise at 10° N	05 43 LMT	July 1
Beginning of Morning Civil Twilight at 10° N	05 20 LMT	July 1
Length of Morning Civil Twilight at 10° N	23 mins.	July 1
Sunrise at 10° N	05 49 LMT	July 31
Beginning of Morning Civil Twilight at 10° N	05 27 LMT	July 31
Length of Morning Civil Twilight at 10° N	22 mins.	July 31
Sunrise at 60° N	02 42 LMT	July 1
Beginning of Morning Civil Twilight at 60° N	01 02 LMT	July 1
Length of Morning Civil Twilight at 60° N	1 hr 40 mins.	July 1
Sunrise at 60° N	03 37 LMT	July 31
Beginning of Morning Civil Twilight at 60° N	02 35 LMT	July 31
Length of Morning Civil Twilight at 60° N	1 hr 02 mins.	July 31

This demonstrates that along a parallel of lat close to the equator there is only a small change in the length of the period of twilight over a 30 day interval, the actual periods being fairly short. However at a higher parallel of lat the change in the length of the period of twilight over the same 30 day interval is quite large, the actual periods being much larger than at the lower parallel of lat. Repeating this exercise for 31 December the length of the period of Morning Civil Twilight at 10° N is found to be 22 mins and at 60° N it is 57 mins. So not only is the length of the twilight period longer at higher lats than at lats near the equator it also varies more between Summer and Winter. A similar pattern of length of twilight periods is to found for Evening Civil Twilight. Fig. 16–12a and b are reproductions of Fig. 16–9a and b with the Twilight Zone shaded in (not to scale) showing how at the higher lats, due to conv, a larger arc of long is in twilight than in the equatorial regions. With the earth rotating at a constant speed the length of the period of twilight will vary with the arc of long that is in twilight, being shortest in the equatorial region and getting longer as lat is increased toward the poles (but excluding the polar regions when they are in either 24 hrs of continual daylight or darkness).

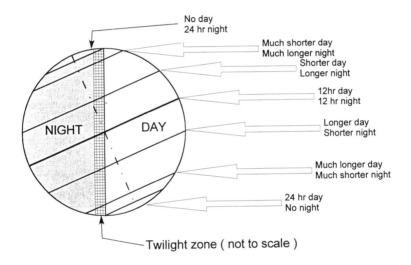

Fig. 16–12 a   The Earth at Perihelion with the N Pole tilted away from the sun, showing the twilight zone.

16.28   The 28 June to 15 August pages introduce another symbol in the TWILIGHT tables. This is an un-enclosed 'hatched' rectangle //// which signifies that at that Lat and Calendar Date the depression of the centre of the sun does not exceed 6° below the visible horizon between Sunset on one

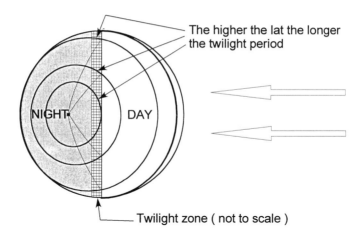

Fig. 16–12b   Plan view of the Twilight Zone showing how the twilight period increases at higher lats.

day and Sunrise on the following day. There is no night as such and twilight exists from Sunset on one day until Sunrise on the following day.

TYPES OF TIME PROBLEMS

16.29   In the Licence Examinations a variety of questions involving the use of some, or all, of the above tables are possible. The questions set are usually fairly straightforward, but they do require the candidate to be careful in reading the questions and methodical in working out the answers. Always enter the Calendar Date and the Time Datum beside all times when working out any time problem and remember that the SUNRISE, SUNSET and CIVIL TWILIGHT tables are all in LMT.

16.30   Below is a list of possible variations of questions involving the SUNRISE, SUNSET and CIVIL TWILIGHT tables only:

Question   Calculation of the length of the period of Morning Civil Twilight for a particular. Lat and Calendar Date.

Method   Extract the appropriate times of the beginning of Morning Civil Twilight and Sunrise from the tables (interpolating if necessary) and subtract the Morning Civil Twilight time from the Sunrise time.

Question   Calculation of the length of the period of Evening Civil Twilight for a particular Lat and Calendar Date.

Method   Extract the appropriate times of the end of Evening Civil

Twilight and Sunset from the tables (interpolating if necessary) and subtract the Sunset time from the end of Evening Civil Twilight time.

Question Calculation of the period of time from Sunset on one day to Sunrise on the next day.

Method Extract the time of Sunset for the first day and the time of Sunrise for the *next* day from the tables (interpolating if necessary, with this type of question attention to the Calendar Dates is essential) and subtract the Sunset time (and Calendar Date) from the Sunrise time (and Calendar Date). Note: This is also the method for calculation of the length of the period of twilight where the //// symbol appears in the TWILIGHT tables.

Question Calculation of the period of daylight from Sunrise to Sunset for a particular Lat and Calendar Date.

Method Extract the appropriate Sunset and Sunrise times from the tables (interpolating if necessary) and subtract the Sunrise time from the Sunset time.

Question Calculation of the period of time from the beginning of Morning Civil Twilight to the end of Evening Civil Twilight for a particular Lat and Calendar Date.

Method Extract the appropriate end of Evening Civil Twilight and beginning of Morning Civil Twilight times from the tables (interpolating if necessary) and subtract the beginning of Morning Civil Twilight time from the end of Evening Civil Twilight time.

16.31 Paragraph 16.19 had an example of a question requiring conversions between LMT, UTC (GMT) and Standard Time and including a flight time. There are many variations that can be played with this type of question and the SUNRISE, SUNSET and TWILIGHT tables can be worked into them as part of the LMT element. It would take many pages to examine every possible variation but the worked example below should give candidates an insight into the way to approach such questions.

Example:
An aircraft is scheduled to depart from San Francisco (California, USA) (37°58' N 102°15' W) on an 11 hrs 35 mins flight to Amsterdam / Schiphol (Holland, the Netherlands) (52°19' N 004°46' E). The ETA is to be 30 mins after Sunrise at Amsterdam / Schiphol on 12 November. Calculate the Local Standard Time and Calendar Date of departure from San Francisco.

Answer:

Stage 1	S/R 52°19' N	07 15 LMT	Nov 12
	Arc to time (4°46' E)	- 00 19 mins	
Stage 2	S/R 52°19' N	06 56 UTC (GMT) Nov 12	
	To arrive 30 mins after S/R	+00 30 mins	
Stage 3	ETA Amsterdam / Schiphol	07 26 UTC (GMT) Nov 12	
	Flight time	– 11 35	
Stage 4	Depart San Francisco	19 51 UTC (GMT) Nov 11	
	Std Time diff (Cal, USA)	– 05 00	
Stage 5	Depart San Francisco	**14 51 LST Cal**	**Nov 11**

Note the logical sequence for solving this particular problem:

Stage 1 Extract the LMT cf Sunrise for 52°19'N on 12 November from the SUNRISE tables, interpolating between N 52° and N 54° (⅙ up OR ⅚ down) and 10 and 13 November (⅔ right OR ⅓ left).

Stage 2 Using the Long of Amsterdam / Schiphol and the CONVER-SION OF ARC TO TIME tables convert the Sunrise time from LMT into UTC (GMT)

Stage 3 Add the 30 mins to the Sunrise time to find the ETA at Amsterdam / Schiphol in UTC (GMT).

Stage 4 Subtract the flight time from the ETA to give the time (and Calendar Date) of departure from San Francisco in UTC (GMT).

Stage 5 Using the STANDARD TIMES tables LIST III apply the conversion for California, USA to convert the departure time from San Francisco from UTC (GMT) into Local Standard Time.

In multi-choice question papers it is common practice to ask about more than one aspect of any calculation involving several steps. For example in the above problem the sort of multi-choice questions asked could be something like:

Q The ETA at Amsterdam / Schiphol is:
a 0626 UTC Nov 12
b 0804 UTC Nov 12
c 0726 UTC Nov 12
d 0704 UTC Nov 12

Q Departure time from San Francisco is:-
a 1451 LST Nov 11
b 1801 LST Nov 12
a 0051 LST Nov 12
b 1351 LST Nov 11

A study of the incorrect answers on offer shows that they have all been obtained by wrong application of a + or a – at some point. Since this is the most common error in this type of calculation it means that a candidate who has made such an error may well find one of the choices matches up with the wrong answer he or she has obtained. Ironically the only time a candidate gets a definite indication that their working is wrong is when their answer is nowhere near any of the multi-choice answers on offer! Where interpolations are involved candidates who find that their answer differs by a min or two from one of the choices, should not waste time reworking, but select that choice as the answer.

ABRIDGED VERSION OF THE AIR ALMANAC EXTRACT USED FOR TRAINING AND EXAMINATION PURPOSES BY THE UK CIVIL AVIATION AUTHORITY.

This extract is Crown copyright and is reproduced by kind permission of the Controller, Her Majesty's Stationery Office.

Note:-

These pages are from an out of date Air Almanac and, apart from the Arc to Time tables, should not be used for operational purposes. Always use the current edition of the Air Almanac for operational purposes. Political changes often lead to changes in the name of a country or state, such changes being incorporated in the Air Almanac as soon as possible after such an event. In the following pages readers will find at least two cases of countries that have changed their name since the time these pages were first printed.

At the time of writing the pages overleaf were in current use for training and examination purposes. The UK CAA does from time to time review its training material and may start to use extracts from a more recent edition of the Air Almanac, however it is the practice of the CAA to give adequate prior warning of any such change. The full current Air Almanac training extract is obtainable from Her Majesty's Stationery Office.

STANDARD TIMES

LIST I—PLACES FAST ON G.M.T. (mainly those EAST OF GREENWICH)

The times given } *added* to G.M.T. to give Standard Time.
below should be } *subtracted* from Standard Time to give G.M.T.

	h m		h m
Admiralty Islands	10	Egypt (United Arab Republic)	02
Afghanistan	04 30	Equatorial Guinea, Republic of	01
Albania*	01	Estonia	03
Amirante Islands	04	Ethiopia	03
Andaman Islands	05 30		
Angola	01	Fernando Póo‡	01
Annobon Island‡	01	Fiji	12
Arabian Emirates, Federation of	04	Finland	02
Australia		France‡ *	01
Australian Capital Territory*	10	French Territory of the Afars and Issas ...	03
New South Wales¹ *	10	Friendly Islands	13
Northern Territory	09 30		
Queensland	10	Gabon	01
South Australia*	09 30	Germany	01
Tasmania*	10	Gibraltar‡	01
Victoria*	10	Gilbert Islands	12
Western Australia	08	Greece*	02
Austria	01	Guam	10
Balearic Islands‡ *	01	Holland (The Netherlands)	01
Bangladesh	06	Hong Kong*	08
Belgium	01	Hungary	01
Benin (Dahomey)	01		
Botswana, Republic of	02	India	05 30
Brunei	08	Indonesia, Republic of	
Bulgaria	02	Bali, Bangka, Billiton, Java,	
Burma	06 30	Lombok, Madura, Sumatra ...	07
Burundi	02	Borneo, Celebes, Flores, Sumba,	
		Sumbawa, Timor	08
Cambodia (Democratic Kampuchea) ...	07	Aru, Kei, Moluccas, Tanimbar,	
Cameroun Republic	01	Irian Jaya	09
Caroline Islands, east of long. E. 160° ...	12	Iran	03 30
west of long. E. 150° ...	10	Iraq	03
Truk, Ponape	11	Israel*	02
Central African Republic	01	Italy*	01
Chad	01		
Chagos Archipelago	05	Japan	09
Chatham Islands‡	12 45	Jordan*	02
China³	08		
Christmas Island, Indian Ocean	07	Kamchatka Peninsula	12
Cocos Keeling Islands	06 30	Kenya	03
Comoro Islands	03	Korea	09
Congo Republic	01	Kuril Islands	11
Corsica‡ *	01	Kuwait	03
Crete *	02		
Cyprus, North*	02	Laccadive Islands	05 30
South*	02	Ladrone Islands	10
Czechoslovakia	01	Laos	07
		Latvia	03
Denmark	01		

* Summer time may be kept in these countries.
‡ The legal time may differ from that given here.
¹ Except Broken Hill Area, which keeps 09ʰ 30ᵐ.
³ All the coast, but some areas may keep summer time.

LIST I—*(continued)*

	h	m		h	m
Lebanon*	02		Saudi Arabia...	03	
Lesotho	02		Schouten Islands	09	
Libya‡	02		Seychelles	04	
Liechtenstein...	01		Sicily*	01	
Lord Howe Island	10		Singapore	07	30
Luxembourg ...	01		Socotra	03	
			Solomon Islands	11	
Macao*	08		Somalia Republic	03	
Malagasy Republic ...	03		South Africa, Republic of ...	02	
Malawi	02		Southern Yemen	03	
Malaysia			South West Africa (Namibia)	02	
Malaya	07	30	Spain‡ *	01	
Sabah, Sarawak	08		Spitsbergen (Svalbard)	01	
Maldive Republic	05		Sri Lanka	05	30
Malta*	01		Sudan, Republic of ...	02	
Manchuria	09		Swaziland	02	
Mariana Islands	10		Sweden	01	
Marshall Islands[1]	12		Switzerland ...	01	
Mauritius	04		Syria* (Syrian Arab Republic)	02	
Monaco‡	01				
Mozambique	02		Taiwan	08	
			Tanzania	03	
Namibia (South West Africa)	02		Thailand	07	
Nauru...	11	30	Tonga Islands	13	
Netherlands, The	01		Truk ...	11	
New Caledonia	11		Tunisia	01	
New Hebrides	11		Turkey*	02	
New Zealand*	12		Tuvalu Islands	12	
Nicobar Islands	05	30			
Niger ...	01		Uganda	03	
Nigeria, Republic of	01		Union of Soviet Socialist Republics[2]		
Norfolk Island	11	30	west of long. E. 40°	03	
Norway	01		long. E. 40° to E. 52° 30'	04	
Novaya Zemlya	05		long. E. 52° 30' to E. 67° 30'	05	
			long. E. 67° 30' to E. 82° 30'	06	
Ocean Island	11	30	long. E. 82° 30' to E. 97° 30'	07	
Okinawa	09		long. E. 97° 30' to E. 112° 30' ...	08	
Oman ...	04		long. E. 112° 30' to E. 127° 30'...	09	
			long. E. 127° 30' to E. 142° 30'...	10	
Pakistan	05		long. E. 142° 30' to E. 157° 30'...	11	
Papua New Guinea ...	10		long. E. 157° 30' to E. 172° 30'...	12	
Pescadores Islands ...	08		east of long. E. 172° 30' ...	13	
Philippine Republic...	08				
Poland	01		Vietnam, Northern ...	07	
			Southern‡	07	
Réunion	04				
Rhodesia	02		Wrangell Island	13	
Romania	02				
Rwanda	02		Yugoslavia	01	
Ryukyu Islands	09				
			Zaire		
Sakhalin	11		Kinshasa, Mbandaka	01	
Santa Cruz Islands ...	11		Orientale, Kivu, Katanga, Kasai	02	
Sardinia*	01		Zambia, Republic of	02	

* Summer time may be kept in these countries.
‡ The legal time may differ from that given here.
[1] Except the islands of Kwajalein and Eniwetok which keep a time 24ʰ slow on that of the rest of the islands.
[2] The boundaries between the zones are irregular; the longitudes given are approximate only.

STANDARD TIMES

LIST II—PLACES NORMALLY KEEPING G.M.T.

Algeria	Great Britain[1]	Ivory Coast	Portugal*	Tangier
Ascension Island	Guinea Bissau‡	Liberia	Principe	Togo Republic
Canary Islands‡ *	Guinea Republic	Madeira	Rio de Oro‡	Tristan da Cunha
Channel Islands[1]	Iceland	Mali	St. Helena	Upper Volta
Faeroes, The	Ifni	Mauritania	São Tomé	Western Sahara
Gambia	Ireland, Northern[1]	(Dakhla)	Senegal	(Moroccan Sector) ‡ *
Ghana	Irish Republic*	Morocco*	Sierra Leone	

* Summer time may be kept in these countries.
‡ The legal time may differ from that given here.
[1] Summer time, one hour in advance of G.M.T., is kept from March 19d 02h to October 29d 02h G.M.T.

LIST III—PLACES SLOW ON G.M.T. (WEST OF GREENWICH)

The times given ⎫ subtracted from G.M.T. to give Standard Time.
below should be ⎭ added to Standard Time to give G.M.T.

	h	m		h	m
Argentina‡	03		Cape Verde Islands‡	01	
Austral Islands[1]	10		Cayman Islands	05	
Azores	01		Chile*	04	
			Christmas Island, Pacific Ocean ...	10	
Bahamas*	05		Colombia	05	
Barbados	04		Cook Islands, except Niue	10	30
Belize*	06		Costa Rica	06	
Bermuda*	04		Cuba*	05	
Bolivia	04		Curaçao Island	04	
Brazil, eastern[2]	03				
Territory of Acre	05		Dominican Republic*	04	
western	04				
British Antarctic Territory[3]	03		Easter Island (I. de Pascua)* ...	07	
			Ecuador	05	
Canada					
Alberta*	07		Falkland Islands[4]	04	
British Columbia*	08		Fanning Island	10	
Labrador*	04		Fernando de Noronha Island ...	02	
Manitoba*	06		French Guiana‡	03	
New Brunswick*	04				
Newfoundland*	03	30	Galápagos Islands	05	
Northwest Territories*			Greenland, Scoresby Sound[5] ...	02	
east of long. W. 68°	04		Angmagssalik and west coast ...	03	
long. W. 68° to W. 85° ...	05		Thule area	04	
long. W. 85° to W. 102° ...	06		Grenada	04	
west of long. W. 102°	07		Guadeloupe	04	
Nova Scotia*	04		Guatemala	06	
Ontario*, east of long. W. 90° ...	05		Guiana, French‡	03	
west of long. W. 90° ...	06		Guyana, Republic of‡	03	
Prince Edward Island*	04				
Quebec*, east of long. W. 63° ...	04		Haiti	05	
west of long. W. 63° ...	05		Honduras	06	
Saskatchewan*					
east of long. W. 106°	06		Jamaica*	05	
west of long. W. 106°	07		Jan Mayen Island	01	
Yukon, east of long. W. 138° ...	08		Johnston Island	10	
west of long. W. 138° ...	09		Juan Fernandez Islands	04	

* Summer time may be kept in these countries.
‡ The legal time may differ from that given here.
[1] This is the legal standard time, but local mean time is generally used.
[2] Including all the coast and Brasilia.
[3] Except South Georgia which keeps 02h.
[4] Except Port Stanley which keeps 03h ‡.
[5] Scoresby Sound may keep 03h in summer.

LIST III—*(continued)*

					h	m
Leeward Islands	...	...	...	...	04	
Low Archipelago	...	...	...	...	10	
Marquesas Islands[1]	...	...	...	...	09	30
Martinique	...	...	...	...	04	
Mexico‡ *[2]	...	...	...	...	06	
Midway Islands	...	...	...	...	11	
Miquelon	...	...	...	...	03	
Nicaragua‡	...	...	...	...	06	
Niue Island	...	...	...	...	11	
Panama Canal Zone	...	...	...	05	
Panama, Republic of	...	...	...	05	
Paraguay*	...	...	...	...	04	
Peru	...	...	...	...	05	
Puerto Rico	...	...	...	...	04	
Rarotonga	...	...	...	...	10	30
St. Pierre and Miquelon	...	...	...	03	
Salvador, El	...	...	...	...	06	
Samoa	...	...	...	...	11	
Society Islands[1]	...	...	...	...	10	
South Georgia	...	...	...	...	02	
Surinam	...	...	...	...	03	30
Tobago	...	...	...	...	04	
Trindade Island, South Atlantic	...		...	02	
Trinidad	...	...	...	...	04	
Tuamotu Archipelago[1]	...	...	...	10	
Tubuai Islands[1]	...	...	...	...	10	
Turks and Caicos Islands*	...	...	...	05	
United States of America						
Alabama[3]	...	...	...	...	06	
Alaska,[3] east of long. W. 137°	...		...	08	
long. W. 137° to W. 141°	...		...	09	
long. W. 141° to W. 161°	...		...	10	
long. W. 161° to W. 172° 30′		...	11	
Aleutian Islands	...	...	...	11	
Arizona	...	...	...	...	07	
Arkansas[3]	...	...	...	...	06	
California[3]	...	...	...	...	08	
Colorado[3]	...	...	...	...	07	
Connecticut[3]	...	...	...	...	05	
Delaware[3]	...	...	...	...	05	
District of Columbia[3]	...	...	...	05	
Florida[3,4]	...	...	...	...	05	
Georgia[3]	...	...	...	...	05	

					h
United States of America *(continued)*					
Hawaii	...	...	...	...	10
Idaho[3,4]	...	...	...	...	07
Illinois[3]	...	...	...	...	06
Indiana[4]	...	...	...	...	05
Iowa[3]	...	...	...	...	06
Kansas[3,4]	...	...	...	...	06
Kentucky[3,4]	...	...	...	...	05
Louisiana[3]	...	...	...	...	06
Maine[3]	...	...	...	...	05
Maryland[3]	...	...	...	...	05
Massachusetts[3]	...	...	...	...	05
Michigan[3,4]	...	...	...	...	05
Minnesota[3]	...	...	...	...	06
Mississippi[3]	...	...	...	...	06
Missouri[3]	...	...	...	...	06
Montana[3]	...	...	...	...	07
Nebraska[3,4]	...	...	...	...	06
Nevada[3]	...	...	...	...	08
New Hampshire[3]	...	...	...	05
New Jersey[3]	...	...	...	...	05
New Mexico[3]	...	...	...	...	07
New York[3]	...	...	...	...	05
North Carolina[3]	...	...	...	05
North Dakota[3,4]	...	...	...	06
Ohio[3]	...	...	...	...	05
Oklahoma[3]	...	...	...	...	06
Oregon[3,4]	...	...	...	...	08
Pennsylvania[3]	...	...	...	...	05
Rhode Island[3]	...	...	...	...	05
South Carolina[3]	...	...	...	05
South Dakota,[3] eastern part	...	06
western part	...	...	07
Tennessee[3,4]	...	...	...	...	06
Texas[3]	...	...	...	...	06
Utah[3,4]	...	...	...	...	07
Vermont[3]	...	...	...	...	05
Virginia[3]	...	...	...	...	05
Washington, D.C.[3]	...	...	...	05
Washington[3]	...	...	...	...	08
West Virginia[3]	...	...	...	05
Wisconsin[3]	...	...	...	...	06
Wyoming[3]	...	...	...	...	07
Uruguay	...	...	...	...	03
Venezuela‡	...	...	...	...	04
Virgin Islands	...	...	...	...	04
Windward Islands	...	...	...	04

* Summer time may be kept in these countries.
‡ The legal time may differ from that given here.
[1] This is the legal standard time, but local mean time is generally used.
[2] Except the states of Sonora, Sinaloa, Nayarit, and the Southern District of Lower California which keep 07ʰ, and the Northern District of Lower California which keeps 08ʰ.
[3] Summer (daylight-saving) time, one hour fast on the time given, is kept in these states from the last Sunday in April to the last Sunday in October, changing at 02ʰ 00ᵐ local clock time.
[4] This applies to the greater portion of the state.

SUNRISE

Lat.	June 28	July 1	4	7	10	13	16	19	22	25	28	31	Aug 3	6	9	12	15
N 72	□	□	□	□	□	□	□	□	□	□	□	□	□	00 49	01 30	01 58	02 21
70	□	□	□	□	□	□	□	□	□	□	00 21	01 11	01 39	02 01	02 20	02 37	02 54
68	□	□	□	□	□	□	□	00 39	01 10	01 32	01 50	02 07	02 22	02 37	02 51	03 04	03 17
66	□	00 13	00 38	00 55	01 10	01 24	01 37	01 50	02 03	02 15	02 27	02 39	02 51	03 03	03 14	25	36
64	01 35	01 40	01 46	01 52	02 00	02 08	02 17	02 26	35	02 44	02 54	03 03	03 13	22	32	41	03 50
62	02 13	02 16	02 20	02 25	31	37	02 44	02 51	02 58	03 06	03 14	22	30	38	46	03 54	04 02
N 60	02 39	02 42	02 45	02 49	02 54	02 59	03 04	03 10	03 17	03 23	03 30	03 37	03 44	03 51	03 58	04 06	04 13
58	02 59	03 01	03 04	03 08	03 12	03 16	21	26	32	38	44	03 50	03 56	04 02	04 09	15	22
56	03 16	18	20	23	27	31	35	40	45	03 50	03 55	04 01	04 06	12	18	24	30
54	30	32	34	37	40	44	48	03 52	03 56	04 01	04 06	11	16	21	26	31	37
52	42	44	46	49	03 52	03 55	03 58	04 02	04 06	10	15	19	24	29	33	38	43
N 50	03 53	03 54	03 57	03 59	04 02	04 05	04 08	04 11	04 15	04 19	04 23	04 27	04 31	04 35	04 40	04 44	04 49
45	04 15	04 17	04 18	04 20	23	25	28	31	34	37	40	43	47	04 50	04 54	04 57	05 01
40	33	34	36	38	40	42	44	46	04 49	04 51	04 54	04 57	04 59	05 02	05 05	05 08	11
35	04 48	04 49	04 51	04 52	04 54	04 56	04 57	04 59	05 01	05 04	05 06	05 08	05 10	13	15	17	19
30	05 01	05 02	05 03	05 05	05 06	05 08	05 09	05 11	13	14	16	18	20	22	23	25	27
N 20	05 23	05 24	05 25	05 26	05 27	05 28	05 29	05 30	05 31	05 33	05 34	05 35	05 36	05 37	05 38	05 39	05 40
N 10	42	05 43	05 43	05 44	05 45	05 46	05 47	05 48	05 48	05 49	05 49	05 50	05 50	05 50	05 51	05 51	05 51
0	05 59	06 00	06 01	06 01	06 02	06 02	06 02	06 02	06 03	06 03	06 03	06 03	06 03	06 02	06 02	06 02	06 01
S 10	06 17	17	18	18	18	18	18	18	18	17	17	16	15	15	14	12	11
20	35	35	36	36	36	35	35	34	34	33	32	30	29	27	26	24	22
S 30	06 56	06 56	06 56	06 56	06 56	06 55	06 54	06 53	06 52	06 50	06 48	06 46	06 44	06 42	06 40	06 37	06 34
35	07 09	07 08	07 08	07 08	07 07	07 06	07 05	07 04	07 02	07 00	06 58	06 56	06 53	06 50	47	44	41
40	23	23	22	22	21	19	18	16	14	12	07 09	07 06	07 03	07 00	06 56	06 53	49
45	07 39	39	39	38	36	35	33	31	28	25	22	19	15	11	07 07	07 03	06 58
50	08 00	07 59	07 59	07 57	07 56	07 54	07 51	48	45	42	38	34	29	25	20	14	07 09
S 52	08 10	08 09	08 08	08 07	08 05	08 03	08 00	07 57	07 53	07 49	07 45	07 41	07 36	07 31	07 25	07 20	07 14
54	21	20	19	17	15	13	09	08 06	08 02	07 58	07 53	48	43	38	32	26	20
56	33	33	31	29	27	24	20	16	12	08 07	08 02	07 57	07 51	45	39	33	26
58	08 48	08 47	08 45	43	40	37	33	28	24	18	13	08 07	08 01	07 54	47	40	33
S 60	09 05	09 04	09 02	08 59	08 56	08 52	08 48	08 43	08 37	08 31	08 25	08 18	08 11	08 04	07 56	07 49	07 41

SUNSET

Lat.	June 28	July 1	4	7	10	13	16	19	22	25	28	31	Aug 3	6	9	12	15
N 72	□	□	□	□	□	□	□	□	□	□	□	□	□	23 08	22 33	22 06	21 43
70	□	□	□	□	□	□	□	□	□	□	23 29	22 52	22 27	22 06	21 46	21 29	21 12
68	□	□	□	□	□	□	□	23 22	22 56	22 35	22 18	22 01	21 46	21 31	21 17	21 03	20 49
66	□	23 44	23 25	23 10	22 56	22 43	22 31	22 18	22 06	21 54	21 42	21 30	21 18	21 07	20 55	20 43	31
64	22 29	22 26	22 21	22 15	22 08	22 01	21 53	21 44	21 36	26	21 17	21 07	20 57	20 47	37	27	17
62	21 53	21 50	21 47	21 43	21 38	21 33	27	20	21 13	21 05	20 57	20 49	41	32	23	14	20 05
N 60	21 27	21 25	21 23	21 20	21 16	21 11	21 06	21 01	20 55	20 48	20 41	20 34	20 27	20 19	20 11	20 03	19 55
58	21 07	21 05	21 03	21 01	20 58	20 54	20 50	20 45	39	34	28	21	15	20 08	20 01	19 53	46
56	20 50	20 49	20 47	20 45	43	39	36	31	27	22	16	10	20 04	19 58	19 52	45	38
54	36	35	34	32	30	27	23	20	15	11	20 06	20 01	19 55	50	44	38	31
52	24	23	22	20	18	16	13	09	20 06	20 02	19 57	19 52	47	42	37	31	25
N 50	20 13	20 12	20 11	20 10	20 08	20 06	20 03	20 00	19 57	19 53	19 49	19 45	19 40	19 35	19 30	19 25	19 19
45	19 51	19 50	19 50	19 49	19 47	19 46	19 43	19 41	38	35	32	29	25	21	19 17	19 12	19 07
40	33	33	32	32	30	29	27	26	23	21	18	15	12	19 09	19 05	19 01	18 57
35	18	18	18	17	16	15	14	13	11	19 09	19 07	19 04	19 02	18 59	18 56	18 52	49
30	19 05	19 05	19 05	19 05	19 04	19 03	19 02	19 01	19 00	18 58	18 56	18 54	18 52	50	47	44	42
N 20	18 43	18 43	18 43	18 43	18 43	18 43	18 43	18 43	18 42	18 41	18 40	18 39	18 38	18 36	18 35	18 33	18 31
N 10	24	25	24	25	26	26	26	25	25	24	24	23	22	21	20	19	18
0	18 07	18 07	18 08	18 08	18 09	18 09	18 10	18 10	18 10	18 10	18 10	18 10	18 10	18 09	18 09	18 08	18 08
S 10	17 49	17 50	17 51	17 52	17 52	17 53	17 54	17 54	17 55	17 56	17 56	17 56	17 57	17 57	17 58	17 58	17 58
20	31	32	33	34	35	36	37	38	39	40	41	43	44	45	45	46	47
S 30	17 10	17 11	17 12	17 14	17 15	17 16	17 18	17 20	17 21	17 23	17 25	17 27	17 29	17 30	17 32	17 34	17 35
35	16 58	16 59	17 00	17 02	17 03	17 05	17 07	17 09	17 11	13	16	18	20	22	24	26	28
40	44	45	16 46	16 48	16 50	16 52	16 54	16 57	16 59	17 02	17 04	17 07	17 10	12	15	18	21
45	27	28	30	32	34	37	39	42	45	16 48	16 51	16 55	16 58	17 01	17 05	17 08	12
50	16 06	16 08	10	13	15	18	21	25	28	32	36	40	44	16 48	16 52	16 56	17 01
S 52	15 56	15 58	16 00	16 03	16 06	16 09	16 12	16 16	16 20	16 24	16 28	16 33	16 37	16 42	16 46	16 51	16 56
54	45	47	15 50	15 52	15 56	15 59	16 03	16 07	11	15	20	25	30	35	40	45	50
56	33	35	38	41	44	48	15 52	15 56	16 01	16 06	11	16	22	27	33	38	44
58	18	21	23	27	31	35	39	44	15 50	15 55	16 01	16 07	12	18	25	31	37
S 60	15 01	15 04	15 07	15 10	15 15	15 20	15 25	15 30	15 36	15 42	15 49	15 55	16 02	16 09	16 15	16 22	16 29

MORNING CIVIL TWILIGHT

Lat.	June 28	July 1	4	7	10	13	16	19	22	25	28	31	August 3	6	9	12	15
N 72	h m	h m	h m	h m	h m	h m	h m	h m	h m	h m	h m	h m	h m	////	///	////	////
70	=	=	=	=	=	=	=	//	=	=	////	////	////	////	////	////	////
68	=	=	=	=	=	=	=	////	////	////	////	////	////	////	////	01 10	01 39
66	=	////	////	////	////	////	////	////	////	////	////	////	00 45	01 19	01 4?	02 01	02 18
64	////	////	////	////	////	////	////	////	////	00 3?	01 08	01 30	01 48	02 04	02 1?	32	02 45
62	////	////	////	////	////	00 24	00 53	01 12	01 28	01 43	01 56	02 09	02 21	3?	02 44	02 54	03 05
N 60	00 55	01 02	01 09	01 18	01 27	01 36	01 46	01 56	02 06	02 16	02 25	02 35	02 45	02 54	03 03	03 12	03 21
58	01 44	01 48	01 52	01 57	02 03	02 10	02 17	02 24	32	02 47	02 55	03 03	03 11	19	27	35
56	02 14	02 16	02 20	02 24	29	34	39	02 45	02 52	02 58	03 05	03 12	19	25	32	39	40
54	36	38	41	02 44	02 48	02 53	02 58	03 03	03 08	03 14	20	26	32	38	44	50	03 56
52	02 53	02 56	02 58	03 01	03 05	03 09	03 13	17	22	27	32	37	43	48	03 54	03 59	04 05
N 50	03 08	03 10	03 13	03 15	03 19	03 22	03 26	03 30	03 34	03 39	03 43	03 48	03 53	03 58	04 03	04 08	04 13
45	03 38	03 39	03 41	03 44	03 46	03 49	03 52	03 55	03 59	04 02	04 00	04 09	04 13	04 17	21	25	29
40	04 00	04 02	04 03	04 05	04 07	04 10	04 12	04 15	04 17	20	23	26	29	32	36	39	42
35	18	20	21	23	25	26	29	31	33	35	38	40	43	45	48	04 50	04 53
30	34	35	04 36	04 37	04 39	04 41	04 42	04 44	04 46	04 48	04 50	04 52	04 54	04 56	04 58	05 00	05 02
N 20	04 59	04 59	05 00	05 01	05 03	05 04	05 05	05 06	05 08	05 09	05 10	05 11	05 12	05 14	05 15	05 16	05 17
N 10	05 19	05 20	20	21	22	23	24	24	25	26	27	27	28	28	28	29	29
0	37	38	38	39	39	40	40	41	41	41	41	41	41	41	40	40	40
S 10	05 54	05 54	05 55	05 55	05 55	05 55	05 56	05 56	05 56	05 55	05 55	05 54	05 53	05 53	05 52	05 51	50
20	06 11	06 11	06 12	06 12	06 12	06 11	06 11	06 11	06 10	06 09	06 08	06 07	06 06	06 04	06 03	06 01	05 59
S 30	06 30	06 30	06 30	06 30	06 30	06 29	06 28	06 27	06 26	06 25	06 23	06 21	06 19	06 17	06 15	06 12	06 09
35	40	41	40	40	39	39	38	36	35	33	31	29	26	24	21	18	15
40	06 52	06 52	06 52	06 51	06 50	06 49	06 48	46	45	42	40	37	34	31	28	25	21
45	07 00	07 05	07 05	07 04	07 03	07 02	07 00	06 58	06 56	06 53	06 50	47	43	40	36	32	27
50	21	21	21	19	18	16	14	07 12	07 00	07 05	07 02	06 58	54	50	45	40	35
S 52	07 29	07 29	07 28	07 27	07 25	07 23	07 21	07 18	07 15	07 11	07 07	07 03	06 59	06 54	06 49	06 44	06 39
54	37	37	36	34	32	30	28	25	21	17	13	09	07 04	06 59	54	48	42
56	46	46	44	43	41	38	36	32	28	24	20	15	10	07 04	06 59	53	47
58	07 56	07 56	07 54	07 53	07 50	48	44	41	36	32	27	22	16	10	07 04	06 58	51
S 60	08 08	08 07	08 05	08 04	08 01	07 58	07 54	07 50	07 45	07 41	07 35	07 29	07 23	07 17	07 10	07 03	06 56

EVENING CIVIL TWILIGHT

Lat.	June 28	July 1	4	7	10	13	16	19	22	25	28	31	August 3	6	9	12	15
N 72	h m	h m	h m	h m	h m	h m	h m	h m	h m	h m	h m	=	=	////	///	////	////
70	=	=	=	=	=	=	=	=	=	=	////	////	////	////	////	////	23 51
68	=	=	=	=	=	=	////	////	////	////	////	////	////	////	23 32	22 50	22 23
66	=	////	////	////	////	////	////	////	////	////	////	////	23 15	22 46	22 23	22 04	21 47
64	////	////	////	////	////	////	////	////	23 24	22 57	22 37	22 20	22 04	21 49	21 35	21
62	////	////	////	////	////	23 30	23 12	22 55	22 40	22 26	22 13	22 01	21 48	21 36	25	21 13	21 02
N 60	23 09	23 03	22 57	22 49	22 41	22 32	22 23	22 14	22 04	21 55	21 45	21 35	21 25	21 16	21 06	20 56	20 46
58	22 21	22 19	22 15	22 11	22 05	21 58	21 51	21 46	21 39	32	23	21 15	21 07	20 59	20 50	20 50	33
56	21 52	21 50	21 48	21 44	21 41	21 36	31	25	19	21 13	21 06	20 59	20 52	45	37	29	21
54	30	29	27	24	21	17	21 13	21 08	21 03	20 58	20 52	46	39	33	26	19	11
52	21 12	21 11	21 10	21 08	21 05	21 02	20 58	20 54	20 49	45	39	34	28	22	16	10	20 03
N 50	20 57	20 57	20 55	20 53	20 51	20 48	20 45	20 42	20 38	20 33	20 29	20 24	20 18	20 13	20 07	20 01	19 55
45	28	28	27	25	24	22	20	19	20 17	20 13	20 10	20 06	20 02	19 58	19 54	19 49	19 44	39
40	20 06	20 05	20 05	20 04	20 03	20 01	19 59	19 57	19 55	19 52	19 49	19 46	42	39	35	31	26
35	19 48	19 47	19 47	19 47	19 46	19 44	43	41	39	37	35	32	29	26	23	19	16
30	32	32	32	32	31	30	29	28	26	25	23	20	18	19 15	19 13	19 10	19 07
N 20	19 08	19 08	19 08	19 08	19 08	19 07	19 07	19 06	19 05	19 04	19 03	19 01	19 00	18 58	18 56	18 54	18 52
N 10	18 47	18 48	18 48	18 48	18 48	18 48	18 48	18 48	18 47	18 47	18 47	18 46	18 45	18 45	43	42	41	40
0	29	30	30	31	31	31	32	32	32	32	32	32	31	31	30	30	29
S 10	18 12	18 13	18 14	18 14	18 15	16	16	17	17	18	18	19	19	19	19	19	19
20	17 55	17 56	17 57	17 58	17 59	18 00	18 01	18 02	18 03	18 04	18 05	18 06	18 07	18 07	18 08	18 09	10
S 30	17 36	17 37	17 38	17 40	17 41	17 42	17 44	17 45	17 47	17 49	17 50	17 52	17 54	17 55	17 57	17 57	18 00
35	26	27	28	30	31	33	35	36	38	40	42	44	46	48	50	52	17 54
40	14	15	17	18	20	22	24	26	29	31	33	36	38	41	43	46	49
45	17 01	17 02	17 04	17 05	17 08	17 10	17 12	15	17	20	23	26	29	32	36	39	42
50	16 45	16 46	16 48	16 50	16 53	16 55	16 58	17 01	17 04	08	11	15	19	23	26	30	34
S 52	16 37	16 39	16 41	16 43	16 46	16 49	16 52	16 55	16 59	17 02	17 06	17 10	17 14	17 18	17 22	17 27	17 31
54	29	31	33	35	38	41	45	48	52	16 56	17 00	17 04	09	13	18	23	27
56	20	22	24	27	30	33	37	41	45	49	10 54	16 58	17 03	08	13	18	23
58	16 10	12	14	17	21	24	28	32	37	42	46	52	16 57	17 02	08	13	19
S 60	15 58	16 01	16 03	16 06	16 10	16 14	16 18	16 23	16 28	16 33	16 38	16 44	16 50	16 56	17 02	17 08	17 14

SUNRISE

Lat.	Nov 19	22	25	28	Dec 1	4	7	10	13	16	19	22	25	28	31	Jan 3
	h m	h m	h m	h m	h m	h m	h m	h m	h m	h m	h m	h m	h m	h m	h m	h m
N 72	■	■	■	■	■	■	■	■	■	■	■	■	■	■	■	■
70	10 14	10 40	11 19	■	■	■	■	■	■	■	■	■	■	■	■	■
68	09 30	09 45	10 00	10 16	10 33	10 52	11 14	■	■	■	■	■	■	■	■	■
66	09 01	09 12	09 23	09 34	09 45	09 55	10 05	10 14	10 22	10 28	10 32	10 35	10 35	10 33	10 30	10 25
64	08 39	08 48	08 57	09 06	09 15	09 23	09 30	09 36	09 42	09 47	09 50	09 52	09 53	09 52	09 51	09 48
62	21	29	37	08 45	08 52	08 59	09 05	09 10	09 15	09 19	22	24	24	24	23	22
N 60	08 07	08 14	08 21	08 28	08 34	08 40	08 45	08 50	08 54	08 58	09 00	09 02	09 03	09 03	09 03	09 01
58	07 54	08 01	08 07	13	19	24	29	33	37	40	08 43	08 45	08 46	08 46	08 46	08 45
56	43	07 49	07 55	08 01	08 06	08 11	15	19	23	26	28	30	31	32	32	31
54	34	40	45	07 50	07 55	07 59	08 03	08 07	08 10	13	15	17	19	19	19	19
52	26	31	36	40	45	49	07 53	07 56	07 59	08 02	08 04	08 06	08 07	08 08	08 08	08 08
N 50	07 18	07 23	07 28	07 32	07 36	07 40	07 43	07 47	07 50	07 52	07 54	07 56	07 57	07 58	07 59	07 58
45	07 02	07 06	07 10	07 14	17	21	24	27	29	32	34	35	37	38	38	38
40	06 49	06 53	06 56	06 59	07 02	07 05	07 08	07 10	07 13	15	17	18	20	21	22	22
35	38	41	44	46	06 49	06 52	06 54	06 57	06 59	07 01	07 03	07 04	07 06	07 07	07 08	07 08
30	28	30	33	35	38	40	43	45	47	06 49	06 50	06 52	06 53	06 54	06 55	06 50
N 20	06 11	06 13	06 15	06 16	06 18	06 20	06 22	06 24	06 26	06 28	06 29	06 31	06 32	06 33	06 35	06 36
N 10	05 56	05 57	05 58	06 00	06 01	06 03	06 04	06 06	06 07	06 09	06 10	06 12	06 13	06 15	06 16	17
0	42	42	43	05 44	05 45	05 46	05 48	05 49	05 50	05 52	05 53	05 55	05 56	05 58	05 59	06 01
S 10	28	28	28	28	29	30	31	32	33	34	35	37	39	40	42	05 43
20	05 12	05 12	05 11	05 11	05 12	05 12	05 13	05 13	05 14	05 15	05 17	05 18	05 20	05 21	23	25
S 30	04 54	04 53	04 52	04 52	04 51	04 51	04 51	04 52	04 52	04 53	04 55	04 56	04 58	04 59	05 01	05 03
35	44	42	41	40	39	39	39	39	40	41	42	43	45	46	04 48	04 51
40	32	30	28	27	26	25	25	25	25	26	27	28	29	31	34	30
45	18	04 15	04 13	04 11	04 09	04 08	04 07	04 07	04 07	04 08	04 10	04 11	04 13	04 15	04 17	04 19
50	04 00	03 57	03 54	03 51	03 49	03 47	03 46	03 45	03 45	03 45	03 46	03 47	03 49	03 51	03 54	03 57
S 52	03 52	03 48	03 45	03 42	03 39	03 37	03 37	03 36	03 35	03 34	03 34	03 35	03 36	03 38	03 40	03 43
54	43	39	35	31	29	26	24	23	22	22	23	24	26	28	31	34
56	32	28	23	10	16	03 13	03 11	03 09	03 09	03 08	03 09	03 10	03 12	03 14	17	21
58	21	15	03 10	03 06	03 02	02 58	02 55	02 53	02 52	02 52	02 52	02 53	02 55	02 57	03 01	03 05
S 60	03 00	03 00	02 54	02 49	02 44	02 40	02 37	02 34	02 32	02 31	02 31	02 32	02 34	02 37	02 41	02 45

SUNSET

Lat.	Nov 19	22	25	28	Dec 1	4	7	10	13	16	19	22	25	28	31	Jan 3
	h m	h m	h m	h m	h m	h m	h m	h m	h m	h m	h m	h m	h m	h m	h m	h m
N 72	■	■	■	■	■	■	■	■	■	■	■	■	■	■	■	■
70	13 15	12 51	12 13	■	■	■	■	■	■	■	■	■	■	■	■	■
68	14 00	13 47	13 33	13 19	13 04	12 47	12 27	■	■	■	■	■	■	■	■	■
66	29	14 19	14 10	14 01	13 52	13 44	13 37	13 30	13 26	13 22	13 21	13 21	13 24	13 29	13 35	13 43
64	14 51	14 43	36	29	14 22	14 17	14 12	14 05	14 05	14 04	14 03	14 04	14 06	14 10	14 15	14 21
62	15 09	15 02	14 56	14 50	14 45	14 41	37	34	32	31	32	33	35	38	14 42	14 47
N 60	15 23	15 18	15 12	15 08	15 03	15 00	14 57	14 55	14 54	14 53	14 53	14 55	14 57	14 59	15 03	15 07
58	36	31	26	22	19	16	15 13	15 12	15 11	15 10	15 11	15 12	15 14	15 17	20	24
56	46	42	38	35	32	29	27	26	25	25	26	27	29	31	34	38
54	15 56	15 52	48	45	43	41	39	38	38	38	39	40	42	44	47	15 50
52	16 04	16 01	15 58	15 55	15 53	15 51	49	48	49	49	15 51	15 52	15 55	15 58	16 01	
N 50	16 12	16 09	16 06	16 03	16 01	16 00	15 59	15 58	15 58	15 58	15 59	16 01	16 02	16 05	16 07	16 10
45	28	26	24	22	21	20	16 19	16 19	16 19	16 19	16 20	21	23	25	28	30
40	41	39	38	37	30	35	35	35	36	37	38	40	42	44	16 47	
35	16 53	16 51	16 50	16 49	16 49	16 48	16 48	16 48	16 49	16 50	16 51	16 52	16 54	16 56	16 58	17 00
30	17 03	17 01	17 01	17 00	17 00	17 00	17 01	17 01	17 02	17 04	17 05	17 07	17 09	17 10	13	
N 20	17 20	17 19	17 19	17 19	17 19	17 20	17 20	17 21	17 22	17 23	17 25	17 26	17 28	17 29	17 31	17 33
N 10	35	35	35	36	37	37	38	39	41	42	17 43	17 45	17 46	17 48	17 50	17 51
0	17 49	17 50	17 51	17 52	17 53	17 54	17 55	17 56	17 58	17 59	18 01	18 02	18 04	18 05	18 07	18 08
S 10	18 03	18 05	18 06	18 07	18 09	18 10	18 12	18 14	18 15	18 17	18	20	21	23	24	25
20	19	21	23	25	26	28	30	32	34	36	37	18 39	18 40	18 41	18 43	18 44
S 30	18 37	18 39	18 42	18 44	18 47	18 49	18 51	18 54	18 56	18 58	18 59	19 01	19 02	19 03	19 04	19 05
35	47	18 50	18 53	18 56	18 59	19 02	19 04	19 06	19 09	19 11	19 12	14	15	16	17	18
40	18 59	19 03	19 06	19 09	19 13	16	18	22	26	27	29	30	31	32	32	
45	19 14	18	22	25	29	32	36	19 39	19 41	19 44	19 45	19 47	19 48	19 49	19 50	19 50
50	31	36	41	45	50	19 54	19 57	20 01	20 03	20 06	20 08	20 10	20 11	20 12	20 12	20 11
S 52	19 40	19 45	19 50	19 55	19 59	20 04	20 07	20 11	20 14	20 17	20 19	20 21	20 21	20 22	20 22	20 22
54	19 49	19 55	20 00	20 05	20 10	15	19	23	26	29	31	33	34	34	34	34
56	20 00	20 06	12	18	23	28	33	37	40	20 43	20 45	20 47	20 48	20 49	20 48	20 47
58	12	19	25	32	38	20 43	20 48	20 53	20 57	21 00	21 02	21 04	21 05	21 05	21 05	21 03
S 60	20 29	20 34	20 41	20 48	20 55	21 01	21 07	21 12	21 17	21 20	21 23	21 25	21 25	21 25	21 24	21 22

MORNING CIVIL TWILIGHT

Lat.	November				December											Jan.
	19	22	25	28	1	4	7	10	13	16	19	22	25	28	31	3
	h m	h m	h m	h m	h m	h m	h m	h m	h m	h m	h m	h m	h m	h m	h m	h m
N 72	08 51	09 05	09 20	09 34	09 48	10 02	10 15	10 27	10 38	10 48	10 54	10 57	10 57	10 53	10 46	10 38
70	25	08 37	08 48	08 59	09 09	09 19	09 28	09 36	09 43	09 48	09 52	09 54	09 55	09 54	09 51	09 47
68	08 06	08 15	25	34	08 42	08 50	08 57	09 04	09 09	09 14	09 17	09 19	09 20	09 20	09 18	09 15
66	07 50	07 58	08 06	08 14	22	29	35	08 40	08 45	08 49	08 52	08 54	08 55	08 55	08 54	08 52
64	37	44	07 52	07 59	08 05	08 11	17	22	26	29	32	34	35	35	34	33
62	26	33	39	45	07 51	07 57	08 02	08 06	08 10	13	16	18	19	19	19	18
N 60	07 16	07 23	07 29	07 34	07 40	07 45	07 49	07 53	07 57	08 00	08 02	08 04	08 05	08 06	08 06	08 05
58	08	14	19	24	29	34	38	42	45	07 48	07 51	07 52	07 54	07 54	07 54	07 54
56	07 01	07 06	11	16	21	25	29	32	36	38	40	42	43	44	44	44
54	06 54	06 59	07 04	08	13	17	20	24	27	29	32	33	35	35	36	35
52	48	53	06 57	07 01	07 05	09	13	16	19	21	23	25	26	27	28	27
N 50	06 42	06 47	06 51	06 55	06 59	07 02	07 06	07 09	07 11	07 14	07 16	07 18	07 19	07 20	07 20	07 20
45	30	34	38	41	44	06 47	06 50	06 53	06 56	06 58	07 00	07 02	07 03	07 04	07 05	07 05
40	20	23	26	29	32	35	38	40	42	44	06 46	06 48	06 49	06 50	06 51	06 52
35	11	13	16	19	21	24	26	29	31	33	34	36	38	39	40	40
30	06 02	06 05	06 07	06 10	06 12	06 14	06 16	18	20	22	24	26	27	28	29	30
N 20	05 48	05 49	05 51	05 53	05 55	05 56	05 58	06 00	06 02	06 04	06 05	06 07	06 08	06 09	06 11	06 12
N 10	34	35	36	37	39	40	42	05 43	05 45	05 46	05 48	05 49	05 51	05 52	05 54	05 55
0	20	20	21	22	23	24	25	26	28	29	31	32	34	35	37	38
S 10	05 05	05 05	05 05	05 06	05 06	05 07	05 08	05 09	05 10	05 11	05 13	05 14	05 16	05 17	05 19	20
20	04 48	04 48	04 48	04 47	04 47	04 48	04 48	04 49	04 50	04 51	04 52	04 53	04 55	04 57	04 59	05 00
S 30	04 28	04 27	04 26	04 25	04 24	04 24	04 24	04 25	04 25	04 26	04 27	04 28	04 30	04 32	04 34	04 36
35	16	04 14	04 12	04 11	04 10	04 10	04 10	04 10	04 10	04 11	04 12	04 13	04 15	04 17	19	21
40	04 01	03 59	03 57	03 55	03 54	03 53	03 52	03 52	03 52	03 53	03 54	03 55	03 57	03 59	04 01	04 04
45	03 43	40	38	35	33	32	31	30	30	30	31	32	34	36	03 39	03 42
50	21	17	13	03 10	03 07	03 04	03 03	03 01	03 01	03 01	03 01	03 01	03 03	03 04	03 07	03 13
S 52	03 09	03 05	03 00	02 57	02 53	02 51	02 49	02 47	02 46	02 46	02 46	02 47	02 49	02 52	02 55	02 58
54	02 57	02 51	02 46	42	38	35	32	30	29	28	28	29	31	34	37	41
56	42	35	30	24	02 20	02 15	02 12	02 09	02 07	02 06	02 06	02 07	02 09	02 12	02 16	02 20
58	24	02 16	02 09	02 02	01 56	01 50	01 46	01 42	01 39	01 37	01 36	01 37	01 39	01 42	01 47	01 53
S 60	02 01	01 52	01 42	01 33	01 24	01 16	01 07	00 59	00 53	00 49	00 47	00 47	00 49	00 54	01 01	01 10

EVENING CIVIL TWILIGHT

Lat.	November				December											Jan.
	19	22	25	28	1	4	7	10	13	16	19	22	25	28	31	3
	h m	h m	h m	h m	h m	h m	h m	h m	h m	h m	h m	h m	h m	h m	h m	h m
N 72	14 38	14 20	14 13	14 01	13 49	13 37	13 27	13 17	13 09	13 02	12 59	12 59	13 02	13 09	13 19	13 31
70	15 04	14 54	14 45	14 36	14 28	14 20	14 14	14 08	14 04	14 02	14 01	14 02	14 04	14 09	14 47	14 53
68	24	15 16	15 08	15 01	14 55	14 49	14 44	14 41	14 38	14 36	14 36	14 37	14 39	14 43	14 47	14 53
66	40	33	26	20	15 15	15 11	15 07	15 04	15 02	15 01	15 01	15 03	15 05	15 08	15 12	15 17
64	15 53	47	41	36	32	28	25	23	21	21	21	22	24	27	31	35
62	16 04	15 58	15 54	15 49	46	42	40	38	37	37	37	39	41	43	15 46	15 51
N 60	16 13	16 09	16 04	16 01	15 57	15 55	15 53	15 51	15 50	15 50	15 51	15 52	15 54	15 57	16 00	16 03
58	22	17	14	10	16 08	16 05	16 04	16 02	16 02	16 02	16 03	16 04	16 06	16 08	11	15
56	29	26	22	19	17	15	13	13	12	12	13	14	16	19	21	25
54	36	33	30	27	25	23	22	21	21	21	22	24	25	28	30	33
52	42	39	36	34	32	31	30	29	29	29	30	32	34	36	39	41
N 50	16 48	16 45	16 43	16 41	16 39	16 38	16 37	16 36	16 37	16 37	16 38	16 39	16 41	16 43	16 46	16 48
45	17 00	16 58	16 56	16 55	16 53	16 52	16 52	16 52	16 52	16 53	16 54	16 55	16 57	16 59	17 01	17 04
40	10	17 09	17 07	17 06	17 06	17 05	17 05	17 05	17 06	17 06	17 07	17 08	17 09	17 11	17 13	17 17
35	20	18	17	17	16	16	16	17	17	18	19	21	22	24	26	28
30	28	27	27	26	26	26	26	26	27	28	29	30	31	33	35	37
N 20	17 43	17 43	17 43	17 43	17 43	17 44	17 45	17 45	17 46	17 48	17 49	17 50	17 52	17 53	17 55	17 57
N 10	17 57	17 57	17 58	17 58	17 59	18 00	18 01	18 02	18 03	18 05	18 06	18 08	18 09	18 11	18 12	18 14
0	18 11	18 12	18 13	18 14	18 15	16	17	19	20	22	23	25	26	28	29	30
S 10	26	27	29	30	32	33	35	37	38	18 40	18 41	18 43	18 44	18 46	18 47	18 48
20	18 43	18 45	18 47	18 49	18 51	18 53	18 55	18 57	18 58	19 00	19 02	19 03	19 05	19 06	19 07	19 08
S 30	19 03	19 06	19 09	19 11	19 14	19 16	19 19	19 21	19 23	19 25	19 27	19 28	19 30	19 31	19 32	19 32
35	16	19	22	25	28	31	33	36	38	40	19 42	19 44	19 45	19 46	19 47	19 47
40	30	34	38	19 41	19 45	19 48	19 51	19 54	19 56	19 58	20 00	20 02	20 03	20 04	20 05	20 05
45	19 48	19 53	19 57	20 01	20 05	20 09	20 12	20 16	20 18	20 21	23	25	26	26	27	27
50	20 11	20 17	20 22	27	32	37	41	44	20 48	20 50	20 53	20 54	20 55	20 56	20 56	20 55
S 52	20 23	20 29	20 35	20 40	20 45	20 50	20 55	20 59	21 03	21 06	21 08	21 10	21 11	21 11	21 11	21 10
54	36	42	20 49	20 55	21 01	21 07	21 12	21 16	20	23	26	27	28	29	28	27
56	20 51	20 58	21 06	21 13	20	26	32	21 37	21 42	21 45	21 48	21 50	21 51	21 50	21 49	21 47
58	21 09	21 18	27	21 36	21 44	21 51	21 59	22 05	22 10	22 15	22 18	22 20	22 20	22 20	22 18	22 15
S 60	21 32	21 43	21 55	22 06	22 17	22 27	22 39	22 48	22 57	23 04	23 08	23 10	23 09	23 09	23 03	22 56

CONVERSION OF ARC TO TIME

°	h m	°	h m	°	h m	°	h m	°	h m	°	h m	′	m s
0	0 00	60	4 00	120	8 00	180	12 00	240	16 00	300	20 00	0	0 00
1	0 04	61	4 04	121	8 04	181	12 04	241	16 04	301	20 04	1	0 04
2	0 08	62	4 08	122	8 08	182	12 08	242	16 08	302	20 08	2	0 08
3	0 12	63	4 12	123	8 12	183	12 12	243	16 12	303	20 12	3	0 12
4	0 16	64	4 16	124	8 16	184	12 16	244	16 16	304	20 16	4	0 16
5	0 20	65	4 20	125	8 20	185	12 20	245	16 20	305	20 20	5	0 20
6	0 24	66	4 24	126	8 24	186	12 24	246	16 24	306	20 24	6	0 24
7	0 28	67	4 28	127	8 28	187	12 28	247	16 28	307	20 28	7	0 28
8	0 32	68	4 32	128	8 32	188	12 32	248	16 32	308	20 32	8	0 32
9	0 36	69	4 36	129	8 36	189	12 36	249	16 36	309	20 36	9	0 36
10	0 40	70	4 40	130	8 40	190	12 40	250	16 40	310	20 40	10	0 40
11	0 44	71	4 44	131	8 44	191	12 44	251	16 44	311	20 44	11	0 44
12	0 48	72	4 48	132	8 48	192	12 48	252	16 48	312	20 48	12	0 48
13	0 52	73	4 52	133	8 52	193	12 52	253	16 52	313	20 52	13	0 52
14	0 56	74	4 56	134	8 56	194	12 56	254	16 56	314	20 56	14	0 56
15	1 00	75	5 00	135	9 00	195	13 00	255	17 00	315	21 00	15	1 00
16	1 04	76	5 04	136	9 04	196	13 04	256	17 04	316	21 04	16	1 04
17	1 08	77	5 08	137	9 08	197	13 08	257	17 08	317	21 08	17	1 08
18	1 12	78	5 12	138	9 12	198	13 12	258	17 12	318	21 12	18	1 12
19	1 16	79	5 16	139	9 16	199	13 16	259	17 16	319	21 16	19	1 16
20	1 20	80	5 20	140	9 20	200	13 20	260	17 20	320	21 20	20	1 20
21	1 24	81	5 24	141	9 24	201	13 24	261	17 24	321	21 24	21	1 24
22	1 28	82	5 28	142	9 28	202	13 28	262	17 28	322	21 28	22	1 28
23	1 32	83	5 32	143	9 32	203	13 32	263	17 32	323	21 32	23	1 32
24	1 36	84	5 36	144	9 36	204	13 36	264	17 36	324	21 36	24	1 36
25	1 40	85	5 40	145	9 40	205	13 40	265	17 40	325	21 40	25	1 40
26	1 44	86	5 44	146	9 44	206	13 44	266	17 44	326	21 44	26	1 44
27	1 48	87	5 48	147	9 48	207	13 48	267	17 48	327	21 48	27	1 48
28	1 52	88	5 52	148	9 52	208	13 52	268	17 52	328	21 52	28	1 52
29	1 56	89	5 56	149	9 56	209	13 56	269	17 56	329	21 56	29	1 56
30	2 00	90	6 00	150	10 00	210	14 00	270	18 00	330	22 00	30	2 00
31	2 04	91	6 04	151	10 04	211	14 04	271	18 04	331	22 04	31	2 04
32	2 08	92	6 08	152	10 08	212	14 08	272	18 08	332	22 08	32	2 08
33	2 12	93	6 12	153	10 12	213	14 12	273	18 12	333	22 12	33	2 12
34	2 16	94	6 16	154	10 16	214	14 16	274	18 16	334	22 16	34	2 16
35	2 20	95	6 20	155	10 20	215	14 20	275	18 20	335	22 20	35	2 20
36	2 24	96	6 24	156	10 24	216	14 24	276	18 24	336	22 24	36	2 24
37	2 28	97	6 28	157	10 28	217	14 28	277	18 28	337	22 28	37	2 28
38	2 32	98	6 32	158	10 32	218	14 32	278	18 32	338	22 32	38	2 32
39	2 36	99	6 36	159	10 36	219	14 36	279	18 36	339	22 36	39	2 36
40	2 40	100	6 40	160	10 40	220	14 40	280	18 40	340	22 40	40	2 40
41	2 44	101	6 44	161	10 44	221	14 44	281	18 44	341	22 44	41	2 44
42	2 48	102	6 48	162	10 48	222	14 48	282	18 48	342	22 48	42	2 48
43	2 52	103	6 52	163	10 52	223	14 52	283	18 52	343	22 52	43	2 52
44	2 56	104	6 56	164	10 56	224	14 56	284	18 56	344	22 56	44	2 56
45	3 00	105	7 00	165	11 00	225	15 00	285	19 00	345	23 00	45	3 00
46	3 04	106	7 04	166	11 04	226	15 04	286	19 04	346	23 04	46	3 04
47	3 08	107	7 08	167	11 08	227	15 08	287	19 08	347	23 08	47	3 08
48	3 12	108	7 12	168	11 12	228	15 12	288	19 12	348	23 12	48	3 12
49	3 16	109	7 16	169	11 16	229	15 16	289	19 16	349	23 16	49	3 16
50	3 20	110	7 20	170	11 20	230	15 20	290	19 20	350	23 20	50	3 20
51	3 24	111	7 24	171	11 24	231	15 24	291	19 24	351	23 24	51	3 24
52	3 28	112	7 28	172	11 28	232	15 28	292	19 28	352	23 28	52	3 28
53	3 32	113	7 32	173	11 32	233	15 32	293	19 32	353	23 32	53	3 32
54	3 36	114	7 36	174	11 36	234	15 36	294	19 36	354	23 36	54	3 36
55	3 40	115	7 40	175	11 40	235	15 40	295	19 40	355	23 40	55	3 40
56	3 44	116	7 44	176	11 44	236	15 44	296	19 44	356	23 44	56	3 44
57	3 48	117	7 48	177	11 48	237	15 48	297	19 48	357	23 48	57	3 48
58	3 52	118	7 52	178	11 52	238	15 52	298	19 52	358	23 52	58	3 52
59	3 56	119	7 56	179	11 56	239	15 56	299	19 56	359	23 56	59	3 56

The above table is for converting expressions in arc to their equivalent in time; its main use in this Almanac is for the conversion of longitude for application to L.M.T. (*added if west, subtracted if east*) to give G.M.T., or vice versa, particularly in the case of sunrise, sunset, etc.

CHAPTER 17

PLOTTING

17.1 With the array of navigation aids to be found on the flight deck of today's commercial aircraft, the need for actually navigating by plotting on a chart is minimal, even if space were available to do so. With the miniaturisation of electronics even quite small executive aircraft can carry an impressive navigation fit. Licence candidates may well feel like asking the questions, 'Why are plotting skills taught? Why should I be examined on something I may never use in practice?' In response to that the following may be said:

> The main purpose of requiring pilots to learn the basic skills of plotting is so that they are more aware of the best ways to use the many navigational aids available to them. It also gives them techniques for cross checking the airborne performance of automated equipment such as Inertial Navigation Systems (INS).
>
> Plotting practise also helps to develop a sense of where one is during a flight. The memory becomes trained as a matter of course to think about time, speed and distance covered. In the (rare) event of a major failure of an aircraft's automated navigation systems the trained mind should be able to take over the navigation task with the minimum of fuss and no panic!

Although the examination calls for plotting a flight on a chart, only a limited number of plotting techniques are required of the candidate. This chapter concentrates on the examination requirements to the exclusion of all other navigation techniques, of which there are many more than those covered below.

17.2 Chapters in Sections 1 and 2 introduced the basic navigation elements and techniques plus the concepts of deduced reckoning (DR) and fuel flow problems. Before launching into plotting on a chart some of these ideas need to be expanded and new items such as Climb and Descent introduced. Items from Chapters 14 and 15 such as revision of TAS to achieve a specific ETA, or calculation of a PNA could also be incorporated into an examination plot. Such additions to a plot would in fact stand on their own as separate questions and should not affect the way the rest of the examination plot is tackled by candidates.

THE BASIC ELEMENTS OF PLOTTING

DEAD RECKONING (DR)

17.3 The term DR can be used to encompass:

DR hdg, the calculated hdg to steer to make good a desired trk for a particular TAS and W/V, (see paragraph 5.14).

DR GS, the expected GS from a particular hdg / TAS and WV combination (see Chapter 5, para 5.12 and 5.14).

DR trk, the expected trk from a particular hdg/TAS and WV combination (see Chapter 5, para 5.12).

DR position, the estimated position of an aircraft at a specified time. This may be for the current time or some minutes ahead of the current time. By projecting from the last known actual position (a fix) along the DR trk at the DR GS for the appropriate time a DR position can be established for a specified time. This is known as **DRing ahead by trk and GS**. The symbol used to signify a DR position is a dot surrounded by a small triangle with the time beside it (see Fig. 17–1).

$$\triangle \ \ 0816$$

Fig. 17–1. The DR position symbol (with its applicable time noted beside it).

The method of DRing ahead by trk and GS only holds good if there has been no change of hdg or TAS since the fix. A change in either or both of these elements could alter the DR trk and/or the DR GS. The technique for DRing ahead where the hdg or TAS has changed at some time since the last fix is outside the licence requirements and therefore should not appear on an examination plot. However candidates should be aware of this limitation whenever DRing ahead during an actual flight.

Before moving on from DR it is important to emphasise that all DR elements are estimated (or expected) values and *not* actual values. A couple of tips about DR GS are worth a mention here, they may or may not prove of value in the examinations but certainly can save time and effort when airborne.

If when DRing ahead at DR trk and DR GS the movement is made for 6 minutes ($^1/_{10}$ of an hour) the distance to move along the DR trk will be $^1/_{10}$ of the DR GS. This is easily found by moving the decimal point one digit to the left (6 min at DR GS 325 kn = 32·5 nm along DR trk). Working in 6 minute steps can save a lot of time and effort!

For very rapid estimation of DR position (needed for some airborne procedures) it is a good idea to be aware of the average distance covered per minute in the aircraft being flown. For example in a light aircraft flying at 123 kn TAS the approximate distance covered per minute (ignoring the WV) is 2 nm. If the last actual fix was 17 minutes ago the current DR position must be somewhere in the vicinity of 2 × 17 = 34 nm down the DR trk from the fix. This rule of thumb way of DRing ahead is not as accurate as using the DR GS but is good enough for some situations as will be shown later in this Chapter.

THE PLOTTING OF POSITION LINES FROM GROUND STATIONS

17.4 A Position Line (P/L) is a line somewhere along which an aircraft was known to be at a certain time. The establishment of the actual position of the aircraft requires at least one other P/L crossing it at the same moment in time and at an angle close to 90°. In visual map reading conditions a P/L could be part of a straight stretch of railway line, major road, or even a coastline. Plotting is more commonly associated with P/Ls obtained from ground located radio stations. The types of ground stations, the information they supply and the procedures for plotting from each are given in paras. 17.5 to 17.8 below. When a P/L is plotted on a chart it is signified with a single arrow-head (pointing outwards) at each end of the line and the time the P/L was obtained written by it. (see Fig. 17–2) A P/L can be any length but when plotted on a chart it should be drawn so as to extend some way either side of the aircraft's DR position since the actual position should not be too far from this position.

Fig. 17–2   *The Position Line (P/L) symbol (with its applicable time noted beside it).*

17.5 Direction Finding (DF) Stations – usually based in Air Traffic Control (ATC) on airfields. These stations take bearings on **Radio Transmissions (RT)** from an aircraft whose pilot is requesting a bearing from the station. Depending on the type of bearing requested it is passed back to the pilot of the aircraft as:

QTE* The (T) bearing of the aircraft from N (T) *at the station.*

QDR* The (M) bearing of the aircraft from N (M) *at the station.*

QDM* The (M) heading to steer to reach the station in zero wind conditions. This is the reciprocal of QDR and is based on N (M) *at the station* and *not* on N (M) at the aircraft which could be different if the aircraft were some distance from the ground station.

QUJ* The (T) heading to steer to reach the station in zero wind conditions. This is the reciprocal of QTE and is based on N (T) *at the station* and *not* on N (T) at the aircraft which could be different (due to conv) if the aircraft were some distance from the ground station. In practice QUJ is rarely used to pass bearings but it is a useful tool in plotting calculations.

On charts the lat and long graticule is based on (T) directions and, apart from Grid navigation, plotting is normally conducted in terms of (T) directions. Of the above four types of bearing only two (QTE and QUJ) are based on N (T), and of these two only QTE is *from* the station. For normal plotting purposes QDM, QDR and QUJ have first to be converted into QTEs before they can be plotted from N (T) at the known position of the ground station. The rules for conversion are:

QUJ + or – 180° = QTE.
QDR + E (or – W) Var *at the station* = QTE.
QDM + or – 180° (= QDR) + E (or – W) Var *at the station* = QTE.
Alternatively
QDM + E (or – W) Var *at the Station* (= QUJ) + or – 180° = QTE.

Since these are radio bearings they will have travelled by the shortest route (i.e. along a GC) between the aircraft and the station. On charts where a straight line can, for all practical purposes, be assumed to be a GC (i.e. Lambert's and Polar Stereographic) the QTE can be plotted as a straight line directly from N (T) at the station. To plot the QTE from the station on a Mercator's chart the GC must first be converted to its RL equivalent before plotting it as a straight line from N (T) at the station. (See Chapter 9 starting at para. 9.16)

17.6 Very High Frequency Omnidirectional Radio Range (VOR) – automatic continual transmission stations of which there are two types, high-powered versions, most of which are located within the Airways System, and low-powered versions which are located as approach aids at some airports. A VOR transmits two signals, the phase difference between them being decoded by a receiver in the aircraft to give either a QDR or QDM based on N (M) *at the station*. The different ways of displaying VOR

---

* These three-letter codes, prefixed with the letter Q, are a relic from the days when air/ground communications were conducted solely in Morse Code by means of a Morse key. To reduce the amount of signals traffic a code known as the 'Q Code' was evolved. A booklet was published containing a different three-letter group for each of a series of standard messages, use of the appropriated group usually only requiring the addition of a few figures to send a message. The increased use of RT eventually did away with the Morse key but the continuing need to restrict the amount of signals traffic meant that some of the more frequently used elements of the Q Code have been retained. These days the most commonly used Q Codes deal with brgs (as above) and Altimeter settings and readings. (See the Instruments and Meteorology syllabi.)

information is part of the Radio syllabus. In plotting the main concern is with use of the end product, a QDR or QDM. The rules for converting QDRs and QDMs into QTEs and for plotting from N (T) at the station on different charts are exactly the same as described in paragraph 17.5 for the DF bearings.

17.7 Non-Directional Beacon (NDB) – radio beacons that transmit a signal radiating in all directions rather like the waves spreading out when a stone is dropped into still water. They are usually located at airfields or points on airway systems and operate on frequencies specifically for use by aircraft. Some transmitters used for public broadcasting may also be used by aircraft provided the frequencies are compatible with the aircraft's direction finding equipment. Apart from transmitting a continual signal the NDB has no further part to play in establishing a position line through the aircraft. Equipment on the aircraft takes a bearing on the incoming signal from the NDB. Depending on the display fit, this is shown as a **Relative Bearing (Rel brg)** measured clockwise round from the fore and aft axis through the nose of the aircraft on a **Relative Bearing Indicator (RBI)** (see Fig. 17–3a), or as a **Magnetic Bearing ((M) brg)** measured clockwise round from N (M) *at the aircraft* on a **Radio Magnetic Indicator (RMI).** (see Fig. 17–3b)

The pointer is indicating the bearing of the NDB it is tuned to clockwise round from the nose of the aircraft

Zero on the indicator dial is aligned with the fore and aft axis of the aircraft with zero indicating the direction of the nose of the aircraft

Fig. 17–3a   A Relative Bearing Indicator (RBI).

The dial is rotated by a remote transmitting magnetic compass system so that the index mark at the top of the dial is pointing at the hdg [M] of the aircraft

The pointer is indicating the bearing of the NDB it is tuned to clockwise round from the local Magnetic N. Many RMIs have a two pointer display enabling the simultaneous display of bearings from two different sources

Fig. 17–3b   A Radio Magnetic Indicator (RMI).

In the case of a Rel brg (see Fig. 17–3a) the information available to the pilot would be:

The Rel brg as displayed on the RBI.

The aircraft's (T) hdg (this may have to be resolved from (C) or (M) hdg as described in Chapter 2, paras 2.2 to 2.6).

The position of the NDB on the chart. This may be printed on the chart or the candidate may have to plot it on the chart from given lat and long co-ordinates. In the latter case care must be taken to plot it in the correct place, if the NDB is marked in the wrong place on the chart it follows that bearings plotted from it will be incorrectly positioned.

The aircraft's DR position (found by DR trk and DR GS since the last fix). The DR position is an essential part of the process as conv between the aircraft and the NDB is going to be needed and without an idea of the approximate long of the aircraft at the time of taking the brg the wrong value could be applied leading to an error in the plotted brg.

Fig. 17–4 shows a Lambert chart with the aircraft and ground position of the NDB marked on. A straight line is drawn from the NDB through the aircraft representing the GC path the radio wave has followed from the beacon to the aircraft. Marked in at the aircraft is the hdg of the aircraft from N (T) at the aircraft and the Rel brg from the nose fore and aft axis clockwise round to the GC. At the NDB's known ground position is indicated the, as yet uncalculated, bearing to be plotted from N (T) at the NDB.

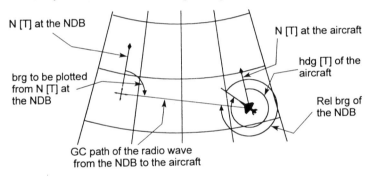

Fig. 17–4   Relative brg of an NDB measured from the nose of an aircraft, situation displayed on a Lambert chart.

The sequence for solving the brg to be plotted from the NDB is as follows:

To the Rel brg from the nose of the aircraft add the (T) hdg of the aircraft. This will give the (T) brg (from N (T) at the aircraft) of the GC *from* the aircraft *to* the NDB. If the answer comes out at more than 360° just subtract 360° from it to give the correct answer.

Any conv between the NDB and the aircraft's DR position must now be corrected. For plotting on Lambert or Polar Stereographic charts the most practical method is to transfer a line parallel to the N (T) meridian at the aircraft's DR position through the position of the NDB to give a Transferred Meridian. (See Chapter 11 para. 11.14 and Figs 11–9 and 11–10) The angle between this Transferred Meridian and N (T) at the NDB being the chart conv between the aircraft's DR position and the NDB.

To the (T) brg of the GC from the aircraft to the NDB add or subtract 180°. This gives the reciprocal brg from N (T) *at the aircraft*. Plot this brg from the Transferred Meridian at the NDB. Fig. 17–5 shows how the situation in Fig. 17–4 is resolved by this method.

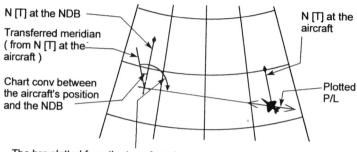

The brg plotted from the transferred meridian is:-
Rel brg of NDB + hdg [T] of the aircraft (- 360° in this case) + or - 180°

Fig. 17–5   Relative brg of an NDB measured from the nose of an aircraft, the plotting solution on a Lambert chart.

For plotting on a Mercator chart the (T) GC brg *from the aircraft* to the NDB *must* be converted to the equivalent (T) RL brg *from the aircraft* to the NDB *before working* out the reciprocal (T) RL brg to be plotted from N (T) at the NDB. Fig. 17–6 shows how the same situation as in Fig. 17–5 would appear on a Mercator chart.

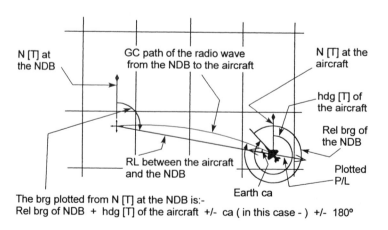

The brg plotted from N [T] at the NDB is:-
Rel brg of NDB + hdg [T] of the aircraft +/- ca (in this case -) +/- 180°

Fig. 17–6   Relative brg of an NDB measured from the nose of an aircraft, plotting solution on a Mercator chart, N hemisphere.

Remember the basic rules for converting GCs to RLs on a Mercator chart:

The ca is *always* applied at the point of measurement. (i.e. At the station for Ground D/F and VOR bearings and at the aircraft for ADF bearings on an NDB.)

The ca is *always* applied from the GC towards the equator and *never* towards the pole.

17.8 Distance Measuring Equipment (DME) – transponder beacons located within the airways system and at airfields. These beacons reply to interrogation signals from the aircraft, the response being displayed on the aircraft's receiver equipment as a range in nm from the ground station. Since the information is a range, the P/L through the aircraft will be an arc of a circle whose centre is the ground position of the DME and whose radius is the range being displayed. In practice DMEs are often co-located with VORs so that interrogation of both at the same time will result in a simultaneous fix being obtained (the curved range P/L from the DME crossing the straight line brg from the VOR at 90°, giving the ideal fix from two P/Ls). Fig. 17–7 shows such a simultaneous co-located VOR / DME fix.

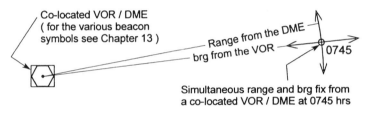

Fig. 17–7   Simultaneous fix from a co-located VOR/DME.

It is worth pointing out situations where the combination of a range P/L from a DME with a P/L from a non co-located source may need a further

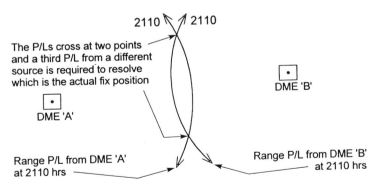

Fig. 17–8   The need for a third P/L to resolve a fix position,
simultaneous ranges from two DME.

P/L (obtained from a third source) to clarify the position of the aircraft. Figs. 17–8 and 17–9 show just such situations. In both cases there are two points where the P/Ls cross and further information is required to ascertain which position is the true one.

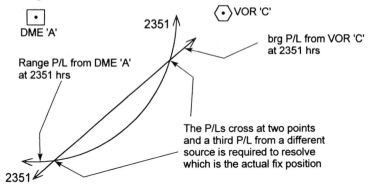

Fig. 17–9   The need for a third P/L to resolve a fix position, simultaneous range from a DME and brg from a non co-located VOR.

CLIMBING AND DESCENDING

17.9 Sometimes a plotting question has a climb and/or a descent in it. Working out a climb or descent is not very different from calculating hdg, GS, time and ETA for a level cruise. Consider the simple trk from 'A' to 'B' shown in Fig. 17–10a. It is required to plan a climb from 2000 ft overhead 'A' up to a cruising level of 26,000 ft and then a descent at the end of the cruise to arrive overhead 'B' at 10,000 ft. Certain items of information are required to enable the calculations to be carried out. These items may appear in questions in several different ways as will be explained later. The first thing to appreciate is that both the climb and the descent are treated as separate legs, even though they have the same trk direction as the cruise. Furthermore the distance from 'A' to the **Top of Climb (TOC)** and from 'B' back to the **Top of Descent (TOD)** have to be worked out and subtracted from the total distance from 'A' to 'B' to find the distance to be flown at the cruising level from TOC to TOD. Fig. 17–10b gives the side view of the situation and has the required elements for each calculation marked in.

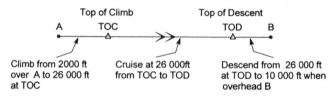

Fig. 17–10a   Plan view of a route with a climb and a descent.

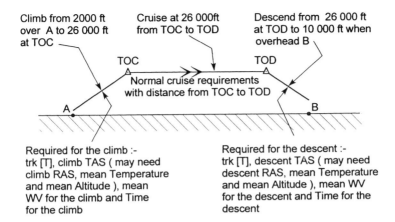

Fig. 17–10b   *Side view of the same route with its climb, cruise and descent.*

17.10   For the climb the required elements are:

Trk (T) which is the same as for the cruise and is measured directly from the chart.

Climbing RAS (for a climb at high levels this could be climbing Mach No). This is usually given in the question.

Mean temperature for the climb to enable **climbing TAS** to be calculated from the climbing RAS. This may be given in the question or have to be calculated as the mean temperature from temperatures given for the top and bottom of the climb (simply add the temperatures algebraically and divide by two).

For example in the case of Fig. 17–10b suppose the temperature at 2000 ft over 'A' was + 6° C and at the cruising level of 26,000 ft it was – 40° C then the mean temperature for the climb would be:

$$(+ 6 – 40) / 2° C = – 34 / 2° C = – 17°C.$$

Sometimes the examination question gives the climbing TAS to use, in which case the above two items are not applicable.

Mean WV for the climb. Like the mean temperature the mean WV may be given in the question or have to be calculated from the mean of the WVs at the top and bottom of the climb. Adding the values together and dividing by two works for the Wind Speed but in certain cases can give the reciprocal of the Wind Direction.

For example there is no problem if the WV at the bottom of the climb were 240/30 and the WV at the top were 280/60, added together would give 520/90 which divided by two gives a **mean WV of 260/45**.

However when the Wind Directions at top and bottom of a climb lie either side of 000°, this method gives a reciprocal mean Wind Direction. For example, if the bottom and top WVs were 340/20 and 040/60 the added figures are 380/80 which when halved give 190/40! The mean speed is correct but the mean direction is patently the reciprocal of the correct answer. In cases where the bottom and top WVs lie either side of 000°, add or subtract 180° to the Wind Direction found by this method (i.e. 190° + or − 180° gives 010° as the mean Wind Direction).

Mean altitude of climb, needed to calculate the mean TAS from the mean RAS and mean temperature. Add together the altitudes at the bottom and top of the climb and divide by two. In the case of the climb in Fig. 17–10b this would be:

$$2000 \text{ ft} + 26,000 \text{ ft} / 2$$
$$= 28,000 \text{ ft} / 2$$
$$= \textbf{14,000 ft.}$$

Climbing time is needed so that, combined with the mean **climbing GS** calculated from the above elements, the **ground distance** from the start of the climb to TOC can be found and plotted on the chart. The time spent on the climb may be given in the question or it may need calculating from a given rate of climb over the altitude change involved. For example in Fig. 17–10b the starting altitude at 'A' is 2000 ft and at TOC it is 26,000ft, if the given rate of climb were 3000 ft per min the climbing time would be:

$$26,000 - 2000 \text{ ft} / 3000 \text{ ft per min}$$
$$= 24,000 \text{ ft altitude change} / 3000 \text{ ft per min}$$
$$= \textbf{8 min.}$$

17.11 **For the descent** the elements are similar to those for the climb. Just substitute the word 'descent' for the word 'climb' and 'TOD' for 'TOC', the distance from TOD to bottom of descent being plotted *from the bottom of descent back along the trk* to find the position of TOD on the chart. A possible variation that can be asked is, starting from a specific TOD, to calculate the rate of descent necessary to arrive overhead a point at a given altitude. The solution is to measure the distance from the position of the specified TOD to the overhead point of the bottom of the descent and use the calculated descent GS to find the descent time. The descent time (in min) divided into the change of altitude (in ft) involved on the descent will give the required rate of descent (in ft per min).

17.12 The calculations involved in preparing a Flight Plan for the route shown in Fig. 17–10b are given below. To demonstrate the process from start to finish different WVs, temperatures and rate of climb to those in the paragraph 17.10 examples will be used. The associated log-keeping procedures will be ignored at this stage, log-keeping is dealt with later in this Chapter.

Example:

An aircraft is to be flown from 'A' to 'B', a distance of 253 nm, trk 090 (T). The aircraft is to climb from 2000 ft overhead 'A' to a cruising altitude of

26,000 ft. Mean RAS for the climb 195 kn, mean rate of climb 2000 ft per min. Cruise RAS 265 kn. The aircraft is to descend from cruising altitude to arrive overhead 'B' at 10,000 ft. Mean RAS for the descent 180 kn, mean rate of descent 1600 ft per min. Forecast WVs and temperatures are:-

At 'A' 2000 ft	WV 150 / 30	temp + 12° C
26,000 ft level	WV 200 / 60	temp – 42° C
At 'B' 10,000 ft	WV 170 / 40	temp – 8° C

Calculate the hdgs and times for the climb, the cruise and the descent.

Answer:
For the climb:
Mean altitude
= (2000 + 26,000) ft / 2   =   28,000 ft / 2   =   **14,000 ft**
Mean temp.
= (+ 12 – 42)° C / 2   =   – 30° C / 2   =   **– 15° C**
Mean WV
= (150 / 30 + 200 / 60) / 2   =   (350 / 90) / 2   =   **175 / 45**
Climbing time
= (26,000 – 2000) ft / 2000 ft per min
= 24,000 ft / 2000 ft per min
= **12 min.**

Fig. 17–11   *The climb, plotting TOC.*

Mean climbing RAS 195 kn, mean altitude 14,000 ft, mean temp –15° C gives a mean climbing **TAS of 238 kn** (see Chapter 4, para. 4.6).
Trk 090 (T), mean climbing TAS 238 kn, mean climbing WV 175 / 45 gives a climbing **hdg of 101 (T)** at a mean climbing **GS of 230 kn** (See Chapter 5, para. 5.14).
Mean climbing GS 230 kn for a climbing time of 12 min gives a distance of **46 nm** along trk from 'A' to the TOC. (see Fig. 17–11)
For the descent:
Mean altitude
= (26,000 + 10,000) ft / 2 = 36,000 ft / 2 = **18,000 ft**
Mean temp
= (- 42 – 8)° C / 2 = – 50° C / 2 = **– 25° C**

Mean WV
= (200 / 60 + 170 / 40) / 2 = (370 / 100) / 2 = **185 / 50**
Descent time
= (26,000 – 10,000) ft / 1600 ft per min
= 16,000 ft / 1600 ft per min
= **10 min**.
Mean descending RAS 180 kn, mean altitude 18 000 ft, mean temp –25° C
gives a mean descending **TAS of 234 kn.**
Trk 090 (T), mean descending TAS 234 kn and mean descending WV
185/50 gives descending **hdg of 102 (T)** at a mean descending **GS of 233 kn.**
Mean descending GS 233 kn for a descending time of 10 min gives a distance of **39 nm** *back* along trk from 'B' *to* the TOD. (See Fig. 17–12).

Fig. 17–12   The descent, plotting TOD.

For the cruise:
Cruise RAS 265 kn, altitude 26,000 ft, temp – 42 C gives a cruise **TAS of
386 kn.** (See Chapter 4, para. 4.7 for TAS > 300 kn.)
Cruise distance from TOC to TOD = Total distance from 'A' to 'B' less the
combined climb and descent distances

$$= 253 - (46 + 39) \, \text{nm}$$
$$= 253 - 85 \, \text{nm}$$
$$= \mathbf{168 \, nm.}$$

Trk 090 (T), cruise TAS 386 kn, WV at 26,000 ft 200 / 60 gives a cruise **hdg
of 099 (T)** at a **GS of 403 kn.**
Cruise distance 168 nm at GS 403 kn gives a **cruise time of 25 min** from levelling off at TOC to starting descent at TOD. (see Fig. 17–13)

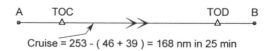

Fig. 17–13   The Cruise, Distance and Time.

Summary of flight plan:
Climb on hdg 101 (T) for **12 min** from 2000 ft overhead 'A' to TOC (49 nm from 'A').
Cruise on **hdg 099 (T)** for **25 min** from TOC to TOD (a distance of 168 nm).
Descent on **hdg 102 (T)** for **10 min** from TOD to 10,000 ft overhead 'B' (a distance of 39 nm).
Total time for flight = 12 + 25 + 10 min = **47 min.** (see Fig. 17–14.)

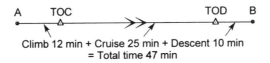

Climb 12 min + Cruise 25 min + Descent 10 min
= Total time 47 min

Fig. 17–14   Total time for the climb, cruise and descent.

THE PLOTTING SEQUENCE

17.13   The basic plotting sequence is an ongoing process which is repeated throughout the flight from start to finish. Expressed in the simplest terms the process consists of the following stages:
Gathering information to up-date the position of the aircraft.
From the latest position reassess TMG, GS and WV.
Assess and implement any alterations needed to hdg and/or ETA as a result of
   changes detected.

THE PLOTTING CHART

17.14   The plotting process is carried out on a plotting chart which has as a minimum a lat and long graticule, isogonals, coastal outlines and the position and identification of ground located radio aids shown. The current charts used for training and examinations in the UK are of A4 size to a scale of 1 : 5,000,000, using what is termed a Minimal Error Conical Projection which is, to all intents and purposes, a Lambert's Projection. One of these charts is used in the demonstration plot later in this Chapter. It must be emphasised that this series of 1 : 5,000,000 plotting charts are not intended for operational use in the air. When the Joint European Licence is introduced the examination charts may well be different from the current UK examination charts but in all probability will still be based on a Lambert's Projection, since this is the predominant projection in use in the European theatre. To back up the visual plot a tabulated log should be kept recording the step by step progress of the flight.

THE NAVIGATION LOG FORM

17.15   Good log-keeping is the secret of good plotting, a well kept log makes it easy to access the latest state of affairs and a well laid out log form can act as an *aide mémoire*; gaps in the columns indicating that a process has not yet been carried out. Log forms can vary in layout but all should have columns for recording items like time, trk, hdg, dev, varn, Alt/FL, temp, RAS / Mach No, TAS, GS, dist, time, ETA, incoming information, etc. While content is essential the actual layout is a matter of personal taste. For example, candidates may find the log form used below (which just happens to be the author's preferred layout) differs in detail from log forms from other sources. For the UK examinations candidates may use whatever type of log form they please. The author strongly advises candidates to choose a log form layout that suits them personally and get plenty of practise in using it. Do not forget to take blank copies with you for use in the examinations. Most log forms have a Time column on the left hand side and an ETA column on the right-hand side. Between these two lie other columns arranged in functional groups. The author's preferred log form layout has the left-hand side dealing with the direction elements first, thus:

Time	Trk	WV/	Hdg	Var	Hdg	Dev	Hdg
	(T)	/drift	(T)		(M)		(C)

In the centre of the log is a wide space (about ⅓ of the total width of the sheet) for **Observations** . The space allows room for calculations of bearings to plot and other items like climbs and /or descents. Between the **Observations** space and the ETA column are the speed, distance and time (to go) elements, thus:

Mach/	Pressure/	TAS	GS	Dist	Time	ETA
No /RAS	Alt /COAT					

Had a log form been used for the calculations of the climb example given in paragraph 17.12 the final result would look something like Fig. 17–15a.

The stages used in completing each line of the log are shown in Fig. 17–15b. Numbers give the sequence of working and arrows indicate the transfer of information from the **Observations** space into specific columns.

PLOTTING THE POSITION OF AN AIRCRAFT

17.16   The established position at which an aircraft is *known* to have been at a particular time (as opposed to a DR position which is an *estimated* position) is known as a **fix**. In plotting, a fix can be established by several

Time	Trk [T]	W V/drift	Hdg [T]	Var	Hdg [M]	Dev	Hdg [C]	Observations	Mach No/RAS	Pressure Alt/COAT	TAS	GS	Dist	Time	ETA
	090	175/45	101					'X' CLIMBING 2000 ↗ 26000FT TOC' MEAN ALT = (2000 + 26000) / 2 = 14000 FT. ALT CHANGE = 26000 - 2000 = 24000 FT AT 2000 FT / MIN = 12 MIN MEAN TEMP = (+12 -42) / 2 = -30 / 2 = -15C. MEAN W V = (150/30 + 200/60) / 2 = 350/90 / 2 = 175/45	195	14000 / -15	233	230	46	12	

Fig. 17–15a   The log sheet, the climb entries

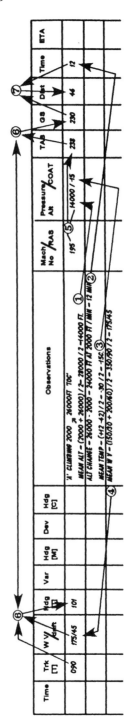

Time	Trk [T]	W V/drift	Hdg [T]	Var	Hdg [M]	Dev	Hdg [C]	Observations	Mach No/RAS	Pressure Alt/COAT	TAS	GS	Dist	Time	ETA
	090	175/45	101					'X' CLIMBING 2000 ↗ 26000FT TOC' MEAN ALT = (2000 + 26000) / 2 = 14000 FT. ALT CHANGE = 26000 - 2000 = 24000 FT AT 2000 FT / MIN = 12 MIN MEAN TEMP = (+12 -42) / 2 = -30 / 2 = -15C. MEAN W V = (150/30 + 200/60) / 2 = 350/90 / 2 = 175/45	195	14000 / -15	233	230	44	12	

Fig. 17–15b   The log sheet, the climb entries showing the sequence of the calculations

different methods. These are described in paragraphs 17.17 to 17.20 along with the symbols used to identify them, by type, on the chart. Fixes should always have the applicable time marked beside them on the chart.

TYPES OF FIX

17.17 **Visual** observation whilst map reading (visual fixes are known as **pinpoints** and are marked on the chart with a dot surrounded by a small circle). It is easier to obtain visual pinpoints at lower altitudes than at high level. Pinpointing requires good visibility and a clear field of view to the ground directly beneath the aircraft, cloud and the restricted downward view from the flight deck of most modern airliners make obtaining visual pinpoints from high altitude almost impossible. Nonetheless pinpoints are sometimes given in training and examination plotting questions, often as a starting point. Candidates should mark the position accurately with the pinpoint symbol and the time of the fix beside it. (see Fig.17–16)

1728 ⊙

Fig. 17–16   The Pinpoint symbol (with its applicable time noted beside it).

17.18 **A radar fix** , as a range and bearing 'to' or 'from' a ground feature displayed on the radar screen. To plot the radar fix the ground feature has to be located on the chart and the bearing plotted 'from' it crossed by the range P/L. Radar fixes are denoted by a cross surrounded by a small circle with the time of the fix beside it. In plotting questions radar fixes are given with Time, Range and Bearing 'to' or 'from' an identified (by lat and long) ground feature . If the bearing given is 'from' the ground feature this is the bearing to plot. If the bearing given is 'to' the ground feature the bearing to plot is the reciprocal of the given bearing (i.e. 'to' brg + or – 180° = 'from' brg). (See Fig. 17–17). Radar signals follow GC paths and the rules for plotting GC brgs must be applied for the type of chart in use. This is especially true at high lats and for long radar ranges.

⊗ 0352

Fig. 17–17   The Radar Fix symbol (with its applicable time noted beside it).

17.19 **A simultaneous fix** from two P/Ls crossing at (or very close to) 90°. One example of this type of fix was given in paragraph 17.8 and Fig. 17–7 where a brg and range were obtained at the same time from a co-located VOR / DME. A simultaneous fix can also be obtained from sources that are not co-located provided the P/Ls cross at or near to 90° at the time they are obtained. The selection of the best stations to interrogate in order to obtain a simultaneous fix requires knowledge of the current DR position of the aircraft in relation to the ground stations in the area. The rough rule-of-thumb for finding the DR position (see para. 17.3) is accurate enough for this purpose. Simultaneous fixes are marked on the chart by plotting the two P/Ls and drawing a small circle round the fix position where the lines cross. The time is recorded against *each* position line *and* the fix. (see Fig. 17–18) Even though in this case it may seem like overkill, writing the relevant time beside *every* item on the plot is a very good habit to get into. Without time tags to identify their place in the sequence of events, fixes, DR positions and P/Ls become almost meaningless and the task of trying to make plotting sense of them almost impossible. The same applies to marking trks and WV vectors with their appropriate arrows.

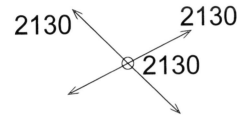

Fig. 17–18   A simultaneous fix with brg P/Ls from two widely separated ground station.

17.20   A running fix made up of P/Ls obtained at different times; the earlier P/Ls being transferred forward (using DR trk and GS) to the time of the later P/L to give a fix for the time of the later P/L. The principle behind this transferring concept is as if the earlier P/Ls are being carried forward on the aircraft's back, along trk at GS for a given time interval. The ideal running fix is made up of three P/Ls which cut each other at approximately 60°. The origin of this type of fix is a nautical one. The reciprocals of three well spaced out brgs taken as a ship sails past a prominent feature (such as a lighthouse, island or headland) being plotted on a chart as P/Ls radiating from the feature's position. The earlier P/Ls are then moved forward (at the ship's equivalent of DR trk and GS) to the time of the last P/L. The result (in a perfect world) being three P/Ls all passing through the same point to fix the ship's position at the time of the last P/L. (see Fig. 17–19) *Note that the transferred P/Ls are annotated with double arrow-heads and are given the time they have been transferred to.*

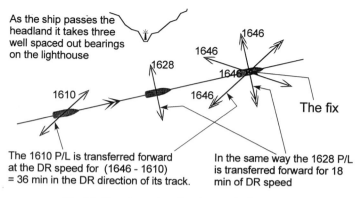

As the ship passes the headland it takes three well spaced out bearings on the lighthouse

1610   1628   1646   1646   1646   1646

The fix

The 1610 P/L is transferred forward at the DR speed for (1646 - 1610) = 36 min in the DR direction of its track.

In the same way the 1628 P/L is transferred forward for 18 min of DR speed

Fig. 17–19   A running fix, the nautical origin.

Two factors can upset the conditions for an ideal running fix:

The accuracy of the brgs taken.

The actual direction and speed of movement of the ship being slightly different from the estimated values used in transferring the P/Ls.

As a result of such error inputs the three P/Ls may produce a small triangle known as a 'cocked hat'. In such cases the centre of the triangle is taken as the fix position thus averaging out the errors. (see Fig. 17–20)

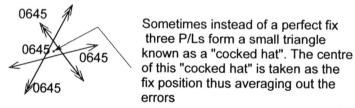

0645   0645   0645   0645

Sometimes instead of a perfect fix three P/Ls form a small triangle known as a "cocked hat". The centre of this "cocked hat" is taken as the fix position thus averaging out the errors

Fig. 17–20   The 'Cocked Hat' fix.

The principle of the running fix can be applied in aviation plotting with the P/Ls being obtained when in transit past a ground station such as a VOR or an NDB. Furthermore, provided the bearings are at, or around, 60° to each other a running fix can be made up from P/Ls obtained from a mixture of sources. (see Fig. 17–21) 'Cocked Hat' fixes also occur in aviation plotting for similar reasons to those mentioned for the shipping fix.

In the example in Fig. 17–21 note how the final fix does not lie on the DR trk. Since the fix is an *actual* position and the DR trk only an *estimated* trk this often happens during a plot and is no cause for alarm. When transferring, as long as a P/L is moved in the *direction* of the DR trk at the DR GS, it will finish up in the right place to give a reasonable fix

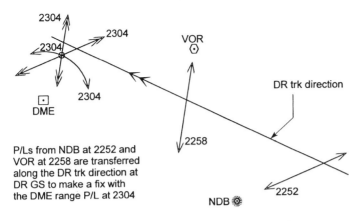

Fig. 17–21   An airborne running fix from mixed sources.

(when combined with other P/Ls) even if the DR trk is displaced well to one side of the actual TMG. A case in point is the transferring of a DME range P/L which is a curve, being the arc of a circle centred on the ground position of the DME station. The only way such a range P/L can be transferred forward is by moving the whole circle in the direction of the DR trk at DR GS for the appropriate time. A construction line is drawn *from* the DME station *in the **direction** of the DR trk* and the station transferred forward *at the DR GS* to the time of the last P/L, the range circle being redrawn from the transferred station to give the transferred range P/L. (See Fig. 17–22)

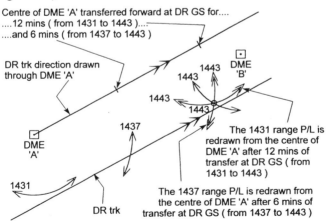

The fix is made up of P/Ls from DME 'A' at 1431 and 1437 (transferred at DR trk and GS to 1443) and a single P/L from DME 'B' at 1443

Fig. 17–22   An airborne running fix from DME stations.

EXAMINATION PLOT

17.21   An examination plot can never be the same as a plot carried out in the air. In the air it is the task of the plotter to get the information needed and also to select which aids to interrogate at any time. In examinations all the plotting information is presented in one go. The candidate has to take this tabulated mass of information and break it into a series of manageable packets. Reading through an examination plotting paper reveals key items of information:

The start point of the plot. Is it an actual position or is it a DR position?
Cruising levels and speeds. Do they change at any point?
Forecast WVs and temperatures.
Is a Climb and / or a Descent to be worked out at any point?
Fixes which have to be plotted. What types are they?
WVs which have to be calculated.
DR positions to be plotted (for alteration of hdg or the assessment of conv).
Alterations of hdg and revision of ETA to be calculated.
Possible pilot navigation requirements.

17.22   The way to approach a plotting examination is to treat it as a series of separate problems that are linked to each other in a string, the most up-to-date information being carried forward from one step to the next in the sequence. This may be modified where examiners find it necessary to ensure that all candidates use the same inputs for a particular plotting process. In such cases instructions will be given in the question paper as to what specific values are to be used in place of information resolved in the previous step. The key to successful plotting is to be methodical. Work towards under-standing the processes and *concentrate on accuracy in the first instance.* Speed will come with practise and experience. Newcomers to plotting who try for speed before acquiring accuracy invariably have troubles with the subject. A well proven sequence to follow is:

Record on the log sheet all the given starting information and plot on the chart the applicable starting point (fix or DR position) with its time beside it.
Having got the start plotted, read ahead only as far as the next major item on the plot.
Compute and plot all the elements to solve this first stage.
Where possible update information (such as WV, TMG, GS, ETA etc.) resulting from completion of the first stage.
Read ahead to the next major item and repeat the process using the most up-to-date information.
Repeat to the end of the plot, remembering to maintain the log and annotate all items on the chart with their correct symbols and times.

17.23   The plot which now follows sets out to use as many aspects of plotting as possible in one exercise. To achieve the maximum number of variables in this plot it has been necessary to select aids which best illustrate plotting methods rather than the more practical options that would be used on a real flight. Also included is some pilot navigation of the type commonly used on airways flying. (see Chapter 7, para. 7.23 and Figs 7–27a, b and c) Questions involving pilot navigation do not as a rule require anything to be plotted on the chart, the log entries usually suffice. Candidates should be on the lookout for any pilot navigation question(s) within the examination plot, if they are not recognised for the simple thing that they are, a lot of time can be wasted on unnecessary plotting.

DEMONSTRATION PLOT

17.24   Candidates will need the following plotting instruments:

Navigation Computer. This must be of the circular slide rule type and not a programmed electronic type (not allowed in examinations).

Straight-edge.

Protractor (square plotter type).

Dividers.

Compasses (continually changing round combined dividers / compasses can waste time in an examination, it is advisable to have one of each).

Pencils (HB for the log and 2H or 3H for the chart work). It is a good idea to have a supply of sharpened pencils to hand *before* the examination starts, sharpening pencils after the examination starts wastes precious time.

Pencil sharpener. Just in case.

Eraser.

The demonstration plot that follows is carried out on UK training and examination chart No 4. *This chart (and its companion charts) are strictly for training and examination purposes only and must **never** be used operationally.* Reproduction of the chart within this publication is with the kind permission of the Aeronautical Charts section of the United Kingdom Civil Aviation Authority.

THE INFORMATION

An aircraft is en route tracking from 'F' (6400N 2200W) to 'M' (5800N 0625W), hdg 122 (T), FL235, temp -35C, RAS 260 kn, DR GS 403 kn.

1310	DR Position 6328N 2015W
1313	VOR 'G' (6400N 1702W) QDM 078
1322	DME 'G' range 73 nm
1331	VOR 'E' (6530N 1400W) QDR 212
	What is the fix position at1331?
1352	NDB 'H' brs 298 RBI (hdg 122 (T))

1358 Ground D/F station 'L' (5900N 0300W) passes QTE 293

1404 VOR 'M' (5800N 0625W) 153 'TO'
What is the fix position at 1404?
What is the mean WV since 1331?

1410 DR position alter hdg for 'M'
What is the hdg (M) to steer?
What is the ETA at 'M'?

1417 Doppler drift and GS, 4S, 425 kn.

1425 Pinpoint overhead 'M'. Alter hdg for 'I' (6030N 0100W), FL230, use WV 020 / 60, temp -30°C, RAS 263 kn.
What is the hdg (M) to steer?
What is the ETA at 'I'?

1451 NDB 'M' brs 183 RBI
NDB 'I' brs 005 RBI
Alter hdg direct for 'I'
What is the new hdg (T)?

1455 DME 'I' range 60 nm.
What is the revised GS and ETA at 'I'?

1506 Overhead 'I' alter hdg for 'J' (6230N 0600E), FL230, use WV 030 / 50, temp -30°C, RAS 263 kn
What is the hdg (M) to steer?
What is the ETA at 'J'?

1515 Message received. 'The aircraft is to descend to arrive at 5000 ft overhead 'J', the descent is to be at 1000 ft per minute and the start of the descent is to be delayed to the latest time that will achieve this objective. WV at 5000 ft at 'J' is 350 / 30 temp + 10° C. Mean TAS for the descent 240 kn.'
What is the position of the Top of Descent (TOD)?
What is the ETA at TOD?
What is the hdg (M) for the descent?
What is the revised ETA for overhead 'J' at 5000 ft?

PROCEDURE FOR THIS PLOT

17.25 From the information at the start and at 1310:

In the first line of the log enter 1310 in the **Time** column and in the **Observations** space enter the DR position information. The appropriate given information is entered in the **RAS**, **Press Alt/temp** and **GS** columns. The TAS is now calculated on the navigation computer and entered in the **TAS** column. In this case a compressibility correction is necessary as the initial TAS > 300 kn. (see Chapter 4, para. 4.7)

The trk from 'F' to 'M' is drawn on the chart and annotated with two arrows in the direction of movement.

The DR position for 1310 is plotted on the chart and indicated with a triangle symbol. The time 1310 is marked on the chart beside the DR position. To plot a given position accurately on a chart with curved parallels and straight meridians use a straight edge to draw in the meridian through the position first, the required latitude can then be measured along this meridian with the aid of dividers and the latitude scale.

17.26   Reading ahead. At 1313, 1322 and 1331 information about three P/Ls is given followed by a request for the position at 1331. This must be calculated and plotted before proceeding beyond 1331:

ENTER 1313 in the **Time** column of the second line on the log form and in the **Observations** space enter the source of the information and what it is.

Carry out the calculations to enable the P/L to be plotted (in this case QDM converted to QTE, see para. 17.5).

Plot the P/L, mark the ends with single arrow-heads to signify it is a P/L and write the time (**1313**) beside it.

This P/L has to be transferred forward in the *direction* of the DR trk (i.e. in the *direction* of the plotted trk from 'F' to 'M') at the DR GS from 1313 to 1331, a period of 18 min. The **GS**, **Dist** and **Time Min** columns are used in calculating and recording the distance the P/L is to be transferred. The process of transferring this P/L is dealt with at the fix time of 1331.

If more than one line is needed to complete the calculations in the **Observations** space mark the **Time** column with a tick to show the information applies to the time above the tick.

ENTER 1322 in the **Time** column of the next line of the log form and in the **Observations** space enter the information details.

Since this is a range from a DME station no calculations are needed prior to plotting the range P/L.

Plot the range P/L (in the region of the DR trk) as the arc of a circle of radius the range from the DME. Mark with P/L arrows and the time (**1322**).

This P/L has to be transferred forward in the *direction* of the DR trk (i.e. in the *direction* of the plotted trk from 'F' to 'M') at the DR GS from 1322 to 1331, a period of 9 min. The **GS**, **Dist** and **Time Min** columns are used in calculating and recording the distance the P/L is to be transferred. The process of transferring this range P/L is dealt with at the fix time of 1331.

ENTER 1331 in the **Time** column of the next line of the log form and in the **Observations** space enter the information details.

Carry out the calculations to enable the P/L to be plotted, in this case QDR converted to QTE (see para. 17.5).

Plot the P/L, mark the ends with single arrow-heads to signify it is a P/L and write the time (**1331**) beside it.

TRANSFER THE 1313 P/L TO 1331. From where the 1313 P/L crosses the DR trk measure the calculated transfer distance forward along the DR trk and put a mark. The transferred P/L must pass through this point and be parallel to the 1313 P/L. With the point of a (sharp) pencil on the transfer mark bring the square plotting protractor up against it and rotate the protractor until the squared grid lines lie parallel over the top of the 1313 P/L. The edge of the protractor is now parallel to the 1313 P/L and passing through the transfer mark ready for the transferred P/L to be drawn along it. Draw the line and mark its ends with double arrows to indicate it is a transferred P/L and give it the time it has been transferred to (**1331** in this case).

TRANSFER THE 1322 RANGE P/L TO 1331. Unlike the 1313 straight P/L the 1322 P/L is part of a circle and to transfer it requires the centre of the circle (the DME station) to be moved in the *direction* of the DR trk at the DR GS and the arc of the circle redrawn from the transferred centre. The square plotting protractor is used to draw a line parallel to the DR trk from the centre of the DME station and the calculated transfer distance is marked off down this line from the DME station. From this mark the original range arc is redrawn to give the transferred range position line (mark its ends with double arrows and give it the transferred time of **1331**).

THE FIX AT 1331. In the ideal case the original 1331 P/L and the two transferred P/Ls should all cross at a common point giving a perfect fix. Errors in plotting sometimes result in a 'cocked hat' (see para. 17.20) in which case the centre of the triangle should be taken to be the fix position.

ENTER THE 1331 FIX position in the log and underline <u>1331</u> in the **Time** column to indicate a fix at that time.

Fig. 17–23 shows the logsheet entries (reduced in size to fit the page) and a corner of the chart with the plot so far.

17.27   Reading ahead the next items are P/Ls at 1352, 1358 and 1404 and a fix to be found at 1404. *Note that there was nothing about finding a WV or TMG at 1331. This is because there is no definite position information available prior to 1331, only an estimated DR position at 1310. A TMG, GS or WV can only be found between established fixes,* **NEVER** *between (an estimated) DR position and (an actual) fix.*

ENTER 1352 in the **Time** column of the next line of the log form and in the **Observations** space enter the information details.
Carry out the calculations to enable the P/L to be plotted. The procedure for converting and plotting an RBI brg of an NDB transmission is to be found at para. 17.7. In this case the DR position at 1352 is in the region of the 12W meridian and the square plotting protractor is used to draw a line parallel to the 12W meridian through the position of NDB 'H' to give the transferred meridian from which the P/L is to be plotted.
Plot the P/L from the transferred meridian and label with the P/L arrows and the time (**1352**).

Time	Trk [T]	W/V / drift	Hdg [T]	Var	Hdg [M]	Dev	Hdg [C]	Observations	Mach No / RAS	Pressure Alt / COAT	TAS	GS	Dist	Time	ETA
1310			122					△ 6328N 2015W	260	23 500 / -35	385	403			
1313								VOR 'G' QDM 078 + 180 = QDR 258							
								-19W VAR = QTE 239 PLOT				✓	121	18	
1322								DME 'G' RNG 73 NM PLOT				✓	60,5	9	
1331								VOR 'E' QDR 212 -18W VAR = QTE 194 PLOT							
✓								✳ 6212N 1540W							

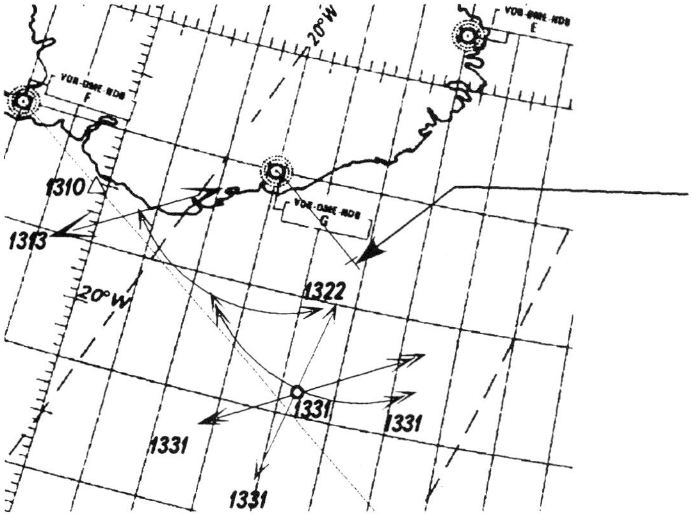
VOR-DME-NDB E
VOR-DME-NDB F
VOR-DME-NDB G
20°W
20°W
1310
1313
1322
1331
1331
1331
1331
Construction for transfer of the
1322 DME range P/L from 'G'
by DR trk (direction) and GS

Fig. 17–23 Demonstration plot, the fix at 1331

This P/L has to be transferred from 1352 to 1404, a time interval of 12 min. Calculate and log the details as before.

ENTER 1358 in the **Time** column of the next line of the log form and in the **Observations** space enter the information details.

Since this is a QTE it can be plotted from N (T) at 'L' with no further calculations required. Mark with the P/L arrows and the time (**1358**).

This P/L has to be transferred from 1358 to 1404, a time interval of 6 min. Calculate and log the details as before.

ENTER 1404 in the **Time** column of the next line of the log form and in the **Observations** space enter the information details.

Carry out the calculations to enable the P/L to be plotted. Whenever a VOR brg is given as 'TO' it is a QDM and if given as 'FROM' it is a QDR (in both cases based on N (M) at the station). This is a similar calculation to the one at 1313, (note that the varn at 'M' is 11W, three-quarters of the way between the 8W and the 12W isogonals on the chart).

Plot the P/L and mark with the P/L arrows and the time (**1404**).

TRANSFER THE 1352 and 1358 P/Ls TO 1404 . The method is the same as used to transfer the 1313 P/L to 1331. Be sure to move the 1352 P/L for 12 min of DR GS and the 1358 P/L for only 6 min of DR GS.

ENTER THE 1404 FIX POSITION in the log and underline <u>1404</u> in the **Time** column.

17.28   At 1404 as well as the fix position the question also wanted the WV since 1331. The 1331 fix and the 1404 fix are both *actual* positions. Since a steady hdg and TAS has been maintained between these two fixes it is a reasonable assumption that a steady TMG and GS have also been maintained between them and these can be extracted from the plot.

DRAW A STRAIGHT LINE joining the 1331 fix to the 1404 fix and extend this line some distance beyond the 1404 fix (the reason for this will be seen later). This is the TMG from 1331 to 1404, mark it with the trk double arrow pointing *from* the 1331 fix *to* the 1404 fix.

MEASURE THE TMG direction from the meridian half way between the two fixes and enter this information in the **Observations** space of the log.

MEASURE THE DISTANCE between the two fixes and enter this information in the **Observations** space of the log along with the time interval between the two fixes.

COMPUTE THE GS from this distance and time interval using the navigation computer (see Chapter 4, para. 4.14) and enter this under the **GS** column.

Fig. 14–24 shows the logsheet entries from 1358 to 1404 (reduced in size to fit the page) and the relevant part of the chart.

Time	Trk [T]	W/V/drift	Hdg [T]	Var	Hdg [M]	Dev	Hdg [C]	Observations	Mach No/RAS	Pressure Alt/COAT	TAS	GS	Dist	Time	ETA
✓								★ 6212N 1540W							
1352								NDB 'H' RBI 298 + 122 - 180 = 240 PLOT FROM TRANSFERRED MERIDIAN				✓	80.6	12	
1358								GRND D/F BRG 'L' QTE 293 PLOT				✓	40.3	6	
1404								VOR 'M' 153 'TO' + 180 - 11W VAR = QTE 322 PLOT							
✓	128	6S	122					★ 5939N 0925W TMG 128 227 NM IN 33 MIN				413	227	33	

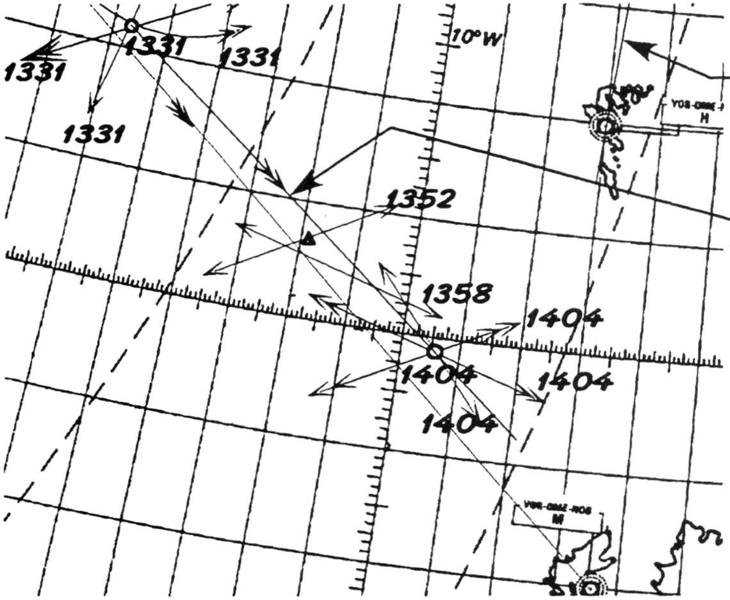

1331
1331
1331
1331
10°W
1352
1358
1404
1404
1404
1404
H
M
Transferred meridian from 1352 DR position
TMG, from the 1331 fix to the 1404 fix, extended beyond the 1404 fix in readiness for DRing ahead

FIG. 17–24 Demonstration plot, plotting the 1404 fix and finding TMG and GS since 1331

All the elements are now available to enable the WV to be found on the navigation computer by the trk and GS method. (see Chapter 5, para. 5.11)

COMPUTE THE WV from hdg, TAS, TMG and GS. Enter this WV in both the **Observations** space and the **WV/drift** column.

17.29   The next item on the question paper is at 1410 asking for an alteration of hdg and revised ETA for 'M'. This involves establishing the DR position at 1410, plotting and measuring the required trk and distance from there to 'M' and finally the computation of hdg, GS, time and ETA.

PLOT THE DR POSITION FOR 1410. As the same hdg and TAS is being flown between 1404 and 1410 as was being flown between 1331 and 1404 it can reasonably be assumed that the TMG and GS will be the same in both cases. On this assumption extension of the TMG (from 1331 to 1404) beyond 1404 to 1410 at the GS found will give the DR position for 1410. Mark the position on the chart with the triangular DR symbol and the time (**1410**).

ENTER 1410 in the **Time** column of the next line of the log form and put a DR triangle symbol in the **Observations** space and the words **ALTER HDG FOR 'M'**.

DRAW A LINE FROM THE DR POSITION TO 'M' and mark it with the double arrow trk symbol pointing towards 'M'. This is the DR trk to reach 'M'.

MEASURE this DR trk direction and distance and enter their values in the **Trk (T)** and **Dist** columns on the 1410 line of the log. Read the mean varn for this trk from the chart and enter it into the **Var** column. Ticks may also be put in the **WV/drift** and **TAS** columns of the 1410 line to indicate no change to their values since the last entry.

COMPUTE HDG (T) AND GS using the navigation computer (see Chapter 5, para. 5.14) and enter the results in the **Hdg (T)** and **GS** columns on the 1410 line of the log. Apply the varn to the hdg (T) to give the hdg (M) and enter this value into the **Hdg (M)** column on the same line.

COMPUTE THE TIME TO GO from the distance to go and the GS (see Chapter 4, para. 4.14) and enter the value in the **Time Min** column on the 1410 line of the log. Add this time to 1410 to give the ETA at 'M', enter it in the **ETA** column.

Fig. 17–25 shows the logsheet entries for 1410 (reduced in size to fit the page) and the relevant part of the chart.

17.30   The Doppler drift and GS at 1417 is used to confirm the calculation of trk (hdg (T) + S Doppler drift) and GS from the 1410 DR position to 'M'. At 1425 the question indicates that the aircraft is fixed as being overhead 'M', with instructions to alter hdg for 'I'. There are changes to the FL, WV, temperature and RAS. In effect all the previous calculations can be ignored from this point on, and a completely new start made.

Time	Trk [T]	W/V /drift	Hdg [T]	Var	Hdg [M]	Dev	Hdg [C]	Observations	Mach No/RAS	Pressure Alt/COAT	TAS	GS	Dist	Time	ETA
✓		000/52						W/V 000/52							
1410	146	✓	142	12W	154			△ ALTER HDG FOR 'M'			✓	426	105	15	1425
1417								DOPPLER DRIFT 4S, GS 425 KN CHECKS OUT							

1410 DR position found by plotting down the extended TMG for 6 min of the mean GS between the 1331 and 1404 fixes.

New DR trk and distance from the 1410 DR position to 'M'.

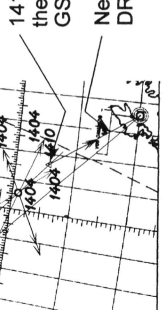

Fig. 17–25   DR'ing ahead and altering hdg for 'M'

ENTER 1425 in the **Time** column of the next line on the log sheet and in the **Observations** space put a pinpoint symbol (a dot with a small circle round it) and the words **'M' ALTER HDG FOR 'I'**. In their appropriate columns enter the new WV, RAS, FL (Pressure Altitude) and temperature. Compute the new TAS (see Chapter 4, para. 4.7, RAS to TAS where TAS > 300 kn) and enter it in the **TAS** column.

DRAW IN THE TRK FROM 'M' TO 'I' on the chart and mark it with the double arrow trk symbol pointing towards 'I'. Read the mean varn for this trk from the chart and enter it into the **Var** column on the 1425 line of the log.

MEASURE the trk direction and distance from 'M' to 'I' and enter their values in the **Trk (T)** and **Dist** columns on the 1425 line of the log.

COMPUTE HDG (T) AND GS using the navigation computer (see Chapter 5, para. 5.14) and enter the results in the **Hdg (T)** and **GS** columns on the 1425 line of the log. Apply the varn to the hdg (T) to give the hdg (M) and enter this value into the **Hdg (M)** column on the same line.

COMPUTE THE TIME TO GO from the distance to go and the GS (see Chapter 4, para. 4.14) and enter the value in the **Time** column on the 1410 line of the log. Add this time to 1425 to give the ETA at 'I', enter it in the **ETA** column.

17.31   At 1451 the RBI shows a back brg of 183° relative on the NDB at 'M' and a forward brg of 005° relative on the NDB at 'I' with instructions to alter hdg directly towards 'I'. This is pure pilot navigation and requires nothing to be plotted on the chart. The reciprocal of the back bearing will give the relative TMG from 'M' and the forward brg the relative required trk to 'I'. The angular difference from the relative TMG to the relative required trk gives the required change of hdg (in degrees) and the direction (Port or Starboard) of that change.

ENTER 1451 in the **Time** column of the next line on the log sheet and in the **Observations** space write **NDB 'M' 183 RBI + 044 -180 = 047 TMG**. On the next line of the **Observations** space write **NDB 'I' 005 RBI + 044 = 049 REQ TRK**. TMG to req trk = 2 S On the next line of the Observations space write **Alter hdg 2S for 'I'**. Enter **046** into the **Hdg (T)** column.

17.32   At 1455 a DME range gives distance to go to 'I' and a GS check and revision of ETA at 'I' is asked for. Subtract distance to go from total length of leg to give distance gone. Subtract start time of leg from 1455 to give time gone. From distance gone and time gone the GS can be computed. From GS and distance to go the time to go can be computed and added to 1455 to give the revised ETA.

ENTER 1455 in the **Time** column of the next line of the log sheet and in the **Observations** space write **DME 'I' rng 60 nm**. On the next line in the Observations space write **224 – 60 = 164 nm gone in 30 min = 328 kn GS**. Enter **328** in the **GS** column and **60** in the **Dist** column.

Time	Trk [T]	W V/drift	Hdg [T]	Var	Hdg [M]	Dev	Hdg [C]	Observations	Mach No/RAS	Pressure Alt/COAT	TAS	GS	Dist	Time	ETA
1425	048	020/60	044	11W	055			⊙ 'M' ALTER HDG FOR 'I'	263	23 000/-30	371	320	224	42	1507
1451								NDB 'M' 183 RBI +044 -180 = 047 TMG							
✓						046		NDB 'I' 005 RBI +044 = 049 REQ TRK							
✓								ALTER HDG 2S FOR 'I' PILOT NAVIGATION							
1455								DME 'I' RNG 60 NM							
✓								224 - 60 = 164 NM GONE IN 30 MIN = 328 KN GS				328	60	11	1506

Apart from plotting the trk from 'M' to 'I' there is no need for further plotting on this leg as all the working is by pilot navigation. Even the DME rng from 'I' at 1455 need not be plotted even though it is shown here

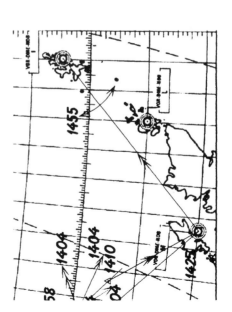

Figure 17-26   Pilot Navigation Leg.

253

COMPUTE THE TIME TO GO from the distance to go and the GS and enter the time in the **Time** column. Add the time to 1455 to give the ETA which is entered in the **ETA** column.

Fig. 17–26 shows the logsheet entries from 1425 to 1455 (reduced in size to fit the page) and the relevant part of the chart.

17.33   At 1506 the aircraft is overhead 'I' and altering hdg for 'J'. RAS, FL and temperature are unchanged (therefore TAS is also unchanged). There is a new WV given and the trk will have to be plotted and its direction and distance measured. Entries in the log follow the same pattern as at the start of the previous leg as do the calculations of hdg, GS and ETA. Figure 17.27 shows the logsheet entries for 1506 (reduced in size to fit the page) and the relevant part of the chart.

17.34   The instructions at 1515 mean that a descent has to be calculated to arrive at 5000 ft over 'J', delaying the start of the descent till the last possible moment. At this point candidates may wish to refer back to paragraphs 17.9 to 17.12 (which covered both climbs and descents) to refresh their memories before proceeding. A run through information shows that there is available:

Altitude at the cruising level (i.e. TOD).
Altitude at bottom of the descent.
The rate of descent in ft / min.
WV and temperature at the cruising level (i.e. TOD).
WV and temperature at the bottom of the descent.
Mean RAS for the descent.
The trk (T) for the descent (the same as the cruise trk (T)).

From this information the following can be calculated and computed:

Mean altitude for the descent (by averaging the altitudes at the top and bottom of the descent).
Total change of altitude in the descent (by subtracting the bottom of descent altitude from the TOD altitude).
Time taken on the descent (total change of altitude / rate of descent).
Mean WV and temperature for the descent (by averaging the WV and temperatures at the top and bottom of the descent).
Mean TAS for the descent (from mean altitude, temperature and RAS).
Mean hdg (T) and mean GS for the descent (from trk (T), mean WV and mean TAS).
Mean hdg (M) for the descent (applying local varn to hdg (T)).
Distance covered on the descent (from mean GS and time taken on the descent).
TOD (by plotting distance covered on the descent from 'J' back along the trk towards 'I').
ETA at TOD (by subtracting distance on the descent from the total leg distance 'I'

Time	Trk [T]	W/V /drift	Hdg [T]	Var	Hdg [M]	Dev	Hdg [C]	Observations	Mach No/RAS	Pressure Alt /COAT	TAS	GS	Dist	Time	ETA
1506	058	030/ 50	054					O/H 'T' ALTER HDG FOR 'J'	263	23 00 / -30	371	326	234	43	1549

This is a straightforward plotting of the required trk, measuring the direction and distance and then computer work to solve hdg, GS, time and ETA

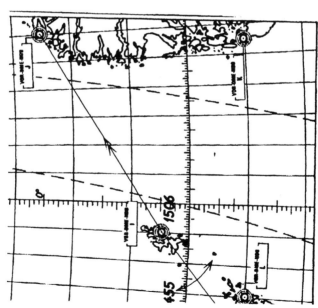

Fig. 17–27   Computing the leg 'T' to 'J'.

to 'J' to give distance from 'I' to TOD and then compute the time from 'I' to
TOD at the cruising GS).
Revised ETA at 5000 ft overhead 'J' (by adding the descent time to the ETA at
TOD).

Fig. 17–28 shows the logsheet entries for this (reduced in size to fit the page)
and the relevant part of the chart. Note how a line was left below the 1506
line (for the calculation of the ETA at the TOD) before the descent calculations were carried out. The whole process is in fact much simpler than the
rather long explanation makes it look. The secret is to be methodical and
keep an organised log, plus plenty of practice. And practice is something
every good pilot knows about.

17.35   Figs. 17–29 and 17–30 on pages 260 and 261 show the complete
logsheet and chart for the exercise just described. Both are shown smaller
than actual size to allow them to fit the page without folding.

17.36   Finally there are two types of peripheral questions that get introduced into plotting examination questions from time to time. These involve
asking for:

The information to be expected from a specified ground-based radio aid when at a
    given position.
The maximum reception range of information from a ground-based radio aid.

In themselves these are not true plotting items but are used by the examiners to check out a candidate's, knowledge of the practical use of radio
aids:

An example of the first case above would have been to ask for the QDR from the
    VOR at 'K' (5902N 0530E) when the aircraft reached the calculated TOD on
    the demonstration plot. To do this plot the TOD and draw a line from 'K'
    through the TOD. Measure the angle of this line from N (T) at 'K' to give the
    QTE and apply the varn at the VOR to convert the QTE to the QDR. On the
    plot the QTE is 342, varn at 'K' 4W gives **QDR 346.**
An example of the second case above would have been to ask for the long of the
    earliest time that a brg could be expected to be to be received from the VOR at
    'M' while on the leg cruising from 'F' to 'M'. To do this the formula for calcu-
    lating the maximum range of a line-of-sight radio transmission has to be
    remembered from the Radio Aids syllabus.

Maximum Range (nm) = $1 \cdot 25 (\sqrt{h1} + \sqrt{h2})$.
Where:
h1 = height of ground transmitter (ft amsl).
h2 = altitude of the aircraft (ft amsl).

Time	Trk [T]	W V/drift	Hdg [T]	Var	Hdg [M]	Dev	Hdg [C]	Observations	Mach No/RAS	Pressure Alt/COAT	TAS	GS	Dist	Time	ETA
1506	058	030/50	054					O/H 'J' ALTER HDG FOR 'J'	263	23 00/-30	371	326	234	43	1549
✓								'J' TO TOD 234 - 82 = 152 NM				✓	152	28	1534
1534		101/40	052					△ TOD 23 000 ↘ 5000 FT	240	14 000/-10	300	273	82	18	1552

Calculation of TOD position and ETA at TOD. Descent hdg, GS, distance and time plus revised ETA at 5000 ft overhead 'J'.

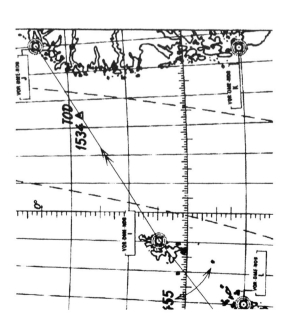

Fig. 17–28 Descent Calculations.

257

In the plot assuming the VOR is at sea level this gives:

Maximum Range (nm) $= 1{\cdot}25 \, (\sqrt{0} + \sqrt{23\,500})$
                                                  $= 1{\cdot}25 \times 153{\cdot}3$
                                                  = 191·6 nm.

When plotted from 'M' back down the trk towards 'F' the maximum range of 191·6 nm cuts the trk at the **11W** meridian.

Time	Trk T	W/V drift	Hdg [T]	Var	Hdg [M]	Dev	Hdg [C]	Observations	Mag No/RAS	Pressure Alt/COAT	TAS	GS	Dist	Time	ETA
1310			122					◁ 6328N 2015W	260	23 500 / -35	385	403			
1313								VOR 'G' QDM 078 + 180 = QDR 258							
✓								-19W VAR = QTE 239 PLOT				✓	121	18	
1322								DME 'G' RNG 73 NM PLOT				✓	60.5	9	
1331								VOR 'E' QDR 212 -18W VAR = QTE 194 PLOT							
✓								✗ 6212N 1540W							
1352								NDB 'W' RBI 298 + 122 - 180 = 240 PLOT FROM TRANSFERRED MERIDIAN				✓	80.6	12	
1358								GRND DVF BRG 'L' QTE 293 PLOT				✓	40.3	6	
1404	128		122					VOR 'M' 153 T0' + 180 - 11W VAR = QTE 322 PLOT			413	227		33	
✓		000/52						✗ 5939N 0925W TMG 128 227 NM IN 33 MIN							
✓								WV 000 / 52							
1410	146	✓	142	12W	154			◁ ALTER HDG FOR 'M'			✓	426	105	15	1425
1417								DOPPLER DRIFT 4S, GS 425 KN CHECKS OUT							
1425	048	020/60	044	11W	055			'M' ALTER HDG FOR 'I'	263	23 000 / -30	371	320	224	42	1507
1451								NDB 'M' 183 RBI +044 -180 = 047 TMG							
✓			046					NDB 'I' BRG 005 RBI +044 = 049 REQ TRK							
✓								ALTER HDG 25 FOR 'I' PILOT NAVIGATION							
1455								DME 'I' RNG 60 NM							
✓								224 - 60 = 164 NM GONE IN 30 MIN = 328 KN GS				328	60	11	1506
1506	058	030/50	054					O/H 'I' ALTER HDG FOR 'J'	263	23 00 / -30	371	326	234	43	1549
✓								'I' TO TOD 234 - 82 = 152 NM				✓	152	28	1534
1534		101/40	052					◁ TOD 23 000 ↘ 5000 FT	240	14 000 / -10	300	273	82	18	1552

Fig. 17.29   Demonstration plot, the log

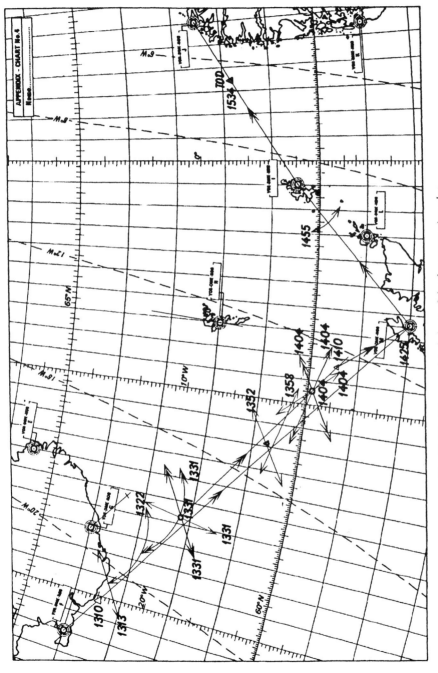

Fig. 17–30   The completed chart of the demonstration plot.

LIST OF ABBREVIATIONS

<	less than
>	more than
ASI	Airspeed Indicator
ATD	Actual Time of Departure
brg	bearing
(C)	Compass (direction)
°C	Degrees Celsius (centigrade temperature)
CA	Closing Angle
ca	conversion angle
CAS	Calibrated Airspeed
ch'lat	change in latitude (another name for d'lat)
ch'long	change in longitude (another name for d'long)
COAT	Correct Outside Air Temperature
Comp. Corr.	Compressibility Correction
conv	convergency
cos	cosine
CP	Critical Point
D	Total Distance of leg in calculation of the Critical Point
d	distance to the Critical Point from the start of the leg
d'lat	difference in latitude
d'long	difference in longitude
Dept	Departure
dev	deviation
DF	Direction Finding (ground station)
DME	Distance Measuring Equipment (ground based radio aid)
DR	Deduced (Dead) Reckoning
E	East (direction)
E	Endurance (can be expressed in time or fuel available)
EAS	Equivalent Airspeed
ETA	Estimated Time of Arrival
ft	feet

g / cub m	grams per cubic metre (atmospheric density)
GC	Great Circle
GMT	Greenwich Mean Time
gnm	ground nautical miles
(G)	Grid (direction)
griv	grivation
GS	Ground Speed
H	Home (as in Groundspeed Home)
hdg	heading
hr	hours (time)
IAS	Indicated Airspeed
IAT	Indicated Air Temperature
Imp Gal	Imperial Gallons (volume)
INS	Inertial Navigation System
ISA	International Standard Atmosphere
kg	kilograms (weight)
km	kilometres (distance)
kn	knots (nautical miles per hour)
kph	kilometres per hour (speed)
lat	latitude
lb	pounds (weight)
LCB	Line of Constant Bearing
LMT	Local Mean Time
long	longitude
lt	litres (volume)
m	metres (distance)
M No	Mach Number
(M)	Magnetic (direction)
mb	millibars (atmospheric pressure)
min	minutes (time)
mph	statute miles per hour (speed)
msl	mean sea level
N	North (direction)
n	constant of the cone
NDB	Non-Directional Beacon (ground based radio aid)
nm	nautical miles (distance)
O	Out or On (as in Groundspeed Out)

P	Port (to the left)
P/L	Position Line
p/o	parallel of origin
PNA	Point of No Alternate
PNR	Point of No Return
RAS	Rectified Airspeed
RBI	Relative Bearing Indicator
RE	Reduced Earth
Rel	Relative (as in Relative bearing)
RL	Rhumb Line
RMI	Radio Magnetic Indicator
RT	Radio Telegraphy
RW	Runway
S	South (direction) or Starboard (to the right)
SAT	Static Air Temperature
sec	secant
SG	Specific Gravity
SP	Standard Parallel
st m	statute miles (distance)
(T)	True (direction)
t	time (in minutes)
TAS	True Airspeed
TAT	Total Air Temperature
TE	Track Error
Th	Time home
TMG	Track Made Good
To	Time out (or on)
TOC	Top Of Climb
TOD	Top Of Descent
trk	track
US Gal	United States Gallons (volume)
UTC	Co-ordinated Universal Time (name now given to GMT)
varn	variation
VOR	Very High Frequency Omni Range (ground based radio aid)
W	West (direction)
WV	Wind Velocity

INDEX